DEEP LEARNING
WITH PYTHON

Travis Booth

TABLE OF CONTENTS

DEEP LEARNING WITH PYTHON
A Hands-On Guide for Beginners

DEEP LEARNING WITH PYTHON
A Comprehensive Guide Beyond The Basics

DEEP LEARNING WITH PYTHON
A Comprehensive Guide for Experts

Other Books by Travis Booth

Machine Learning Series

Machine Learning With Python:
Hands-On Learning for Beginners

Machine Learning With Python:
An In Depth Guide Beyond the Basics

Python Data Analytics Series

Python Data Analytics:
The Beginner's Real World Crash Course

Python Data Analytics:
A Hands-On Guide Beyond the Basics

Python Data Science Series

Python Data Science:
Hands-On Learning for Beginners

Python Data Science:
A Hands-On Guide Beyond the Basics

Bonus Offer: Get the Ebook absolutely free when you purchase the paperback via Kindle Matchbook!

DEEP
LEARNING
WITH PYTHON

A Hands-On Guide for Beginners

Travis Booth

Introduction

———————◆———————

Thank you for purchasing the book "Deep Learning".

Most artificial intelligence problems like image classification, optical character recognition, question answering, transforming text to speech, and speech recognition can be solved using the process of deep learning. It is true that the topic is a complex subject to learn and understand, but it is not difficult for most machine learning algorithms. If you want to find out how to build a deep learning model in Python, you have come to the right place. It is important to learn more about the different subjects mentioned here before you build a deep learning model.

Over the course of the book, you will gather information concerning what deep learning is and how it is different from machine learning. You will also learn about the different neural network architectures that designers use to program a deep learning model. The book provides information on how you can build a deep learning model in Python using Keras. The examples use data sets that are available online. You can download the data from the links mentioned in the book and use these data sets to test your model.

I hope this book includes all the information you are seeking.

Chapter One

The Foundations of Machine Learning

———————•◆•———————

The act of learning itself is difficult to define. In its simplest sense, to learn is to gain knowledge or understanding of a new concept, which can only be acquired through study, experience, or instruction.

There are many correlations that one can draw between human learning or animal learning and machine learning. The techniques used in animal learning are often employed to develop machine-learning concepts. Conversely, certain breakthroughs in machine learning have helped us understand new perspectives in biological, animal learning patterns as well.

To improve the efficiency of a machine, it is often recalibrated structurally. Doing so generally increases its performance and quality of output, and it is, in fact, a method for learning how the machine functions. With machine learning, however, not all such recalibration results in new learning.

For instance, suppose a machine is supposed to predict whether India will win a cricket match against Australia. The engineer or developer can feed some historical information pertaining to both Indian and Australian players, their match statistics and run rates, etc. into the machine, and it can then can use that input to predict an outcome. This is a type of machine learning.

The whole concept behind machine learning is to apply it to something that has artificial intelligence that can process large volumes of information and churn out analyses and results. As such, artificial intelligence and machine learning go hand in hand. Engineers build machines with artificial intelligence to perform the following functions: diagnosis, prediction, and recognition. The engineer can use sample data or historical data to train the machine to predict the desired output; it then uses the training data set that the engineer provides it with to learn how to perform the tasks. The machine identifies patterns in the training data and teaches itself to execute different types of analyses on the data.

Apart from training data, there are various other learning mechanisms that an engineer teaches a machine with artificial intelligence. The most commonly used ones are supervised learning and unsupervised learning.

There are some who deem machine learning to be a questionable exercise; they do not view machines as being capable of anything else beyond performing specific tasks. It is imperative that a machine learns for various reasons, with one of the main reasons being that it paves the way for further understanding of human learning.

Below are a few other advantages that machine learning brings with it.

Advantages of Machine Learning

Due to the sheer volume and magnitude of the tasks, there are some instances where an engineer or developer cannot succeed, no matter how hard they try; in those cases, the advantages of machines over humans are clearly stark.

Identifies Patterns

When the engineer feeds a machine with artificial intelligence a training data set, it will then learn how to identify patterns within the data and produce results for any other similar inputs that the engineer provides the machine with. This is efficiency far beyond that of a normal analyst. Due to the strong connection between machine learning and data science (which is the process of crunching large volumes of data and unearthing relationships between the underlying variables), through machine learning, one can derive important insights into large volumes of data.

Improves Efficiency

Humans might have designed certain machines without a complete appreciation for their capabilities, since they may be unaware of the different situations in which a computer or machine will work. Through machine learning and artificial intelligence, a machine will learn to adapt to environmental changes and improve its own efficiency, regardless of its surroundings.

Completes Specific Tasks

A programmer will usually develop a machine to complete certain tasks, most of which involving an elaborate and arduous program where there is scope for the programmer to make errors of omission. He or she might forget about a few steps or details that they should have included in the program. An artificially intelligent machine that can learn on its own would not face these challenges, as it would learn the tasks and processes on its own.

Helps Machines Adapt to the Changing Environment

With ever-changing technology and the development of new programming languages to communicate these technological advancements, it is nearly impossible to convert all existing programs and systems into these new syntaxes. Redesigning every program from its coding stage to adapt to technological advancements is counterproductive. At such times, it is highly efficient to use machine learning so that they can upgrade and adapt to the changing technological climate all on their own.

Helps Machines Handle Large Data Sets

Machine learning brings with it the capability to handle multiple dimensions and varieties of data simultaneously and in uncertain conditions. An artificially intelligent machine with abilities to learn on its own can function in dynamic environments, emphasizing the efficient use of resources.

Machine learning has helped to develop tools that provide continuous improvements in quality in small and larger process environments.

Disadvantages of Machine Learning

- It is difficult to acquire data to train the machine. The engineer must know what algorithm he or she wants to use to train it, and only then can he or she identify the data set they will need to use to do so. There can be a significant impact on the results obtained if the engineer does not make the right decision.

- It's difficult to interpret the results accurately to determine the effectiveness of the machine-learning algorithm.

- The engineer must experiment with different algorithms before he or she chooses one to train the machine with.

- Technology that surpasses machine learning is being researched; therefore, it is important for machines to constantly learn and transform to adapt to new technology.

Subjects Involved in Machine Learning

Machine learning is a process that uses concepts from multiple subjects. Each of these subjects helps a programmer develop a new method that can be used in machine learning, and all these concepts together form the discipline of the topic. This section covers some of the subjects and languages that are used in machine learning.

Statistics

A common problem in statistics is testing a hypothesis and identifying the probability distribution that the data follows. This allows the statistician to predict the parameters for an unknown data set. Hypothesis testing is one of the many concepts of statistics that are used in machine learning. Another concept of statistics that's used in machine learning is predicting the value of a function using its sample values. The solutions to such problems are instances of machine learning, since the problems in question use historical (past) data to predict future events. Statistics is a crucial part of machine learning.

Brain Modeling

Neural networks, which will be covered later in the book, are closely related to machine learning. Scientists have suggested that nonlinear elements with weighted inputs can be used to create a neural network. Extensive studies are being conducted to assess these elements. Scientists and psychologists alike are trying to gather more information about the human mind through these neural networks. Connectionism, sub-symbolic processing, and brain style computation are a few spheres that are associated with these types of studies.

Adaptive Control Theory

Adaptive control theory is a subject that's closely associated with the control of systems. As mentioned earlier, it is difficult for the system to adapt to a change in the surrounding environment. Adaptive control theory is a part of this subject that deals with methods that help the system adapt to such changes and continue to perform optimally. The idea is that a system should anticipate the changes and modify itself accordingly.

Psychological Modeling

For years, psychologists have tried to understand human learning. The EPAM network is a method that's commonly used to understand human learning. This network is utilized to store and retrieve words from a database when the machine is provided with a function. The concepts of semantic networks and decision trees were only introduced later. In recent times, research in psychology has been influenced by artificial intelligence. Another aspect of psychology called reinforcement learning has been extensively studied in recent times, and this concept is also used in machine learning.

Artificial Intelligence

As mentioned earlier, a large part of machine learning is concerned with the subject of artificial intelligence. Studies in artificial intelligence have focused on the use of analogies for learning purposes and on how past experiences can help in anticipating and accommodating future events. In recent years, studies have focused on devising rules for systems that use the concepts of inductive logic programming and decision tree methods.

Evolutionary Models

A common theory in evolution is that animals prefer to learn how to better adapt to their surroundings to enhance their performance. For example, early humans started to use the bow and arrow to protect themselves from predators that were faster and stronger than them. As far as machines are concerned, the concepts of learning and evolution can be synonymous with each other. Therefore, models used to explain evolution can also be utilized to devise machine learning techniques. The most prominent technique that has been developed using evolutionary models is the genetic algorithm.

Programming Languages

R

R is a programming language that is estimated to have close to 2 million users. This language has grown rapidly to become very popular since its inception in 1990. It is a common belief that R is not only a programming language for statistical analysis but can also be used for multiple functions. This tool is not limited to only the statistical domain. There are many features that make it a powerful language.

The programming language R is one that can be used for many purposes, especially by data scientists to analyze and predict information through data. The idea behind developing R was to make statistical analysis easier.

As time passed, the language began to be used in different domains. There are many people who are adept at coding in R, although they are not statisticians. This situation has arisen since many packages are being developed that help to perform functions like data processing, graphic visualization, and other analyses. R is now used in the spheres of finance, genetics, language processing, biology, and market research.

Python

Python is a language that has multiple paradigms. You can probably think of Python as a Swiss Army knife in the world of coding, since this language supports structured programming, object-oriented programming, functional programming, and other types of programming. Python is the second-best language in the world since it can be used to write programs in every industry and for data mining and website construction.

The creator, Guido Van Possum, decided to name the language Python, after Monty Python. If you were to use some inbuilt packages, you would find that there are some sketches of the Monty Python in the code or documentation. It is for this reason and many others that Python is a language that most programmers love, though engineers or those with a scientific background who are now data scientists would find it difficult to work with.

Python's simplicity and readability make it quite easy to understand. The numerous libraries and packages available on the internet demonstrate that data scientists in different sectors have written programs that are tailored to their needs and are available to download.

Since Python can be extended to work best for different programs, data scientists have begun to use it to analyze data. It is best to learn how to code in Python since it will help you analyze and interpret data and identify solutions that will work best for a business.

Chapter Two

Machine Learning Models

———— ♦ ————

Supervised Machine Learning

An important part of the learning process is when a machine is provided with data about historic events that will help it anticipate any future events. When the training data fed is supervised, this type of learning is called "supervised learning". The data fed essentially includes training examples that consist of inputs and the desired outputs. These desired outputs are also known as supervisory signals. The machine then uses a supervised machine algorithm that creates an inferred function that's used to forecast any events. If the outputs are discrete, the function is called a "classifier", and if the outputs are continuous, the function is known as a "regression function". The function is also used to predict the outputs for future inputs. This algorithm is utilized to create a generalized method to reach the output from the data that was fed in as input. An analogy that can be made in the spheres of human and animal learning is concept learning.

Overview

This type of learning always uses a fixed algorithm. The steps that are involved in the process are listed below.

Step 1

The first step in this process of learning is to determine the type of examples that need to be used to train the machine. This step is extremely crucial since the engineer will need to know what kind of data he needs to use as examples for his machine. For instance, for a speech recognition system, the engineer can use single words, small sentences, or entire paragraphs for training the machine.

Step 2

When the engineer has decided upon the type of data that will be used, he then needs to collate that data and create a training set. This set will be used to represent the possibilities of any function that can be used. He will need to collect the desired inputs and outputs that are to be used for the training process.

Step 3

The next step is to determine how to represent the input data to the machine. This is very important given that the accuracy of the machine depends on the input representation of the function. Normally, the representation is done in the form of a vector. This vector contains information about various characteristic features of the input; however, the vector should not include information on too many features, since this would increase the time taken for training. A larger number of features may also lead to mistakes made by the machine in prediction. The vector needs to contain exactly enough data to predict outputs.

Step 4

Once the engineer has decided what to use as input data, a decision will need to be made about the structure of the function needs to be created. The learning algorithm must also be decided upon. The algorithms that are used are often supported vectors and decision trees.

Step 5

The engineer will now need to complete the design. The algorithm that is chosen needs to be run on the data set that has been used as the training input data. There are some algorithms that need the engineer to identify certain control parameters to verify that the algorithm is running well. These parameters can be estimated by testing on a smaller subset or by using the method of cross-validation.

Step 6

Once the algorithm has run and the function has been generated, its accuracy and effectiveness will need to be calculated; engineers use a testing set for this task. This data set is different from the training data set, and the corresponding outputs to the input data are already known. The test set inputs are sent to the machine, and the outputs obtained are checked with those in the test set.

Some supervised learning algorithms are often used, and each of these has its own strengths and weaknesses. Since there is no definitive algorithm that can be used for all instances, the selection of the learning algorithm is a major step in the procedure.

Issues to Consider in Supervised Learning
With the usage of supervised learning algorithms, there arise a few associated issues. Below we have detailed four major issues in supervised learning:

Bias-Variance Tradeoff

The bias-variance tradeoff is an issue that needs to be kept in mind while working with learning. Let's say you are in a situation where you have some good training sets. When a machine is trained using some training data sets, it gives predictions that are systematically incorrect for certain output. It can be said that the algorithm is biased toward the input data set. A learning algorithm is also sometimes considered to have a high variance for input. This occurs when the algorithm causes the machine to predict different outputs for the input in each training set. The sum of the variance and the bias of the learning algorithm are known as the prediction error for the classifier function. There is a tradeoff that exists between the variance and the bias. A requirement for learning algorithms with low bias is that they need to be flexible enough to accommodate all the data sets. If they are too flexible, the learning algorithms might end up giving varying outputs for each training set, hence increasing the variance. This trade-off will need to be adjusted using supervised learning algorithms, which is done automatically or by using an adjustable parameter.

Function Complexity and Amount of Training Data

The second issue is concerned with deciding on the amount of training data based on the complexity of the classifier or regression function to be generated. Suppose the function to be generated is simple; a learning algorithm that is relatively inflexible with low variance and high bias will be able to learn from a small amount of training data. On many occasions, the function will be complex. This can be the case due to a large number of input features being involved or due to the machine being expected to behave differently for different parts of the input vector. In such cases, the function can only be learned from a large amount of training data. These cases also require the algorithms used to be flexible with low bias and high variance. Therefore, efficient learning algorithms automatically arrive at a tradeoff between the bias and variance depending on the complexity of the function and the amount of training data required.

Dimensionality of the Input Space

Another issue that needs to be dealt with is the dimensionality of the input vector space. If the input vector includes a large number of features, the learning problem will become difficult, even if the function only considers a few of these features as valuable inputs. This is simply because the extra and unnecessary dimensions can lead to confusion and cause the learning algorithm to have high variance. So, when the input dimensions are large, the classifier is adjusted to offset the effects by having low variance and high bias. In practice, an engineer can manually remove the irrelevant features to improve the accuracy and efficiency of the learning algorithm, though this might not always be a practical solution. In recent times, many algorithms have been developed that are capable of removing unnecessary features and retaining only the relevant ones. This concept is known as "dimensionality reduction", and it helps in mapping input data into lower dimensions to improve the performance of the learning algorithm.

Noise in the Output Values

Last but not least, an issue that can arise is the interference of noise (white noise) in the output values provided by the machine. The output values can be incorrect due to this noise that is added to the output values, and these values can also be incorrect due to human error. In such cases, the learning algorithm should not aim to match the training inputs with their exact outputs. Algorithms with a low variance and high bias are the most desirable.

Unsupervised or Reinforcement Learning

Apart from supervised learning, there are other concepts of learning that are gaining importance, with one being unsupervised, or reinforcement, learning. In this technique, the machine is designed to interact with its ambient environment through actions. Based on the environment's response to these actions, the machine receives rewards if the environment reacts positively, or it receives punishments if it reacts negatively. The machine will learn from the reactions; it is taught to react in a manner by which it can maximize rewards and also identify futuristic events. The objective would also be to minimize future punishments. This technique of learning is related to the subjects of control theory in decision theory and engineering in indicators and management sciences.

The main problems in these two subjects are more or less equal, and the solutions are similar as well, but each subject focuses on different aspects of the problem. There is also another technique that uses unsupervised learning and game theory. The idea here is similar to unsupervised learning. The machine produces some actions that affect the surrounding environment, and it receives rewards or punishments depending on the reaction of the environment. However, the main difference is that the environment is not static; it is dynamic and can include other machines as well. These other machines are also capable of producing actions and receiving rewards (or punishments). So, the objective of the machine is to maximize its future rewards (or minimize its future punishments) while taking into account the effects of the other machines in its surroundings.

The application of game theory to such a situation with multiple, dynamic systems is a popular area of research. In the technique of unsupervised learning, the machine receives training inputs, but it does not receive any target outputs or rewards and punishments for its actions. This begs the question: how can the machine possibly learn anything without receiving any feedback from the environment or having information about target outputs? However, the idea is to develop a structure in the machine to build representations of the input vectors in such a manner that they can be used for other applications, such as prediction and decision-making. Essentially, unsupervised learning can be understood as the machine identifying patterns in input data that would normally go unnoticed. Two of the most popular examples of unsupervised learning are dimensionality reduction and clustering. The technique of unsupervised learning is closely related to the fields of information theory and statistics.

How to Evaluate Machine Learning Models

It is important to remember that you can apply a machine learning algorithm to a problem only when you have defined it and prepared your data. Once you do this, you can spend sufficient time running different algorithms to solve the problem, which will help you choose the right algorithm for the problem. You must ensure that you use your time well when you are closer to reaching your goal. This section will help you understand how to test different algorithms and verify if they are the right fit for the problem at hand. It will also help you identify the most effective algorithm that can be used to solve the problem.

Test Harness

You must remember to define the test harness. This is the data that you'll test and train the algorithm against. It's also the performance measure that you will use to assess the accuracy and performance of the model. You must always define the test harness well and use it to evaluate multiple algorithms, which will help you understand the problem better.

You must ensure that you can use the test harness to test an algorithm quickly against an accurate outcome or output of the solved problem. When you test multiple algorithms using a test harness, you must ensure that you have chosen the performance measure. You can use this measure to estimate the accuracy of different algorithms, in turn helping you identify which problems that you should spend time working on and which ones you should no longer consider.

These results will also help you understand if it is easy for the machine to comprehend your problem. If you find that numerous machine learning algorithms are performing poorly on the problem, it could mean that it has not been structured well enough. This could be due to the fact that there is no structure in the data that is selected. Alternatively, it could be that you can use this opportunity to teach the algorithm the right structure.

Performance Measure

You can evaluate the solution to any problem using the performance measure. It's used to test the accuracy of the predictions being made by the model on the training or testing data set, depending on whether you have split the data set.

A performance measure is usually derived based on the problem that you're working on. This means that the measure will be different for a clustering, classification, and regression model. There are many standard performance measures that you can use to obtain some meaningful information about the problem that you've selected. For instance, for a classification problem, the standard performance measure is calculated using the following formula:

(Total correct correlation/total predictions made using the model) * 100

You may want to derive a detailed breakdown of your model's performance. For instance, you may be working on a model that will automatically classify an email as spam or important. For such a problem, you will need to define a method to identify a false classification where an important email is marked as spam.

You do not have to identify or calculate a new performance measure since there are numerous standard performance measures that you can choose from. This means that you can identify the right measure and adapt it to match the requirements of your problem. Look for some similar problems that were solved in the past, and try to use those performance measures for your problem.

Train and Test Data Sets

Once you have manipulated and cleaned the data set, you must split it into a training and testing data set. You will then use the training data set to teach your algorithm and test the performance and accuracy of that algorithm against the testing data set. This could be as simple as splitting the data set using a random split; alternatively, you can use a more complicated method of doing this.

Most trained models are never exposed to test data sets during the training period, and it's for this reason that the predictions the models make on the testing data set can be used to understand the performance of the model. Therefore, you should be certain that you select the right data set that will represent your problem.

Cross-Validation

Another approach that you can use to train and test your data set is the full data set to train an algorithm and the same data set to test the algorithm. One of the methods you can utilize to test the accuracy of the model is cross-validation. For this process, you split the data set into groups of instances of the same size. The model will then be trained using all these blocks of data, aside from the one block that was left out. The model is then tested on the last block, or fold. This process will be repeated multiple times to ensure that each block of data is left out at least once during the training process. The performance measures calculated across all iterations are then averaged to estimate the accuracy and performance of the algorithm.

For instance, when you use a three-fold cross-validation method, you'll be training the model thrice. The following method is used to do this.

- First iteration: Train the model on the folds 1 and 2, and test using 3

- Second iteration: Train the model on folds 2 and 3, and test using 1

- Third iteration: Train the model on folds 3 and 1, and test using 2

Remember that the number of folds in every data set will vary depending on the size. Some of the most common number of folds are 3, 5, 7, and 10. It is important to maintain a balance between the sizes of the data set and how your algorithm represents it.

When you are performing this test for the first time, it's a good idea to stick to a simple split. You should only use cross-validation when you have enough confidence.

Testing Algorithms

Once you have defined both the problem and the test harness that you want to use, you should begin trying different algorithms. It's always a good idea to check the data to ensure that there is some structure within the data set. This will help you identify those algorithms that you can use on the data set you've chosen. When you spot check, you can also work out any issues in the test harness. This will help ensure that you have chosen the right performance measure to use to test the accuracy of the model.

It's ideal to use a random algorithm to check the data set. For this, you can plug in any number generator, which will help you generate the predictions for the data set. This will give you the worst result you could have possibly imagined, and it will be the measure you'll use to improve the other algorithms you choose.

You can select at least ten algorithms to predict the outcome for the problem that you have chosen and assess the accuracy of the model using your test harness. When it comes to standard algorithms, it's ideal to choose the ones that have no special adjustments or configurations. Ensure that the algorithm you decide upon is appropriate for the problem. For example, you should choose a regression algorithm if you are working on a regression problem.

Chapter Three

An Introduction to Neural Networks

————————•◆•————————

Before we delve into the concepts involved in the topic of deep learning, let us first take a look at what neural network architecture is. Engineers built artificial neural networks to help machines process information in the same way as the human brain. The key feature of these networks is how the layers are structured to process any information. Each layer consists of a network of interconnected neurons that process information, and these neurons work together to solve any problem. Since the neural network processes information the same way as the human brain, a machine with neural network architecture is able to learn by example. Engineers can only develop these machines for a specific purpose, such as pattern recognition or data classification. Human beings learn when the brain makes some adjustments to the neuron. Neural networks work in the same way.

Historical Background

Although neural networks were developed before the invention of computers, they suffered a setback since people were not fully adept at using these networks. It is due to this reason that the simulation of neural networks is a recent development. Improvements made to computers have boosted many advances in the development of neural networks. People threw themselves into research when the concept began to gain importance. They were unable to obtain any information regarding how they could use these networks to improve the accuracy and efficiency of machines, which led to a dip in enthusiasm. There were some researchers who continued to study neural networks and worked hard to develop technology that people in the industry would accept.

Warren McCulloch and Walter Pitts developed and produced the first artificial neural network in 1943. This neuron is known as the McCulloch-Pitts neuron. Since the technology to develop the network further was not available to them in that year, they were unable to use the neural network to perform complex tasks.

Why Use Neural Networks?
Every industry today utilizes large volumes of data to improve functions. These data sets have many variables that make it difficult for human beings to understand the patterns within them; neural networks make it easier to identify these hidden patterns in the data set. Some computers also find it difficult to identify the trends in the data set if they do not have neural network architecture. An engineer can train the neural network using large data sets to help it become an expert in the field. They can then use the network to predict the

output for any future input. This gives the engineer a chance to answer some important questions about the future.

Some advantages of neural networks include:

- They use a machine learning technique called supervised machine learning to adapt and learn new tasks.

- They can represent any information provided to it during the learning stage.

- Since neural networks can compute some data in parallel, machines with neural network architecture work faster to provide results.

- If a neural network is partially damaged, it can lead to a dip in performance; however, the network can retain some of its properties even when damaged.

Neural Networks vs. Conventional Computers

Conventional computers and neural networks do not both use the same approach to solve any problem. The former only use algorithms to solve a given problem. Conventional computers can also solve problems if they know what steps to follow to identify the solution. This means that conventional computers often solve problems that human beings can solve, though computers are definitely more useful when they can solve problems that human beings cannot solve.

As mentioned earlier, neural networks function in the same way as the human brain. The neurons in the network are interconnected. The neural networks always work together to solve most problems. Since the network learns by example, the engineer cannot teach the network to perform a specific task. This makes it important for the engineer to choose the training data sets carefully. Otherwise, it's difficult for the machine to learn how it should solve a problem correctly. Since the neural network learns from the data set, it can solve a variety of problems, including those that the engineer does not train the machine to solve. This makes them quite unpredictable.

Computers also solve problems using cognitive approaches. The computer should know the process it needs to follow in order to solve the problem, and this will only work when the engineer provides the machine with the correct instructions, which can be provided to it using a high-level programming language. The computer will then decode the instructions into a language that it can understand. This process helps the engineer predict how a machine will work. If there's an issue with the result, the engineer can be certain that it's due to a hardware or software problem.

Neural networks and conventional computers complement each other. Some tasks like arithmetic calculations are better suited for conventional algorithmic computers, while various complex tasks are more suited for neural networks; however, most require a combination of these approaches to ensure that the machine performs at maximum efficiency.

Types of Neural Networks

Fully Connected Neural Network

The network layer is the most common type of neural network architecture. It has three layers of interconnected neurons. The first layer, which is also known as the input layer, is connected to the hidden layer of neurons, and that is connected to the output layer. The input layer represents the data or information that the engineer provides to the network. How the input layer views the raw data determines the weights that are placed on the neurons in the hidden layer and the weights that are placed on the nodes connecting the neurons in the input layer to the hidden layer. The behavior of the output layer is dependent on the weights placed on the neurons in the hidden one and the weights placed on the nodes connecting the neurons in the hidden layer to the output layer.

This is the structure for a simple neural network, and it is interesting since the hidden layers can choose to represent the data in any form. The weights present on the nodes linking the input layer with the hidden layer determine when the hidden network layer must stay active. The engineer can modify the weights between the input and hidden layers to ensure that the hidden unit will represent what the engineer wants.

It's also easy to differentiate between a single-layer and a multi-layer architecture. In the single-layer architecture, the neurons are connected at their nodes. This means that every layer in the network is connected, in turn increasing the computational power of the network. In the multi-layer architecture, the network is numbered by layers. This means that the layers are interconnected rather than the neurons.

Feed-Forward Networks

The feed-forward network is also known as the top-down or bottom-up network. Signals in the feed-forward network only travel in one direction - from the input to the output. This network does not have a feedback loop, so the output derived from one layer does not affect the output derived from other layers. The network is straightforward in the sense that the input is associated with the output. This is used in pattern recognition.

Convolutional Neural Networks

Convolutional neural networks (CNNs) are similar to fully connected neural networks. They are made up of multiple layers with many neurons, with each neuron in the network being assigned a weight based on the training data that the engineer uses to teach the network. When the neurons receive an input, they perform a dot product and then follow that product with a nonlinearity. So, what is the difference between a convolutional neural network and a fully-connected neural network? A CNN makes the assumption that every input in the training data set is an image that allows the engineer to encode some properties into the network architecture. These make it easier for the network to apply the forward function and reduce the number of instances in the training data set. Most deep learning applications use these types of neural networks.

Feedback Networks

Signals in the feedback network travel in both directions, introducing a loop within the network. These networks are complicated to build but extremely powerful. The state of the feedback network will change until the signals reach a point of equilibrium. The network will remain in this state of equilibrium until the input data set changes. When the engineer feeds a new data set to the machine, the network will need to identify a new equilibrium point. These networks are interactive and recurrent; however, only single-layer networks are referred to as recurrent. We will learn more about recurrent neural networks later on in this chapter.

Perceptrons

The term "perceptrons" was coined in the year 1960 by Frank Rosenblatt when there were significant developments being made in neural network architecture. A perceptron is a type of McCulloch and Pitts model. In this model, every neuron is assigned a fixed or pre-processing weight. A perceptron is similar to the visual system in human beings. These are used only in pattern recognition, although they have the ability to be used for other functions.

Recurrent Neural Networks

In recurrent neural networks, information always goes through a loop. When the network makes a decision, it will consider the current input and also assess what it has learned from the previous inputs. The usual RNN has a short-term memory, but when it is combined with the LSTM (long short-term memory), it has a long-term memory. This is further discussed below.

A good way to illustrate the concepts of RNN is by using an example. Consider that you're using a regular feed-forward neural network and give the network the word "brain" as the input. This network will process that word character-by-character, and by the time it reaches the character "I", it will forget about the first three characters. This makes it impossible to use this model to predict what the next character will be. An RNN can remember the previous characters and also predict the next character since it has an internal memory. It produces outputs and copies those outputs back into the network. This means that the RNNs always add the immediate past information to the present information. Therefore, an RNN network has the following inputs:

- The present data

- The recent data

An engineer must be careful about the training data set he uses to teach the model since it uses the sequences to predict characters in the text. This means that an RNN can perform functions that most other algorithms cannot. A feed-forward neural network will assign weights to the neurons in every layer to produce the output. The RNN applies weight to the current and the previous input data and also tweaks the weights assigned to the neurons.

Generative Adversarial Network

In a generative adversarial network (GAN), two networks are pitted against each other, hence the name. The potential of a GAN is huge since it can learn to mimic any data set or distribution. This means that you can use a GAN to build or create a world that's very similar to your own in many domains, like images, speech, pictures, and prose. The output from these networks is impressive.

In this network, one neural network is known as the generator and the other is known as the discriminator. The first generates the new instances and the second evaluates those instances. The discriminator decides whether or not a new instance belongs to the training data set.

Let's look at the following example. We want to generate handwritten numerals from the MNIST data set. You can download the data set from the following location:

http://yann.lecun.com/exdb/mnist/

The discriminator must identify if a new instance that the generator creates is authentic or not when compared to the MNIST data set.

The generator will continue to develop new instances of data and hope that the discriminator will deem those instances to be authentic, although they are actually fake. The generator must lie without being caught, and the discriminator must identify the fake instances that the generator creates. The steps that the GAN takes are as follows:

- The generator takes random numbers from the data set and returns an image as the output.

- The engineer will feed the generated image into the second network, the discriminator, and a stream of images from the training data set.

The discriminator will label the images with a degree of authenticity "1" and label the fake images "0".

Chapter Four

An Introduction to Deep Learning

------------◆------------

From the first few chapters, you should have gathered that the machine will use a training data set to understand different types of data and use that learning to predict the outcome for new data sets. Google and Facebook are, however, trying to identify words spoken in order to categorize them. They are also trying to help different machines identify the relationship between alternate objects in the training data set and assess that relationship between differing variables or data points.

For example, if you want a computer to interpret "this is an elephant" exactly that way instead of "this is a collection of pixels", you must determine a way to map some features of the elephant to other complex features. For instance, you can convert a line, curve, pixels, sounds of alphabets, and much more if you know how to transform the features of that entity into ones that can be recognized by the machine. It can then use indexing or inference to predict the output. This type of learning is called "deep learning".

Neural networks are used in deep learning models to identify the outputs. In this type of learning, different nodes are used as inputs in the differing layers, and a signal from the input layer is sent to the hidden layers in the network. The hidden layers will then use that input to calculate or derive the output. The work in deep learning is defined by how the human mind learns; it also considers how calculations and computations take place in the cerebral cortex of the human brain.

Every node in the model is assigned a weight. For instance, if you are trying to use the model to identify or classify images, you can assign a weight to every pixel in the image that is used as the input. You should also include the output value that you want the machine to provide in the training data set. An error message is passed to the input layer or the source if the output image is not the same as the one in the training data set. This means that the weights assigned to the nodes will need to be updated.

The changes in these weights will help the user steer the network towards the right output. The signals sent from one side of the neural network to the other help the machine determine the correct values that must be provided as the output. A system can use deep learning either in a supervised or unsupervised mode.

Supervised Modes
The neural network is taught with a training data set. In this type of learning, you will need to provide the output layer with the values that are associated with the input category. When a similar data set

is used as the test data set, the network will look at the output layer and provide the user with the desired output.

Unsupervised Modes

Both the input and the output layers in the network are provided with the examples that you're processing. Since the inner, or hidden, layers of the network are being compressed, most of the features in the data set are overlooked. In this mode of learning, the network will use the values produced by the inner layer as the output.

Scientists and engineers are now spending the time to understand deep learning systems since it helps them identify the features that a network can support. This also helps the engineer or programmer understand how the different features in the data can be combined to derive the necessary output.

The disadvantage of using these techniques is that they are impenetrable. It is hard for most systems to identify and report new features in the data set. This makes it extremely difficult for the model to explain the method it used, which is an ability that a machine must possess. This means that the model can present you with some outputs or inferences that it may be unable to explain. In this case, you will need to dig deeper to understand the model and see how it derived a specific output.

Most engineers and developers help machines learn using different machine learning techniques. Deep learning is one of the many techniques used to help a machine do this by example. It is one of the key technologies used to help a car navigate through the streets without a driver; cars can now identify stop signs, pedestrians, and lampposts. Deep learning is also used in voice control devices like phones, tablets, televisions, and other hands-free devices, like Alexa. Through deep learning, the technology industry can achieve results that were never possible before.

Computer models using deep learning techniques learn to perform classification tasks from text, sound, or images. A machine using deep learning models can achieve a high level of accuracy where human beings cannot, and these machines also perform better than us. Engineers train the machines using large data sets called the training data set and neural network architecture.

How to Obtain Impressive Results Using Deep Learning

Deep learning can attain impressive results due to accuracy. Through deep learning techniques, engineers can ensure that the machines they develop have a higher level of recognition accuracy. This helps it meet the demands of the customer, and it is crucial for devices like driverless cars to have this feature. The recent developments in deep learning have improved machines to a point where they perform some tasks better than human beings, such as the classification of images.

Although deep learning was studied in the early 1980s, there are two reasons why it is a popular machine learning technique now:

- Deep learning uses large volumes of labeled data to train machines. For example, it takes thousands of hours of video and millions of images to train a driverless car to perform well on roads.

- Deep learning also requires computing power. Most machines have a parallel architecture that improves the function of the deep learning technique. When deep learning is combined with cloud computing or clusters, it reduces the time the engineer must spend to train the machine from a few weeks to hours or less.

Examples of Deep Learning

Deep learning techniques and applications are used in a wide range of industries.

Automated Driving

Automotive researchers use deep learning techniques to help machines detect objects like traffic lights and stop signs. In addition to this, the techniques are used to detect pedestrians and other cars, which helps to decrease the number of accidents.

Defense and Aerospace

Deep learning techniques are used to identify safe or unsafe zones for people and troops. These techniques also help machines identify areas of interest using satellite imagery.

Medical Research

Cancer researchers use deep learning techniques to detect cancer cells in the human body. Many teams at UCLA built a microscope that uses deep learning techniques to yield a high-dimensional data set. This microscope can detect cancer cells anywhere in the human body.

Industrial Automation

Deep learning techniques assist organizations in improving the safety of workers around any heavy machinery. The machines using these techniques detect when an object or a person is within an unsafe distance from the machinery.

Electronics

Deep learning techniques are now used in automated speech and hearing translations. For instance, home assistance devices like Alexa that can respond to your voice and understand your preferences by utilizing deep learning algorithms.

How Does Deep Learning Work?

The neural network architecture is used in most deep learning techniques, and it is for this reason that deep learning models are known as deep neural networks. (The concept of neural networks is covered in the previous chapter.) The term "deep" refers to the many hidden layers in the network. A traditional neural network can only have up to two hidden layers, but a deep neural network can have close to 150 of them. Deep learning models use large data sets called the training data set and neural networks to learn features from the data, and due to this, there is no need for the engineer to manually extract features from the data to train the machine.

One of the most common types of deep networks is called the convolutional neural network, or CNN. This type of network is well suited to process two-dimensional data, such as images. A CNN combines the features it has learned with the features in the input data and uses the two-dimensional convolutional layers to process information.

A CNN eliminates the need to extract features from data manually. This means that the engineer does not need to classify the features or identify the images to assist the network in categorizing them. The CNN extracts the features directly from the images or input data. The engineer does not train the data to choose some features from the information provided to it. The CNN learns what features it needs to look for when the engineer feeds it the training data set. It is for this reason that computers or models with CNN are used to classify objects.

A CNN learns to identify the different characteristics and structures of an image. It does this by using the many hidden layers within the network. Every hidden layer identifies complex features of the image, and the complexity increases as the hidden layers increase. For example, the initial hidden layer can detect colors in the image, while the last layer can identify different objects in the background.

Why Deep Learning Is Better than Traditional Learning Methods

Deep learning is a type of machine learning. Let us consider an instance where an engineer is training a machine using a machine learning and deep learning model to categorize images. In machine learning, the engineer trains the model by extracting the relevant features from the training data set and providing that information to the machine. The machine then uses these features to categorize objects present in the images. As mentioned earlier, a deep learning model will identify the features from the training dataset. In addition to this, deep learning also performs "end-to-end" learning. In this process, the network is given the training data set and is asked to perform a task, like classification, and the network learns to do this without the help of the engineer.

Another difference is that shallow learning algorithms converge with the increase in data, while a deep learning algorithm will scale with data. In other words, the hidden layers in the deep neural network continue to learn and improve in their functioning as the size of the data set increases. Shallow learning algorithms refer to those machine-learning algorithms that plateau at a specific performance level when the engineer adds more training data or examples to the network.

Therefore, in machine learning, the engineer must provide the machine with a classifier and feature to sort images, while with deep learning, the machine learns to perform these functions by itself.

Choosing Between Deep Learning and Machine Learning

Machine learning algorithms offer different models and techniques that the engineer can choose from depending on the application, the type of problem the machine should solve, and the data that it's processing. Deep neural networks require a huge volume of data that the engineer can use to train the model, as well as a graphics processing units, or GPUs, which will process the data quickly.

When you need to choose between deep neural networks and machine learning, you should consider whether you have labeled data and a high-performance GPU. If you do not have either, you should stick to machine learning algorithms. Since deep learning is more complex, you'll need at least a few thousand variables to ensure that the algorithm provides the necessary output. If you have GPU with high performance, you can be certain that the model will analyze the data quickly.

Chapter Five

How to Create and
Train Deep Learning Models

———————•♦•———————

This chapter provides information on the three ways an engineer can train a deep learning model to classify objects, including training from scratch, transfer learning, and feature extraction.

Training from Scratch

If you want to train the deep neural network from scratch, you should collate a large volume of labeled data. You must then design the network to ensure that it will learn all the features in the data set. This is a good practice for new applications or for ones that have multiple output categories. Most engineers do not use this approach since the network will take a few days or weeks to learn the process due to the large volume of training data.

Transfer Learning

Most engineers train deep learning networks using the transfer learning approach. In this process, a pre-existing or pre-trained model is fine-tuned. You can start with networks like GoogleNet and AlexNet and feed these networks with new data containing some unknown classes. You're also able to make a few tweaks to the network, which will allow the network to perform new tasks. Therefore, you will not require large volumes of data to train the network, in turn reducing the computation time to a few hours or minutes.

If you want to use transfer learning to train a model, you will need an interface that allows you to connect to the pre-existing network. This will help you enhance and modify the network to perform the task. Software like MATLAB has functions and tools that you can use for this very purpose.

Feature Extraction

This is a specialized and slightly less common approach to training a deep neural network. Every layer in the network needs to identify the different features in the large data set. You can extract these features from the network at any time during the training process; they can be used to train support vector machines or a machine learning model.

Chapter Six

Applications of Deep Learning

————————• ◆ •————————

Automatic Colorization of Images

You can now use deep learning networks to automatically add color to black and white photographs. A deep learning network will identify the objects in the image and their context within the photograph, then adding color to the image using that information. This is a highly impressive feat. This capability increases the use of large convolutional and high-quality neural networks like ImageNet. This approach involves the use of supervised layers and CNNs to recreate an image by adding color to it.

Adding Sound to Silent Movies

In this task, the deep neural network must develop or recreate sounds that will match a silent video. Let's look at the following example. We need the network to add sounds to a video where people are playing drums. The engineer will provide the network with close to 1,000 videos with the sound of the drum striking many surfaces. The network will identify the different sounds and associate the video frames from the silent video or movie with the pre-recorded sounds and then select the sound from the database that matches the video in the scene. This system is then evaluated using a Turing test for which human beings were asked to differentiate between the real and synthesized video. Both CNN and LSTM neural networks are used to perform this application.

Automatic Translation

Deep neural networks can translate words, phrases, or sentences from one language to another automatically. This application has existed for a long time now, but the introduction to deep neural networks has helped it achieve great results in certain areas of the translation of images and text.

For the translation of a text, the engineer does not have to feed the deep neural network with a pre-processing sequence. This allows the algorithm to identify the dependencies between the words in a sentence and map them to a new language. The stacked networks in a large LDTM recurrent neural network are used for this purpose.

You may have guessed from previous sections of the chapter that a CNN is used to verify if an image has letters and then finding where those letters are in the scene. Once the network identifies these letters, it can transform them into text, translate the text into a different language, and recreate the image with the translated text. This process is known as instant visual translation.

Object Detection and Classification in Images

In this application, the deep neural network identifies and organizes the objects in an image by classifying the images into a set of previously known objects. Very large CNNs have been used to achieve accurate results when compared to the benchmark examples of the problem.

Automatic Handwriting Generation

For this application, the engineer must feed the deep neural network with a few handwriting examples. This helps the network generate a new handwriting for a given word, phrase, or sentence. The data set that the engineer feeds the network should provide a sequence of coordinates that the writer uses when writing with a pen. From this data set, the network identifies and establishes a relationship between the movement of the pen and the letters in the data set. The network can then generate new handwriting examples. What is fascinating is that the network can learn different styles and mimic them whenever necessary.

Automatic Text Generation

For automatic text generation, the engineer will feed the network with a data set that only includes text. The network learns it and can generate new text character-by-character or word-by-word. The network can learn how to punctuate, spell, form sentences, differentiate between paragraphs, and capture the style of the text from the data set.

An engineer will use large recurrent neural networks to perform this task. The network establishes the relationship between the items in the many sequences in the data set and then generates new text. Most engineers choose the LSTM recurrent neural network to generate text since these networks use a character-based model and generate only one character at a time.

Automatic Image Caption Generation

As the name suggests, when given an image, the model must describe the contents of the image and generate a caption. In 2014, many deep-learning algorithms used the models for object detection and object classification in images to generate a caption. Once the model detects objects in the image and categorizes them, it will need to label those objects and form a coherent sentence. This is an impressive application of deep learning. The models used for this application utilize large CNNs to detect the objects in the images and a recurrent neural network like the LSTM to generate a coherent sentence using the labels.

Automatically Playing a Game

This is an application where a machine learns how it can play a game using only the pixels on the screen. Engineers use deep reinforcement models to train a machine to play a computer game. DeepMind, which is now a part of Google, works primarily on this application.

Chapter Seven

Activation Functions Used to Develop Deep Learning Models

————•◆•————

A n activation function is an important feature of every artificial neural network. These functions decide whether a neuron in a layer should be used while creating the output. It also decides if the information that the neuron receives is worth using in the calculation or if it should be ignored. The activation function is a nonlinear transformation that's done over the input layer. The output from the input layer is sent as an input to the other layers in the network.

Popular Activation Functions

Binary Step Function
A binary step function is a threshold-based classifier that determines whether the network should include a neuron in the calculation process. If the output value from the neuron is higher than a given threshold, the neuron is activated; otherwise, it should remain deactivated.

The function is defined as: $f(x) = 1, x>=0$.

The binary function is a simple example of an activation function. This function can be used when you need to create a binary classifier.

Sigmoid Function

The sigmoid function is an activation function that most engineers use when they develop a deep neural network. The examples in the book use a sigmoid activation function to activate the layers of the neural network. The function is of the form: $f(x) = 1/(1+e^{-x})$.

The sigmoid function is smooth, nonlinear, and continuously differentiable. When saying that the function is nonlinear, we mean that you receive a nonlinear output when you multiply neurons that have a sigmoid function. The output values for a sigmoid function lie in the range [0,1] where 0 and 1 are included, and the curve of the function has an S shape.

Tanh

The tanh and sigmoid functions are similar, but the tanh function is only a scaled version. It's scaled using the following function: $tanh(x) = 2sigmoid(2x)-1$.

Alternatively, you can write the function in the following way: $tanh(x)=2/(1+e^{-2x})-1$. The tanh function is symmetric, unlike the sigmoid function. This solves the problem of the values derived as the output having the same sign. Like the sigmoid function, the tanh function is differentiable and continuous at all points. Since the function is nonlinear, it makes it easy for the engineer to backpropagate the errors.

ReLU

The rectified linear unit, or ReLU, function is defined as follows: $f(x)=max(0,x)$. Most engineers use this function to design networks. The ReLU function is nonlinear, which means that you can backpropagate errors and activate many layers of neurons. The advantage of the ReLU function is that it does not activate every neuron in the network. This means that if the output from one neuron is negative, it will deactivate that neuron and convert the output to zero. In this situation, the network is sparse, which makes it easier to compute the problem.

Choosing the Right Activation Function

Now that you have come to understand a few different activation functions, you should know which one is best to use in a given situation. You can make your choice regarding which activation you require depending on the properties of the problem.

A sigmoid function and its combinations work if you want to solve a classification problem. Stay away from the sigmoid and activation functions if you want to avoid the vanishing gradient problem.

Chapter Eight

An Introduction to Python

---◆---

Running Python

Python is a software program that can be installed and run on multiple operating systems, including Mac OS X, or OS/2, Linux, Unix, and Windows. If you are running Python on GNU/Linux or Mac OS X, you may already have the software installed in the system. It's recommended to use this type of system since it already has Python set up as an integral part. The programs in this book will work on any operating system.

Installing on Windows

If you are using Windows, you'll need to install Python and configure certain settings correctly before you start working on the examples given in this book. To do that, you must refer to specific instructions provided for your operating system on the following Python web pages:

- http://wiki.python.org/moin/BeginnersGuide/Download

- http://www.python.org/doc/faq/windows/

- https://wiki.python.org/moin/BeginnersGuide

You will first need to download the official installer. Alternative versions for AMD and Itanium machines are available at http://www.python.org/download/. This file, which has a .msi extension, must be saved at a location where you can find it easily. You can then double-click on this file to start the Python installation wizard, which will help you through the process. It's best to choose the default settings if you are uncertain of the answers.

Installing on Other Systems

You may choose to install Python on other systems if you want to take advantage of the latest versions of the software. The instructions for Unix-like and Linux systems can be found at the following links:

- https://docs.python.org/2/using/unix.html

If you're using OS X, your instructions can be found here:

- https://www.python.org/downloads/mac-osx/

- https://docs.python.org/3/using/mac.html

Choosing the Right Version

Different installers include different numbers after the word "Python" which refer to the version number. If you look at the archives on multiple websites, the version numbers will range from 2.5.2 to 3.0, where the former is an old but usable version of Python and the latter is the latest version. The Python team released the version 2.6 at the same time that it released the version 3.0, since there are some people who may still want to stick to version 2 of Python; these people most likely wish to continue to write code the old way while also getting benefits like general fixes and some of the new features introduced in version 3.0.

The Python language is continuously evolving. Version 3.0 has become the norm and has evolved into version 3.1.1, and the newer versions of 3.0 are refinements of version 3.0. Version 3.0 includes several changes to the programming language that is incompatible with version 2.0. You needn't worry about programming using different versions of Python since there is only a subtle difference in the language, or syntax.

There may be some differences when running Python on other operating systems, which will be pointed out in the book wherever necessary. Otherwise, the codes in the book will work in the same way across different operating systems. This is one of the many great features of Python. For the most part, this book will concentrate on the fun part - learning how to write programs using Python. If you wish to know more about Python, you can read the documentation prepared by the developers, which is free and well written. It can be found using this link: http://www.python.org/doc/.

Python Keywords

The following words (also called keywords) are the base of the Python language. You cannot use these words to name an identifier or a variable in your program since they are considered the core words of the language. They cannot be misspelled and must be written in the same way for the interpreter to understand what you want the system to do. Some of the words listed below have a different meaning, which will be covered in later chapters.

- False
- None
- assert
- True
- as
- break
- continue
- def
- import
- in
- is
- and
- class
- del

- for
- from
- global
- raise
- return
- else
- elif
- not
- or
- pass
- except
- try
- while
- with
- finally
- if
- lambda
- nonlocal
- yield

Understanding the Naming Convention

Let's talk about the words that you can use and those you cannot. Every variable name must always begin with an underscore or a letter. Some variables can contain numbers, but they cannot start with one. If the interpreter comes across a set of variables that begin with a number instead of quotation marks or a letter, it will only consider that variable as a number. You should never use anything other than an underscore, number, or letter to identify a variable in your code. You must also remember that Python is a case-sensitive language; therefore false and False are two different entities. The same can be said for vvariable, Vvariable, and VVariable. As a beginner, you must make a note of all the variables you use in your code. This will also help you find something easier in your code.

Creating and Assigning Values to Variables

Every variable is created in two stages; the first stage is used to initialize the variable and the second is used to assign a value to that variable. In the first step, you must create a variable and name it appropriately to stick a label on it, and in the second step, you must put a value in the variable. These steps are performed using a single command in Python that utilizes the equal-to sign. When you must assign a value, you should write the following code:

Variable = value

Every section of the code that performs some function, like an assignment, is called a statement. The part of the code that can be evaluated to obtain a value is called an expression. Let us take a look at the following example:

Length = 14

Breadth = 10

Height = 10

Area_Triangle = Length * Breadth * Height

Any variable can be assigned a value, or an expression, like the assignment made to Area_Triangle in the example above.

Every statement must be written in a separate line. If you write the statements down the way you would write down a shopping list, you are doing it the right way. Every recipe begins in the same way with a list of ingredients and the proportions along with the equipment that you need to use to complete your dish. The same happens when you write a Python code; you first define the variables you want to use and then create functions and methods to use on those variables.

Recognizing Different Types of Variables

The interpreter in Python recognizes different types of variables - sequences or lists, numbers, words or string literals, booleans, and mappings. These variables are often used in Python programs. A variable None has a type of its own called NoneType. Before we look at how words and numbers can be used in Python, we must first look at the dynamic typing features.

Working with Dynamic Typing

When you assign a value to a variable, the interpreter will decide the type of value the variable is, which is called "dynamic typing". Unlike other languages, Python does not require the user to declare the types of the variables being utilized in the program. This can be considered both a blessing and a curse. The advantage is that you do not have to worry about the variable type when you write the code, and you only need to worry about the way the variable behaves.

Dynamic typing in Python makes it easier for the interpreter to handle user input that's unpredictable. The interpreter for Python accepts different forms of user input to which it assigns a dynamic type. This means that a single statement can be used to deal with numbers, words, or other data types, and the user does not have to always know what data type the variable must be. Not needing to declare variables before you use them makes it tempting to introduce variables at random places in your scripts. You must remember that Python won't complain unless you try to use a variable before you have actually assigned it a value, but it's really easy to lose track of what variables you are using and where you set up their values in the script.

There are two really sensible practices that will help keep you sane when you start to create large numbers of different variables. One is to set up a bunch of default values at the start of each section if you're sure of where you will need to use them. It is always a good idea to group all the variables together. The other is to keep track of the expected types and values of your variables, keeping a data table in your design document for each program that you're writing.

The API in Python will need to keep track of the variable type for a few reasons. The machine will need to set some memory aside to store this information. The different data types in Python take up different volumes of space. The second reason is that keeping track of types helps to avoid and troubleshoot errors. Once Python has decided what type a variable is, it will flag up a TypeError if you try to perform an inappropriate operation on that data. Although this might at first seem to be an unnecessary irritation, you'll discover that this can be an incredibly useful feature of the language, as the following command-line example shows:

```
>>> b = 3

>>> c = 'word'

>>> trace = False

>>>

b + c
```

Traceback (most recent call last):

File "", line 1, in <module>

TypeError: unsupported operand type(s) for +: 'int' and 'str'

>>> c - trace

Traceback (most recent call last):

File "", line 1, in <module>

TypeError: unsupported operand type(s) for -: 'str' and 'bool'

The program above attempts to perform the operation on data types that are incompatible. You're not allowed to add a number to a word or take a yes/no answer away from it. It is necessary to convert the data to a compatible type before trying to process it. You can add words together or take numbers away from each other just like you can in real life, but you can't do arithmetic on a line of text. Python will alert you if there is some error in your logic using tracebacks. In this case, it gives you the TypeError. This error will let you know that you must rewrite the code to ensure that you let the compiler know what type of information you should put in. This information is dependent on the output that you want to obtain.

The purpose of data types is to allow you to represent information that exists in the real world (the world that exists outside your computer) as opposed to the virtual world inside. (We can have the existential conversation about what is real and what is not some other time.) The previous example uses variables of type int (whole numbers) and type str (text). It will quickly become apparent that these basic data types can only represent the simplest units of information; you may need to use quite a complicated set of words, numbers, and relationships to describe even the simplest real-world entity in virtual-world terms.

Python provides a variety of ways to combine these simple data types to create more complex data types, which we'll come to later in the book. First, you need to know about the fundamental building blocks that are used to define your data and the basic set of actions you can use to manipulate the different types of values.

The None Variable

A predefined variable called None is a special value in Python. It has a type of its own and is useful when you need to create a variable without defining or specifying a value to it. When you assign values such as "" and 0, the interpreter will define the variable as the str or int variable.

Information = None

A variable can be assigned the value None using the statement above. The next few examples will use real-world information that will be modeled into a virtual form using some fantasy characters. This example uses some statistics to represent a few attributes of the characters in order to provide data for the combat system. You can use this example to automate your database and your accounts. So, let's take a look at some of the characters in the example.

In the program, hello_world.py, you saw how you can get a basic output using the print () function. This function can be used to print out the value of the variable and a literal string of characters. Often, each print statement must start on a new line, but several values can be printed on a single line by using a comma to separate them; print () can then be used to concatenate all the variables into a single line only separated by spaces.

>>> *Race = "Goblin"*

>>> *Gender = "Female"*

>>> *print (Gender, Race)*

Female Goblin

Different segments of information can be combined into a single line using multiple methods. Some of these methods are more efficient when compared to others. Adjacent strings that are not separated will be concatenated automatically, but this is not a function that works for most variables.

>>> *print ("Male" "Elf")*

The expression above will give you the following output: "MaleElf".

However, when you enter the following code,

>>> *print ("Male" Race)*

You will receive the following error:

File "<stdin>", line 1

print ("Male" Race)

^

SyntaxError: invalid syntax

This approach cannot be used since you can't write a string function as a variable and a string together since this is just a way of writing a single line string.

It is straightforward to assign any number to variables.

Muscle = 8

Brains = 13

If any variable begins with a number, the interpreter will view that variable as a number, even if there are some other characters used in that variable. It is for this reason that you should never name a variable starting with a number. There are a few points that you will need to keep in mind before you work with numbers.

Computers Only Take Zeros and Ones

The information on any computer is stored only as a binary value - zero or one. A machine will always store and process any volume of data using switches that are labeled as zero or one.

Deep Learning Libraries in Python

In this section, you will learn about the different libraries in Python that you can use when you build a deep neural network. The list of libraries in this chapter is not exhaustive.

Keras

Keras is a modular and minimalist neural network library that uses either TensorFlow or Theano as its backend. Keras allows you to experiment quickly, which means that you can obtain results for many problems fast. It is easy to build a neural network in Keras since it includes some of the best optimizers, normalizers, and activation functions. Keras focuses more on convolutional neural networks.

In Keras, you can construct graph-based and sequence-based networks, which makes it easier to implement architectures like SqueezeNet and GoogleNet. The only problem with Keras is that it does not allow the engineer to train multiple networks or layers in parallel as it does not support a multi-GPU environment. The examples in later chapters use the Keras libraries to build a neural network in Python.

Theano

If Theano was not developed, it would have been difficult for engineers to experiment with higher-level abstraction problems. At its very core, Theano is a library that an engineer can utilize to define, optimize, and evaluate complex mathematical expressions that include multi-dimensional arrays. Theano can achieve this since it supports the use of GPUs. Experts believe that Theano is a building block for neural networks in Python. Therefore, it can be integrated with different libraries to build better and more complex models.

TensorFlow

TensorFlow is similar to Theano. It's an open source library that's used for numerical computation that was developed by a research team in Google's machine intelligence organization. Through TensorFlow, an engineer can distribute the computing function of the network between multiple GPUs. You can use TensorFlow as a backend for Keras when you build deep neural networks in Python.

Chapter Nine

How to Clean Data Using Python

———————•◆•———————

Most engineers and data scientists spend too much of their time cleaning a data set and manipulating that data into a format that they can use to train the machines. There are many data scientists who argue that the cleaning of data constitutes at least 80% of the job. Therefore, if you are stepping into this field, you must learn how to deal with missing data, messy data, inconsistent formatting, outliers, and malformed records.

In this chapter, we will look at how to use the NumPy and Pandas libraries to clean data sets. We will look at the following points:

- How to drop columns in a data frame

- How to change the index in a data frame

- How to clean the columns using .str()

- How to use the functioning DataFrame.applymap() to clean the complete data set

- How to rename columns with recognizable labels

- How to skip unnecessary rows

We'll be using the following data sets:

- BL-Flickr-Images-Book.csv – This is a csv file which has information about the books in the British Library

- university_towns.txt – This is a text file that contains information about college towns in the US

- olympics.csv_– This is a csv file that provides a summary of the countries that participated in the Summer and Winter Olympics

These data sets can be downloaded from the GitHub repository for Python. Let us first import the NumPy and Pandas libraries to begin with the cleaning of data.

>>>

>>> import pandas as pd

>>> import numpy as np

Dropping Columns in a Data Frame

You will see that most categories of data in the data set can be used for analysis. For instance, you are probably looking at a database that contains student information, including their personal information, but you only want to focus on the analysis of their grades. In this instance, the personal information is not necessary or important to you. You can remove these categories to reduce the amount of space that is taken up by the data set, thereby improving the performance of the program.

When you use Pandas, you can remove any unwanted row or column in a data frame using the drop() function. Let us now look at an example where we remove columns from a data frame. Before we do this, we will need to create a data frame of the BL-Flickr-Images-Book.csv file.

First, let's create a data frame out of the CSV file 'BL-Flickr-Images-Book.csv'. In the following example, we will be passing the path to pd.read.csv. This means that all the data sets from the csv file are saved in the folder named "Datasets" in the current working directory.

>>>

>>> df = pd.read_csv('Datasets/BL-Flickr-Images-Book.csv')

>>> df.head()

Identifier	Edition Statement	Place of Publication \
0 206	NaN	London

1	216	NaN	London; Virtue & Yorston
2	218	NaN	London
3	472	NaN	London
4	480	A new edition, revised, etc.	London

	Date of Publication	Publisher \
0	1879 [1878]	S. Tinsley & Co.
1	1868	Virtue & Co.
2	1869	Bradbury, Evans & Co.
3	1851	James Darling
4	1857	Wertheim & Macintosh

	Title	Author \
0	Walter Forbes. [A novel.] By A. A	A. A.
1	All for Greed. [A novel. The dedication signed...	A., A. A.
2	Love the Avenger. By the author of "All for Gr...	A., A. A.
3	Welsh Sketches, chiefly ecclesiastical, to the...	A., E. S.

4 [The World in which I live, and my place in it... A., E. S.

                    Contributors Corporate Author \

0   FORBES, Walter.   NaN

1 BLAZE DE BURY, Marie Pauline Rose - Baroness   NaN

2 BLAZE DE BURY, Marie Pauline Rose - Baroness   NaN

3   Appleyard, Ernest Silvanus.   NaN

4   BROOME, John Henry.   NaN

    Corporate Contributors Former owner Engraver Issuance type \

0   NaN   NaN   NaN monographic

1   NaN   NaN   NaN monographic

2   NaN   NaN   NaN monographic

3   NaN   NaN   NaN monographic

4   NaN   NaN   NaN monographic

                    Flickr URL \

0 http://www.flickr.com/photos/britishlibrary/ta...

1 http://www.flickr.com/photos/britishlibrary/ta...

2 http://www.flickr.com/photos/britishlibrary/ta...

3 http://www.flickr.com/photos/britishlibrary/ta...

4 http://www.flickr.com/photos/britishlibrary/ta...

                    Shelfmarks

0   British Library HMNTS 12641.b.30.

1   British Library HMNTS 12626.cc.2.

2   British Library HMNTS 12625.dd.1.

3   British Library HMNTS 10369.bbb.15.

4   British Library HMNTS 9007.d.28.

We use the head() method to look at the first five entries. You will see that some of the columns provide information about the various books which will help the library, but that information is not descriptive about the books. These columns include Edition Statement, Corporate Author, Corporate Contributors, Former owner, Engraver, Issuance type, and Shelfmarks.

To drop these columns, use the code below:

```
>>>

>>> to_drop = ['Edition Statement',
...           'Corporate Author',
...           'Corporate Contributors',
...           'Former owner',
...           'Engraver',
...           'Contributors',
...           'Issuance type',
...           'Shelfmarks']


>>> df.drop(to_drop, inplace=True, axis=1)
```

In the section above, we have listed the columns that we want to remove from the data set. For this, we will use the drop() function on the object and pass the axis parameter as one and the inplace parameter as true. This will tell the Pandas directory that you want to change the object directly, and the directory should look for all the values in the column of the object that should be dropped.

When you look at the data frame now, you will see that the columns that you don't want to use have been removed.

>>>

>>> df.head()

	Identifier	Place of Publication	Date of Publication \
0	206	London	1879 [1878]
1	216	London; Virtue & Yorston	1868
2	218	London	1869
3	472	London	1851
4	480	London	1857

	Publisher	Title \
0	S. Tinsley & Co.	Walter Forbes. [A novel.] By A. A
1	Virtue & Co.	All for Greed. [A novel. The dedication signed...
2	Bradbury, Evans & Co.	Love the Avenger. By the author of "All for Gr...
3	James Darling	Welsh Sketches, chiefly ecclesiastical, to the...

4   Wertheim & Macintosh [The World in which I live, and my place in it...

	Author	Flickr URL
0	A. A.	http://www.flickr.com/photos/britishlibrary/ta...
1	A., A. A.	http://www.flickr.com/photos/britishlibrary/ta...
2	A., A. A.	http://www.flickr.com/photos/britishlibrary/ta...
3	A., E. S.	http://www.flickr.com/photos/britishlibrary/ta...
4	A., E. S.	http://www.flickr.com/photos/britishlibrary/ta...

You can also choose to remove the columns by using the columns parameter instead of specifying which labels the directory needs to look at and which axis should be considered.

```
>>>
```

```
>>> df.drop(columns=to_drop, inplace=True)
```

This is a readable and a more intuitive syntax. It's apparent what we are doing here. If you know the columns that you want to retain, you can pass them through the argument usecols in the pd.read.csv function.

Changing the Index of a Data Frame

The Index function in Pandas will allow you to extend the functionality of arrays in the NumPy directories. The function will also enable you to slice and label the data with ease. It is always a good idea to use a unique value to identify a field in the data set. For instance, you can expect that a librarian will always input the unique identifier for every book if he or she needs to search for the record.

```
>>>

>>> df['Identifier'].is_unique

True
```

You can use the set_index method to replace the existing index using a column.

```
>>>

>>> df = df.set_index('Identifier')

>>> df.head()
```

	Place of Publication	Date of Publication \
206	London	1879 [1878]
216	London; Virtue & Yorston	1868
218	London	1869

| 472 | London | 1851 |
| 480 | London | 1857 |

Publisher \

206	S. Tinsley & Co.
216	Virtue & Co.
218	Bradbury, Evans & Co.
472	James Darling
480	Wertheim & Macintosh

| Title | Author \ |

206	Walter Forbes. [A novel.] By A. A	A. A.
216	All for Greed. [A novel. The dedication signed...	A., A. A.
218	Love the Avenger. By the author of "All for Gr...	A., A. A.
472	Welsh Sketches, chiefly ecclesiastical, to the...	A., E. S.
480	[The World in which I live, and my place in it...	A., E. S.

206	http://www.flickr.com/photos/britishlibrary/ta...
216	http://www.flickr.com/photos/britishlibrary/ta...
218	http://www.flickr.com/photos/britishlibrary/ta...
472	http://www.flickr.com/photos/britishlibrary/ta...
480	http://www.flickr.com/photos/britishlibrary/ta...

Every record in the data frame can be accessed using the loc[] function. This function will allow you to give every element in the cell an index based on the label. This means that you can give the record an index regardless of its position.

>>>

>>> df.loc[206]

Place of Publication	London
Date of Publication	1879 [1878]
Publisher	S. Tinsley & Co.
Title	Walter Forbes. [A novel.] By A. A
Author	A. A.

Flickr URL   http://www.flickr.com/photos/britishlibrary/ta...

Name: 206, dtype: object

The number 206 is the first label for all the indices. If you want to access the label based on its position, you can use df.iloc[0]. This function will give the element an index according to its position. .loc[] is a class instance, and it has a special syntax that does not follow the rules of a Python instance.

In the previous sections, the index used was RangeIndex. This function labeled the elements using integers and this is analogous to the steps performed by the in-built function range. When you pass a column name to the set_index function, you'll need to use the values in Identifier to change the index. If you looked closely, you will have noticed that we now use the object returned by the df = df.set_index(...) method as the variable. This is because this method does not make any changes directly to the object, but it does return a modified copy of that object. If you want to avoid this, you should schedule the inplace parameter.

df.set_index('Identifier', inplace=True)

Tidying up Fields in the Data

We have now removed all the unnecessary columns in the data frame and changed the indices to the data frame to something that's more sensible. This section will explain how to work on specific columns alone and format them to help you gain a better understanding. It will also assist you in enforcing some consistency. We will be cleaning the fields Place of Publication and Date of Publication. When you inspect the data set further, you will notice that every data type is currently dtype. This object is similar to the str type in Python. This data type can encapsulate every field that can't be labeled as categorical or numerical data. It makes sense to use this since we will be working with data sets that have a bunch of messy strings.

```
>>>

>>> df.get_dtype_counts()

object  6
```

You can enforce some numeric value to the Date of Publication field. This will allow you to perform other calculations down the road.

```
>>>

>>> df.loc[1905:, 'Date of Publication'].head(10)
```

Identifier

1905	1888
1929	1839, 38-54
2836	[1897?]
2854	1865

2956	1860-63
2957	1873
3017	1866
3131	1899
4598	1814
4884	1820

Name: Date of Publication, dtype: object

Every book can only have a single date of publication. This means that we must do the following:

Remove the extra dates in the square brackets.

Convert the date ranges to the "start date" wherever they are present.

If we are uncertain about some dates, remove them and replace them with NaN from the NumPy directory.

Convert the string nan to the NaN value.

You can take advantage of the regular expression by synthesizing these patterns. This will allow you to extract the year of publication.

>>>

regex = r'^(\d{4})'

You can find the four digits at the start of the string by utilizing the regular expression above. This is enough for us. The example used in the section above is a raw string. This means that the backslash in this string cannot be used as an escape character. This is standard practice when it comes to regular expressions. (4) in the above string will repeat the rule four times while \d represents a digit. The ^ depicts the start of the string, and the parentheses will denote the capturing group. This signals to the Pandas directory that we only want to extract a portion of the regular expression. Let's now run this regular expression, or regex, across the data frame.

>>>

>>> extr = df['Date of Publication'].str.extract(r'^(\d{4})', expand=False)

>>> extr.head()

Identifier

206	1879
216	1868
218	1869
472	1851
480	1857

Name: Date of Publication, dtype: object

This column still has dtype, which is a string object. You can obtain the numerical version of that object using the pd.to.numeric function.

```
>>>

>>> df['Date of Publication'] = pd.to_numeric(extr)

>>> df['Date of Publication'].dtype

dtype('float64')
```

This will show you that at least one value is missing from ten values. This shouldn't worry you since you can now perform functions on all the valid values in the data frame.

```
>>>

>>> df['Date of Publication'].isnull().sum() / len(df)

0.11717147339205986
```

This is now done.

In the above section, you will have noticed that the df['Date of Publication'].str is used to access some string operations in the Pandas directory. This attribute performs functions on compiled regular expressions or Python strings. If you want to clean the Place of Publication field, you will need to combine the str method from the Pandas directories with the np.where function from the NumPy directories. This means that you will be creating a vectorized form of the IF loop in Excel. The syntax is as follows:

```
>>>

>>> np.where(condition, then, else)
```

In the above section, the term condition can hold a boolean mask or an array-like object. The then value is to be looked at if the condition is true, and the else section is looked at if the condition is false. The .where() method will take every cell or element, and check that element against the condition. If the value of the condition is True, the context in the condition will hold true, while the else condition is run if the condition is False. This can also be nested into a complex if-then statement, which will allow you to compute the values that are based on many conditions.

```
>>>

>>> np.where(condition1, x1,

np.where(condition2, x2,

np.where(condition3, x3, ...)))
```

Since the Place of Publication column has only string values, we will be using these two functions to clean it. The contents of the column are given below:

```
>>>
```

```
>>> df['Place of Publication'].head(10)
```

Identifier

206	London
216	London; Virtue & Yorston
218	London
472	London
480	London
481	London
519	London
667	pp. 40. G. Bryan & Co: Oxford, 1898
874	London]
1143	London

Name: Place of Publication, dtype: object

You'll notice that for some rows, there's some unnecessary information surrounding the place of publication. If you look at the values closely, you can see that this is only for some rows, especially for those rows where the place of publication is "Oxford" or "London".

Let's now look at two different entries:

>>>

>>> df.loc[4157862]

Place of Publication   Newcastle-upon-Tyne

Date of Publication   1867

Publisher   T. Fordyce

Title   Local Records; or, Historical Register of
rema...

Author   T. Fordyce

Flickr URL
    http://www.flickr.com/photos/britishlibrary/ta...

Name: 4157862, dtype: object

>>> df.loc[4159587]

Place of Publication   Newcastle upon Tyne

Date of Publication   1834

Publisher   Mackenzie & Dent

Title   An historical, topographical and descriptive v...

Author   E. (Eneas) Mackenzie

Flickr URL   http://www.flickr.com/photos/britishlibrary/ta...

Name: 4159587, dtype: object

The books in the list above were published at the same time and in the same place, but there is one that has a hyphen while the other does not. You can use the str.contains() function to clean this column in one shot. Use the code below to clean these columns:

```
>>>
>>> pub = df['Place of Publication']
>>> london = pub.str.contains('London')
>>> london[:5]
```

Identifier

206	True
216	True
218	True
472	True
480	True

Name: Place of Publication, dtype: bool

>>> oxford = pub.str.contains('Oxford')

These can be combined using the method np.where.

>>>

df['Place of Publication'] = np.where(london, 'London',

np.where(oxford, 'Oxford',

pub.str.replace('-', ' ')))

>>> df['Place of Publication'].head()

Identifier

206   London

216   London

218   London

472   London

480   London

Name: Place of Publication, dtype: object

In the above example, the np.where() function is the nested structure. The condition in this structure is a series of boolean values that are obtained using the function str.contains(). The contains() method allows Python to look for an entity in the substring of a string or an iterable. This method is similar to the in keyword. The replacement that you will need to use is a string that will represent the place of publication. You can also replace a hyphen using a space. This can be done using the str.replace() function, and the column can be reassigned in the data frame. It is true that there is a lot more messy data in the data frame, but we will look at these columns for now.

Let's now take a look at the first five rows in the data frame, which looked better than they did when we started,

>>>

>>> df.head()

	Place of Publication	Date of Publication	Publisher \
206	London	1879	S. Tinsley & Co.
216	London	1868	Virtue & Co.
218	London	1869	Bradbury, Evans & Co.
472	London	1851	James Darling
480	London	1857	Wertheim & Macintosh

Title	Author
206	Walter Forbes. [A novel.] By A. A AA
216	All for Greed. [A novel. The dedication signed... A. A A.
218	Love the Avenger. By the author of "All for Gr... A. A A.
472	Welsh Sketches, chiefly ecclesiastical, to the... E. S A.
480	[The World in which I live, and my place in it... E. S A.

	Flickr URL
206	http://www.flickr.com/photos/britishlibrary/ta...
216	http://www.flickr.com/photos/britishlibrary/ta...
218	http://www.flickr.com/photos/britishlibrary/ta...
472	http://www.flickr.com/photos/britishlibrary/ta...
480	http://www.flickr.com/photos/britishlibrary/ta...

Cleaning the Entire Data Set Using the applymap()

In some instances, you will notice that the "mess" is not only in one column, but can be found across the data set. There will be some times when you'll need to apply a function to every element or cell in a data frame. You can use the applymap() function to apply one function to every cell or element in the data frame. This is similar to the map() function.

Review the following example where we create a data frame using the university_towns.txt file.

$ head Datasets/univerisity_towns.txt

Alabama[edit]

Auburn (Auburn University)[1]

Florence (University of North Alabama)

Jacksonville (Jacksonville State University)[2]

Livingston (University of West Alabama)[2]

Montevallo (University of Montevallo)[2]

Troy (Troy University)[2]

Tuscaloosa (University of Alabama, Stillman College, Shelton State)[3][4]

Tuskegee (Tuskegee University)[5]

Alaska[edit]

In the above section, you'll see that every periodic state name is followed by a university town in that state (for example, StateA TownA1 TownA2). If you pay attention to the way the names of the states are written, you will see that each one of them has the "[edit]" substring. You can create a list of tuples in the form (State, City) and wrap that list using a data frame.

```
>>>

>>> university_towns = []
>>> with open('Datasets/university_towns.txt') as file:
    for line in file:
        if '[edit]' in line:
            # Remember this `state` until the next is found
            state = line
        else:
            # Otherwise, we have a city; keep `state` as last-seen
            university_towns.append((state, line))


>>> university_towns[:5]
[('Alabama[edit]\n', 'Auburn (Auburn University)[1]\n'),
 ('Alabama[edit]\n', 'Florence (University of North Alabama)\n'),
```

('Alabama[edit]\n',   'Jacksonville   (Jacksonville   State
University)[2]\n'),

('Alabama[edit]\n', 'Livingston (University of West Alabama)[2]\n'),

('Alabama[edit]\n', 'Montevallo (University of Montevallo)[2]\n')]

This list can be wrapped using a data frame, and the columns can be set to "RegionName" and "State". The Pandas directory will consider every element in the list and set the left value to State and the right value to RegionName. The data frame will now look like this:

>>>

>>> towns_df = pd.DataFrame(university_towns,

columns=['State', 'RegionName'])

>>> towns_df.head()

	State	RegionName
0	Alabama[edit]\n	Auburn (Auburn University)[1]\n
1	Alabama[edit]\n Alabama)\n	Florence (University of North
2	Alabama[edit]\n University)[2]\n	Jacksonville (Jacksonville State

3	Alabama[edit]\n Alabama)[2]\n	Livingston (University of West
4	Alabama[edit]\n Montevallo)[2]\n	Montevallo (University of

The strings could have been fixed or cleaned in the loop above. The Pandas directory makes it easier to do this. All you need is the name of the town and the state, and you can remove everything else. We can use the .str() method in this instance, but you can also use the applymap() method to map every element in the data frame to a Python callable. To understand what we mean by the term "element", you must look at the example given below:

>>>

	0	1
0	Mock	Dataset
1	Python	Pandas
2	Real	Python
3	NumPy	Clean

In the above example, every cell is considered an element. Therefore, the applymap() function will look at each of these cells independently and apply the necessary function. Let's now define that function:

```
>>>

>>> def get_citystate(item):

if ' (' in item:

return item[:item.find(' (')]

elif '[' in item:

return item[:item.find('[')]

else:

.return item
```

The applymap() function in the Pandas directory only takes one parameter. This parameter is the function, also called the callable, which can be applied to every element.

```
>>>

>>> towns_df = towns_df.applymap(get_citystate)
```

We'll first need to define a function in Python that will pick an element as a parameter from the data frame. A check will then be performed within the function to determine whether the element contains a "(" or "[" - or neither. Based on the value of the check, the values are mapped to that element by the function. The applymap() function will then be called on the object. If you look at the data frame now, you'll see that it is neater than before.

```
>>>

>>> towns_df.head()
```

	State	RegionName
0	Alabama	Auburn
1	Alabama	Florence
2	Alabama	Jacksonville
3	Alabama	Livingston
4	Alabama	Montevallo

In the above section of the code, the applymap() method looked at every element in the data frame and passed that element to the function, after which the returned value was used to replace the original value. It is this simple.

The applymap() method is both a convenient and versatile method. However, this method can take some time to run for large data sets. This is because it maps every individual element to a Python callable. So, it is always a good idea to use vectorized operations that use the NumPy or Cython directories.

There are times when you'll have data sets that have some unnecessary or unimportant information in the first or last rows or column names that are difficult to understand. For example, there can be some definitions or footnotes in the data set which are not necessary for you to use. In cases such as these, you should skip those rows or rename the columns so you can remove the unnecessary information or work with sensible labels.

Let's first review the first few rows in the Olympics.csv data set before we go over how this can be accomplished.

```
$ head -n 5 Datasets/olympics.csv

0,1,2,3,4,5,6,7,8,9,10,11,12,13,14,15

,? Summer,01 !,02 !,03 !,Total,? Winter,01 !,02 !,03 !,Total,? Games,01 !,02 !,03 !,Combined total

Afghanistan (AFG),13,0,0,2,2,0,0,0,0,0,13,0,0,2,2

Algeria (ALG),12,5,2,8,15,3,0,0,0,0,15,5,2,8,15

Argentina (ARG),23,18,24,28,70,18,0,0,0,0,41,18,24,28,70
```

Now, we'll read it into a Pandas data frame:

```
>>>

>>> olympics_df = pd.read_csv('Datasets/olympics.csv')

>>> olympics_df.head()
        0          1   2  3     4    5        6   7  8 \
0     NaN   ? Summer  01 ! 02 ! 03 ! Total ? Winter  01 ! 02 !
```

1	Afghanistan (AFG)	13	0		0	2	2	0	0
	0								
2	Algeria (ALG)	12	5		2	8			15
	3	0	0						
3	Argentina (ARG)	23	18		24	28	70		
18	0	0							
4	Armenia (ARM)	5	1	2	9	12	6	0	0

	9	10	11	12	13	14	15
0	03 !	Total	? Games	01 !	02 !	03 !	Combined total
1	0 0	13	0	0	2		2
2	0 0	15	5	2	8		15
3	0 0	41	18	24	28		70
4	0 0	11	1	2	9		12

This is certainly messy. Every column is indexed at zero and is the string form of the integer. The row that you are using to set the names of the other columns is at the Olympics_df.iloc[0]. This is because the file that we're using starts the indexing at 0 and ends at 15.

If you want to go to the source of the data set, you will see that Nan above a column will represent Country, "? Summer" will represent the Summer Games, "01!" represents Gold, etc. Therefore, we will need to do the following:

Skip the first row and set the index as zero for the headers.

Rename all the columns.

You can pass some parameters in the read.csv() function if you want to skip some rows and set the index for the headers as one. The function read.csv does use a lot of parameters, but in this instance, we only need to remove the first row (which has the index zero).

```
>>>

>>> olympics_df = pd.read_csv('Datasets/olympics.csv', header=1)

>>> olympics_df.head()
```

	Unnamed: 0	? Summer	01 !	02 !	03 !	Total	? Winter \
0	Afghanistan (AFG)	13	0	0	2	2	0
1	Algeria (ALG)	12	5	2	8	15	3
2	Argentina (ARG)	23	18		24	28	70
	18						
3	Armenia (ARM)	5	1	2	9	12	6

4 Australasia (ANZ) [ANZ]   2   3 4   5   12
        0

	01 !.1	02 !.1	03 !.1	Total.1	?	Games	01 !.2	02 !.2	03 !.2 \
0	0		0	0	0		13	0	0	2
1	0	0	0	0		15	5	2	8	
2	0	0	0	0		41	18	24	28	
3	0		0	0	0		11	1	2	9
4	0		0	0	0		2	3	4	5

Combined total

	Combined total
0	2
1	15
2	70
3	12
4	12

The data set no longer has any unnecessary rows, and the correct names have been used for all fields. You should see how the Pandas library has changed the name of the Countries column from NaN to Unnamed: 0.

To rename the columns, we will use the rename() method in the data frame. This will allow you to relabel any axis in the data set using a mapping. In this instance, we will need to use dict. We must first define the dictionary, which will map the existing names of the columns to the usable names which are present in the dictionary.

```
>>>

>>> new_names = {'Unnamed: 0': 'Country',

'? Summer': 'Summer Olympics',

'01 !': 'Gold',

'02 !': 'Silver',

'03 !': 'Bronze',

'? Winter': 'Winter Olympics',

'01 !.1': 'Gold.1',

'02 !.1': 'Silver.1',

'03 !.1': 'Bronze.1',

'? Games': '# Games',

'01 !.2': 'Gold.2',
```

'02 !.2': 'Silver.2',

'03 !.2': 'Bronze.2'}

We will now call upon the rename() function on the object.

>>>

>>>   olympics_df.rename(columns=new_names, inplace=True)

If you want changes to be made directly to the object, you should set inplace to true. Let's see if this works for us:

>>>

>>> olympics_df.head()

Country	Summer Olympics	Gold	Silver	Bronze	Total \
0	Afghanistan (AFG) 13	0	0	2	2
1	Algeria (ALG) 12	5	2	8	15
2	Argentina (ARG) 23	18	24	28	70
3	Armenia (ARM) 5	1	2	9	12
4	Australasia (ANZ) [ANZ] 2 12	3	4	5	

Winter Olympics	Gold.1	Silver.1	Bronze.1	Total.1	# Games	Gold.2 \
0	0	0	0	0	13	0
1	3	0	0	0	15	5
2	18	0	0	0	41	18
3	6	0	0	0	11	1
4	0	0	0	0	2	3

Silver.2	Bronze.2	Combined	total
0	0	2	2
1	2	8	15
2	24	28	70
3	2	9	12
4	4	5	12

In this chapter, you've gathered information on how you can remove any unnecessary fields in a data set and how you can set an index for every field in the data set to make it easier for you to access that field.

You've also learned how you can use the applymap() function to clean the complete data set and to use the .str() accessor to clean specific object fields. It's important to know how to clean data since it is a big part of data analytics, and you should now know how you can use NumPy and Pandas to clean different data sets.

Chapter Ten

How to Manipulate Data Using Python

———◆———

In this chapter, we'll learn more about how we can use the NumPy and Pandas libraries to manipulate data.

Starting with Numpy

Load the library and check its version, just to make sure we aren't using an older version

> import numpy as np:
>
> np.__version__
>
> '1.12.1'

Create a list comprising numbers from 0 to 9:

> L = list(range(10))

The style of handling lists that involves converting integers to string is known as list comprehension.

List comprehension offers a versatile way to handle list manipulations tasks easily. We'll learn about them in future tutorials. We have provided an example below.

[str(c) for c in L]

['0', '1', '2', '3', '4', '5', '6', '7', '8', '9']

[type(item) for item in L]

[int, int, int, int, int, int, int, int, int, int]

Creating Arrays

Arrays created in NumPy are always homogeneous in nature. This means that they can only hold variables of the same data type.

Creating arrays:

np.zeros(10, dtype='int')

array([0, 0, 0, 0, 0, 0, 0, 0, 0, 0])

Creating a 3 row x 5 column matrix:

np.ones((3,5), dtype=float)

array([[1., 1., 1., 1., 1.],

[1., 1., 1., 1., 1.],

[1., 1., 1., 1., 1.]])

Creating a matrix with a predefined value:

```
np.full((3,5),1.23)

array([[ 1.23,  1.23,  1.23,  1.23,  1.23],
       [ 1.23,  1.23,  1.23,  1.23,  1.23],
       [ 1.23,  1.23,  1.23,  1.23,  1.23]])
```

Create an array with a set sequence:

```
np.arange(0, 20, 2)

array([0, 2, 4, 6, 8,10,12,14,16,18])
```

Create an array of even space between the given range of values:

```
np.linspace(0, 1, 5)

array([ 0., 0.25, 0.5 , 0.75, 1.])
```

Create a 3x3 array with mean 0 and standard deviation 1 in a given dimension:

```
np.random.normal(0, 1, (3,3))

array([[ 0.72432142, -0.90024075,  0.27363808],
```

[0.88426129, 1.45096856, -1.03547109],

[-0.42930994, -1.02284441, -1.59753603]])

Create an identity matrix:

np.eye(3)

array([[1., 0., 0.],

[0., 1., 0.],

[0., 0., 1.]])

 Set a random seed:

np.random.seed(0)

 x1 = np.random.randint(10, size=6) #one dimension

x2 = np.random.randint(10, size=(3,4)) #two dimension

x3 = np.random.randint(10, size=(3,4,5)) #three dimension

 print("x3 ndim:", x3.ndim)

print("x3 shape:", x3.shape)

```
print("x3 size: ", x3.size)
```

('x3 ndim:', 3)

('x3 shape:', (3, 4, 5))

('x3 size: ', 60)

Array Indexing

You must remember that indexing in Python always begins at zero.

```
x1 = np.array([4, 3, 4, 4, 8, 4])
```

```
x1
```

array([4, 3, 4, 4, 8, 4])

Assess value to index zero:

```
x1[0]
```

4

Assess fifth value:

```
x1[4]
```

8

Get the last value:

x1[-1]

4

Get the second last value:

x1[-2]

8

In a multidimensional array, we need to specify row and column index:

x2

array([[3, 7, 5, 5],

[0, 1, 5, 9],

[3, 0, 5, 0]])

1st row and 2nd column value:

x2[2,3]

0

3rd row and last value from the 3rd column:

x2[2,-1]

0

Replace value at 0,0 index:

x2[0,0] = 12

x2

array([[12, 7, 5, 5],

[0, 1, 5, 9],

[3, 0, 5, 0]])

Array Slicing

Let's now see how we can access a range of elements or multiple elements in an array.

x = np.arange(10)

x

array([0, 1, 2, 3, 4, 5, 6, 7, 8, 9])

From start to 4th position:

x[:5]

array([0, 1, 2, 3, 4])

From 4th position to end:

x[4:]

array([4, 5, 6, 7, 8, 9])

From 4th to 6th position:

x[4:7]

array([4, 5, 6])

Return elements at even place:

x[: : 2]

array([0, 2, 4, 6, 8])

Return elements from first position step by two:

x[1::2]

array([1, 3, 5, 7, 9])

Reverse the array:

x[::-1]

array([9, 8, 7, 6, 5, 4, 3, 2, 1, 0])

Array Concatenation

There will be times when you'll need to combine multiple arrays. Instead of typing the elements manually, you can concatenate them to make it easier to handle such tasks.

You can concatenate two or more arrays at once:

x = np.array([1, 2, 3])

y = np.array([3, 2, 1])

z = [21,21,21]

np.concatenate([x, y,z])

array([1, 2, 3, 3, 2, 1, 21, 21, 21])

You can also use this function to create 2-dimensional arrays:

grid = np.array([[1,2,3],[4,5,6]])

np.concatenate([grid,grid])

array([[1, 2, 3],

[4, 5, 6],

[1, 2, 3],

[4, 5, 6]])

Using its axis parameter, you can define row-wise or column-wise matrix:

np.concatenate([grid,grid],axis=1)

array([[1, 2, 3, 1, 2, 3],

[4, 5, 6, 4, 5, 6]])

Until now, we have only used the concatenation function on arrays that have the same dimension. So, what should you do if you want to combine a one-dimensional array with a two-dimensional array? You should use the np.hstack or np.vstack in such instances. Let's take a look at how this can be accomplished.

x = np.array([3,4,5])

grid = np.array([[1,2,3],[17,18,19]])

np.vstack([x,grid])

array([[3, 4, 5],

[1, 2, 3],

[17, 18, 19]])

Similarly, you can add an array using np.hstack:

z = np.array([[9],[9]])

np.hstack([grid,z])

array([[1, 2, 3, 9],

[17, 18, 19, 9]])

You can use some predefined conditions or positions to split the array.

x = np.arange(10)

x

array([0, 1, 2, 3, 4, 5, 6, 7, 8, 9])

```
x1,x2,x3 = np.split(x,[3,6])

print x1,x2,x3

[0 1 2] [3 4 5] [6 7 8 9]


grid = np.arange(16).reshape((4,4))

grid

upper,lower = np.vsplit(grid,[2])

print (upper, lower)

(array([[0, 1, 2, 3],

  [4, 5, 6, 7]]), array([[ 8,  9, 10, 11],

  [12, 13, 14, 15]]))
```

Apart from the functions used above, there are many mathematical ones in the NumPy directories that you can use. Some examples are sum, divide, abs, multiple, mod, power, log, sin, tan, cos, mean, min, max, and var. These functions can be used to perform some arithmetic calculations. You should refer to the NumPy documentation to understand them.

We will now delve into the Pandas directories. You must ensure that you read every line carefully to ensure that you perform data manipulation well.

Let's Start with Pandas

Load library - pd is just an alias. We have used pd because it's short and literally abbreviates pandas.

You can use any name as an alias.

import pandas as pd

Create a data frame; dictionary is used here where keys get converted to column names and values to row values:

```
data = pd.DataFrame({'Country':
['Russia','Colombia','Chile','Equador','Nigeria'],

'Rank':[121,40,100,130,11]})

data
```

Country		Rank
0	Russia	121
1	Colombia	40
2	Chile	100
3	Ecuador	130
4	Nigeria	11

We can do a quick analysis of any data set using:

data.describe()

Rank

count 5.000000

mean 80.400000

std   52.300096

min   11.000000

25%   40.000000

50%   100.000000

75%   121.000000

max   130.000000

You must remember that the method describe() will give you the summary statistics of the integer or double variables alone. If you want to obtain the complete information about the data set, you should use the info() function.

Among other things, it shows the data set has 5 rows and 2 columns with their respective names.

data.info()

```
<class 'pandas.core.frame.DataFrame'>

RangeIndex: 5 entries, 0 to 4

Data columns (total 2 columns):

Country          5 non-null object

Rank             5 non-null int64

dtypes: int64(1), object(1)

memory usage: 152.0+ bytes
```

Let's create another data frame.

```
data = pd.DataFrame({'group':['a', 'a', 'a', 'b','b', 'b', 'c', 'c','c'],'ounces':[4, 3, 12, 6, 7.5, 8, 3, 5, 6]})

data
```

group ounces

0   a   4.0

1   a   3.0

2   a   12.0

3   b   6.0

4	b	7.5
5	b	8.0
6	c	3.0
7	c	5.0
8	c	6.0

Let's sort the data frame by ounces - inplace = True will make changes to the data.

data.sort_values(by=['ounces'],ascending=True,inplace=False)

	group	ounces
1	a	3.0
6	c	3.0
0	a	4.0
7	c	5.0
3	b	6.0
8	c	6.0
4	b	7.5
5	b	8.0

| 2 | a | 12.0 |

You can now sort the data using multiple columns.

```
data.sort_values(by=['group','ounces'],ascending=[True,Fals
e],inplace=False)
```

group ounces

2	a	12.0
0	a	4.0
1	a	3.0
5	b	8.0
4	b	7.5
3	b	6.0
8	c	6.0
7	c	5.0
6	c	3.0

We often get a data set that has duplicate rows, and these rows are only noise. It is for this reason that you must remove any such inconsistencies in the data set before you train the model. Let us now see how we can remove the duplicate rows.

Create another data with duplicate rows:

data = pd.DataFrame({'k1':['one']*3 + ['two']*4,
'k2':[3,2,1,3,3,4,4]})

data

	k1	k2
0	one	3
1	one	2
2	one	1
3	two	3
4	two	3
5	two	4
6	two	4

Sort values:

data.sort_values(by='k2')

	k1	k2
2	one	1
1	one	2

0	one	3
3	two	3
4	two	3
5	two	4

Remove duplicates:

data.drop_duplicates()

	k1	k2
0	one	3
1	one	2
2	one	1
3	two	3
5	two	4

In the above example, we have matched the values in the rows across all the columns to remove any duplicates. You can also remove them based on specific columns. Let's now remove all the duplicate values in the K1 column.

data.drop_duplicates(subset='k1')

	k1	k2

0	one	3
3	two	3

Now we'll learn how we can categorize the rows using some predefined criteria. This will happen quite a bit when you process data, especially that data where you will need to categorize some variables. For instance, let's assume that you have a column that includes the names of all the countries in it. You want to place those countries into their respective continents, and because of this, you will need to create a new variable.

You should follow the steps provided below:

data = pd.DataFrame({'food': ['bacon', 'pulled pork', 'bacon', 'Pastrami','corned beef', 'Bacon', 'pastrami', 'honey ham','nova lox'],

'ounces': [4, 3, 12, 6, 7.5, 8, 3, 5, 6]})

data

	food	ounces
0	bacon	4.0
1	pulled pork	3.0
2	bacon	12.0
3	Pastrami	6.0

4	corned beef	7.5
5	Bacon	8.0
6	pastrami	3.0
7	honey ham	5.0
8	nova lox	6.0

We'll now create some new variables that will indicate what type of animal will act as the source of food for another. For this, we will first need to map the food to the animals using the dictionary. We can then use the map function to map the values in the dictionary to the keys. Let's take a look at how this can be done:

```
meat_to_animal = {

'bacon': 'pig',

'pulled pork': 'pig',

'pastrami': 'cow',

'corned beef': 'cow',

'honey ham': 'pig',

'nova lox': 'salmon'

}
```

```python
def meat_2_animal(series):

if series['food'] == 'bacon':

return 'pig'

elif series['food'] == 'pulled pork':

return 'pig'

elif series['food'] == 'pastrami':

return 'cow'

elif series['food'] == 'corned beef':

return 'cow'

elif series['food'] == 'honey ham':

return 'pig'

else:

return 'salmon'
```

Create a new variable:

```
data['animal']                                      =
data['food'].map(str.lower).map(meat_to_animal)

data
```

	food	ounces	animal
0	bacon	4.0	pig
1	pulled pork	3.0	pig
2	bacon	12.0	pig
3	Pastrami	6.0	cow
4	corned beef	7.5	cow
5	Bacon	8.0	pig
6	pastrami	3.0	cow
7	honey ham	5.0	pig
8	nova lox	6.0	salmon

Another way of doing it is to convert the food values to the lower case and apply the function:

```
lower = lambda x: x.lower()

data['food'] = data['food'].apply(lower)

data['animal2'] = data.apply(meat_2_animal, axis='columns')
```

data

	food	ounces	animal	animal2
0	bacon	4.0	pig	pig
1	pulled pork	3.0	pig	pig
2	bacon	12.0	pig	pig
3	pastrami	6.0	cow	cow
4	corned beef	7.5	cow	cow
5	bacon	8.0	pig	pig
6	pastrami	3.0	cow	cow
7	honey ham	5.0	pig	pig
8	nova lox	6.0	salmon	salmon

You can use the assign function to create another variable. This chapter will teach you some new functions that you'll need to keep in mind. You will also find out why it's important to understand the Pandas directory well.

```
data.assign(new_variable = data['ounces']*10)
```

food   ounces   animal   animal2
new_variable

	food	ounces	animal2	animal2	
0	bacon	4.0	pig	pig	40.0
1	pulled pork	3.0	pig	pig	30.0
2	bacon	12.0	pig	pig	120.0
3	pastrami	6.0	cow	cow	60.0
4	corned beef	7.5	cow	cow	75.0
5	bacon	8.0	pig	pig	80.0
6	pastrami	3.0	cow	cow	30.0
7	honey ham	5.0	pig	pig	50.0
8	nova lox	6.0	salmon	salmon	60.0

Let us now remove the animal2 column from the data frame:

```
data.drop('animal2',axis='columns',inplace=True)

data
```

	food	ounces	animal
0	bacon	4.0	pig
1	pulled pork	3.0	pig
2	bacon	12.0	pig
3	Pastrami	6.0	cow

4	corned beef	7.5	cow
5	Bacon	8.0	pig
6	pastrami	3.0	cow
7	honey ham	5.0	pig
8	nova lox	6.0	salmon

There are times when you will find some missing values in the data set. You can choose to input a missing value in the data set with any random number. There is a probability of there being outliers in the data set, and you can use some dummy or default values as a substitute to those values. Let's see how we can replace them in the data set.

The series function from pandas are used to create arrays:

data = pd.Series([1., -999., 2., -999., -1000., 3.])

data

0	1.0
1	-999.0
2	2.0
3	-999.0
4	-1000.0

5   3.0

dtype: float64

Replace -999 with NaN values:

    data.replace(-999, np.nan,inplace=True)

    data

0   1.0

1   NaN

2   2.0

3   NaN

4   -1000.0

5   3.0

        dtype: float64

We can also replace multiple values at once:

    data = pd.Series([1., -999., 2., -999., -1000., 3.])

    data.replace([-999,-1000],np.nan,inplace=True)

data

0   1.0

1   NaN

2   2.0

3   NaN

4   NaN

5   3.0

  dtype: float64

Now, take a look at how we can rename the rows and columns:

data = pd.DataFrame(np.arange(12).reshape((3, 4)),index=['Ohio', 'Colorado', 'New York'],columns=['one', 'two', 'three', 'four'])

data

	one	two	three	four
Ohio	0	1	2	3
Colorado	4	5	6	7
New York	8	9	10	11

Using rename function:

```
data.rename(index = {'Ohio':'SanF'},
columns={'one':'one_p','two':'two_p'},inplace=True)
```

data

	one_p	two_p	three	four
SanF	0	1	2	3
Colorado	4	5	6	7
New York	8	9	10	11

You can also use string functions:

```
data.rename(index = str.upper,
columns=str.title,inplace=True)
```

data

	One_p	Two_p	Three	Four
SANF	0	1	2	3
COLORADO	4	5	6	7
NEW YORK	8	9	10	11

We will need to split or categorize the continuous variables.

```
ages = [20, 22, 25, 27, 21, 23, 37, 31, 61, 45, 41, 32]
```

We'll now divide the ages into smaller segments, or bins, like 18-25, 26-35,36-60, and 60 and above.

Understand the output - '(' means the value is included in the bin, '[' means the value is excluded:

bins = [18, 25, 35, 60, 100]

cats = pd.cut(ages, bins)

cats

[(18, 25], (18, 25], (18, 25], (25, 35], (18, 25], ..., (25, 35], (60, 100], (35, 60], (35, 60], (25, 35]]

Length: 12

Categories (4, object): [(18, 25] < (25, 35] < (35, 60] < (60, 100]]

To include the right bin value, we can do:

pd.cut(ages,bins,right=False)

[[18, 25), [18, 25), [25, 35), [25, 35), [18, 25), ..., [25, 35), [60, 100), [35, 60), [35, 60), [25, 35)]

Length: 12

Categories (4, object): [[18, 25) < [25, 35) < [35, 60) < [60, 100)]

The Pandas library intrinsically assigns an encoding to categorical variables:

cats.labels

array([0, 0, 0, 1, 0, 0, 2, 1, 3, 2, 2, 1], dtype=int8)

Let's check how many observations fall under each bin:

pd.value_counts(cats)

(18, 25]   5

(35, 60]   3

(25, 35]   3

(60, 100]   1

dtype: int64

We can also pass a name to every label.

bin_names = ['Youth', 'YoungAdult', 'MiddleAge', 'Senior']

new_cats = pd.cut(ages, bins,labels=bin_names)

pd.value_counts(new_cats)

Youth   5

MiddleAge   3

YoungAdult 3

Senior   1

dtype: int64

Additionally, we can calculate their cumulative sum:

pd.value_counts(new_cats).cumsum()

Youth   5

MiddleAge   3

YoungAdult 3

Senior   1

dtype: int64

Let's learn more about how we can group data and create pivots using the Pandas directories. It's important to learn how to create a pivot table since it's one of the easiest analysis methods that you can use on any data set that you work with.

df = pd.DataFrame({'key1' : ['a', 'a', 'b', 'b', 'a'],

'key2' : ['one', 'two', 'one', 'two', 'one'],

'data1' : np.random.randn(5),

'data2' : np.random.randn(5)})

df

data1	data2	key1	key2
0	0.973599	0.001761	a
1	0.207283	-0.990160	a
2	1.099642	1.872394	b
3	0.939897	-0.241074	b
4	0.606389	0.053345	a

Calculate the mean of data1 column by key1:

grouped = df['data1'].groupby(df['key1'])

grouped.mean()

key1

a   0.595757

b   1.019769

Name: data1, dtype: float64

Now, let's look at how to slice the data frame.

```
dates = pd.date_range('20130101',periods=6)

df = pd.DataFrame(np.random.randn(6,4),index=dates,columns=list('ABCD'))

df
```

```
                   A         B         C         D
2013-01-01  1.030816 -1.276989  0.837720 -1.490111
2013-01-02 -1.070215 -0.209129  0.604572 -1.743058
2013-01-03  1.524227  1.863575  1.291378  1.300696
2013-01-04  0.918203 -0.158800 -0.964063 -1.990779
2013-01-05  0.089731  0.114854 -0.585815  0.298772
2013-01-06  0.222260  0.435183 -0.045748  0.049898
```

Get first n rows from the data frame:

```
df[:3]
```

```
                   A         B         C         D
```

2013-01-01 1.030816 -1.276989 0.837720 -1.490111

2013-01-02 -1.070215-0.209129 0.604572 -1.743058

2013-01-03 1.524227 1.863575   1.291378
     1.300696

Slice based on date range:

df['20130101':'20130104']

        A   B   C   D

2013-01-01 1.030816 -1.276989 0.837720 -1.490111

2013-01-02 -1.070215-0.209129 0.604572 -1.743058

2013-01-03 1.524227 1.863575   1.291378
     1.300696

2013-01-04 0.918203 -0.158800 -0.964063 -1.990779

Slicing based on column names:

df.loc[:,['A','B']]

        A   B

2013-01-01 1.030816 -1.276989

2013-01-02 -1.070215-0.209129

2013-01-03 1.524227 1.863575

2013-01-04 0.918203 -0.158800

2013-01-05 0.089731 0.114854

2013-01-06 0.222260 0.435183

Slicing based on both row index labels and column names:

df.loc['20130102':'20130103',['A','B']]

     A B

2013-01-02 -1.070215-0.209129

2013-01-03 1.524227 1.863575

Slicing based on index of columns:

df.iloc[3] #returns 4th row (index is 3rd)

A 0.918203

B -0.158800

C -0.964063

D -1.990779

Name: 2013-01-04 00:00:00, dtype: float64

Returns a specific range of rows:

df.iloc[2:4, 0:2]

	A	B
2013-01-03	1.524227	1.863575
2013-01-04	0.918203	-0.158800

Returns specific rows and columns using lists containing columns or row indexes:

df.iloc[[1,5],[0,2]]

	A	C
2013-01-02	-1.070215	0.604572
2013-01-06	0.222260	-0.045748

You can also perform boolean indexing using the values in the columns. This will help you filter the data set based on some conditions. These conditions must be pre-defined.

df[df.A > 1]

	A	B	C	D
2013-01-01	1.030816	-1.276989	0.837720	-1.490111
2013-01-03	1.524227	1.863575	1.291378	1.300696

We can copy the data set:

```
df2 = df.copy()

df2['E']=['one', 'one','two','three','four','three']

df2
```

	A	B	C	D	E
2013-01-01	1.030816	-1.276989	0.837720	-1.490111	one
2013-01-02	-1.070215	-0.209129	0.604572	-1.743058	one
2013-01-03	1.524227	1.863575	1.291378	1.300696	two
2013-01-04	0.918203	-0.158800	-0.964063	-1.990779	three
2013-01-05	0.089731	0.114854	-0.585815	0.298772	four
2013-01-06	0.222260	0.435183	-0.045748	0.049898	three

Select rows based on column values:

```
df2[df2['E'].isin(['two','four'])]
```

	A	B	C	D	E
2013-01-03	1.524227	1.863575	1.291378	1.300696	two

2013-01-05 0.089731 0.114854   -0.585815   0.298772
   four

Select all rows except those with two and four:

  df2[~df2['E'].isin(['two','four'])]

          A   B   C   D   E

  2013-01-01 1.030816 -1.276989 0.837720 -1.490111
      one

  2013-01-02 -1.070215-0.209129 0.604572 -1.743058 one

  2013-01-04 0.918203 -0.158800   -0.964063   -1.990779
  three

  2013-01-06 0.222260 0.435183   -0.045748   0.049898
      three

You can also select columns using a query method. In this method, you will need to enter a criterion.

List all columns where A is greater than C:

  df.query('A > C')

  A   B   C   D

  2013-01-01 1.030816 -1.276989 0.837720 -1.490111

2013-01-03 1.524227 1.863575   1.291378
    1.300696

2013-01-04 0.918203 -0.158800 -0.964063 -1.990779

2013-01-05 0.089731 0.114854   -0.585815
    0.298772

2013-01-06 0.222260 0.435183   -0.045748 0.049898

Using OR condition:

df.query('A < B | C > A')

A   B   C   D

2013-01-02 -1.070215-0.209129 0.604572 -1.743058

2013-01-03 1.524227 1.863575   1.291378
    1.300696

2013-01-05 0.089731 0.114854   -0.585815
    0.298772

2013-01-06 0.222260 0.435183   -0.045748 0.049898

A pivot table is useful to analyze the data set since you customize the format. Excel is a tool that's utilized popularly because of the option to use a pivot table, which allows users to analyze data quickly.

Create a data frame:

```
data = pd.DataFrame({'group': ['a', 'a', 'a', 'b','b', 'b', 'c', 'c','c'],

        'ounces': [4, 3, 12, 6, 7.5, 8, 3, 5, 6]})

data
```

group ounces

0	a	4.0
1	a	3.0
2	a	12.0
3	b	6.0
4	b	7.5
5	b	8.0
6	c	3.0
7	c	5.0
8	c	6.0

Calculate the means of each group:

```
data.pivot_table(values='ounces',index='group',aggfunc=np.
mean)
```

group

a   6.333333

b   7.166667

c   4.666667

Name: ounces, dtype: float64

Calculate the count by each group:

data.pivot_table(values='ounces',index='group',aggfunc='count')

group

a   3

b   3

c   3

Name: ounces, dtype: int64

We have now become familiar with the basics of the Pandas library using the example above. We will review a real-life data set and see how we can use the information that we have gathered in this chapter to explore it.

Chapter Eleven

Python Environment for Deep Learning

---◆---

This chapter will provide you with information on the environment that you need to set up to use Python for deep learning. You must install the following software to build deep learning algorithms in Python:

- Python 2.7+

- Matplotlib

- SciPy with NumPy

- Theano

- Keras

- TensorFlow

Experts recommend that you install Python, Matplotlib, SciPy, and NumPy through the Anaconda distribution since it comes with all the packages. You must ensure that the different software you download is installed correctly. To import the libraries from the software listed above into Python, type the commands below in the command line program in Python.

$ python

Python 3.6.3 |Anaconda custom (32-bit)| (default, Oct 13 2017, 14:21:34)

[GCC 7.2.0] on Linux

Now, you should import the necessary libraries in Python and print their version numbers in the output window.

import numpy

print numpy.__version__

You will receive the version number of the installed software.

Installation of Keras, TensorFlow, and Theano

Before you install the packages from Keras, TensorFlow, and Theano, you should confirm that your machine has pip installed. Pip is the package management system in Anaconda.

You should type in the following command in Python to confirm if the pip has been installed:

$ pip

When Python confirms that the pip has been installed, you need to install Keras and TensorFlow using the command provided below.

$pip install theano

$pip install tensorflow

$pip install keras

To confirm if Theano has been installed in Python, you should type the following code:

$python –c "import theano: print (theano.__version__)"

Once you obtain the version number of Theano that has been installed in your system, you should confirm if TensorFlow has been installed in Python. You can do this by running the code below in Python:

$python   –c   "import   tensorflow: print tensorflow.__version__"

You should now confirm if Keras has been installed correctly in your system. Type the following line in Python to verify the same.

$python –c "import keras: print keras.__version__"

Using TensorFlow backend:

You will receive the version number of TensorFlow that is installed in your system.

Chapter Twelve

Regression Problem Using Keras

————————◆————————

In this chapter, you will learn more about how you can develop and evaluate a neural network model in Keras to solve a regression problem. Once you are completed with this chapter, you will know how to do the following:

- Load the CSV data set into Keras and make it available for use.

- Create a neural network model to solve the regression problem.

- Use scikit-learn in Keras and evaluate the model using the method of cross-validation.

- Prepare the data set well to improve the accuracy and predictions of the model.

- Tune or improve the network topology for different models using Keras.

In this chapter, we will be looking at the Boston house prices data set. You can download this data set from the following location:

https://www.kaggle.com/vikrishnan/boston-house-prices. Download the data set it into your current working directory, and rename the file to housing.csv.

You'll look at thirteen different properties of the houses in the suburbs in Boston. These properties are numerical in nature, and the problem is concerned with modeling the price of the houses in thousands of dollars. This is an example of a regression predictive model. The input variables include proportion of non-retail business land, crime rate, chemical concentration in soil, and more.

This problem has been studied well by most people working with machine learning. This is because the data set is easy to work with since both the input and output variables are numerical. You can work with close to 506 instances in this problem.

The performance of the model is evaluated using the mean squared error (MSE), and the expected output is around $4,500 or 20 in squared thousands of dollars. This is a good target to aim for in the neural network model.

Develop the Baseline Model

Using this section, you can create or develop a baseline model that you can use to solve the regression problem. Let's first begin by including the objects and functions that we will be using to solve this problem.

```
import numpy

import pandas

from keras.models import Sequential

from keras.layers import Dense

from keras.wrappers.scikit_learn import KerasRegressor

from sklearn.model_selection import cross_val_score

from sklearn.model_selection import KFold

from sklearn.preprocessing import StandardScaler

from sklearn.pipeline import Pipeline
```

You can now load the data set into the local directory using a file.

The data set that you have downloaded is not in the CSV format from the location you have downloaded the file from. The attributes in the data set are separated using whitespaces. You should use the Pandas library to load it onto the system. It's a good idea to split the input variables as X and the output variables as Y since that will make it easier for you to build the model in Keras using scikit-learn.

load data set

```
dataframe          =          pandas.read_csv("housing.csv",
delim_whitespace=True, header=None)
```

```
dataset = dataframe.values
```

split into input (X) and output (Y) variables

```
X = dataset[:,0:13]

Y = dataset[:,13]
```

You can create and evaluate a neural network model in Keras with scikit-learn by using some handy wrapper objects that you can call from the Keras library. It's always a good idea to do this since scikit-learn is excellent at evaluating a model. This will also allow you to use different data preparation and model evaluation techniques by writing few lines of code.

Every Keras wrapper uses a function as an argument, and this function should be the one that you use to create the neural network model that you wish to evaluate.

The function that we'll be using to create the model is defined below. This is a sample model that has 13 neurons, which is the same as the number of attributes in the input. It also has one hidden layer that is fully connected. This network will use practices like rectifier activation to activate the hidden layer. The output layer does not require any activation function since this is a regression problem, and we only want to ensure that the right numbers are being predicted and that there's no transformation required for the data.

In the model below, we will be using the ADAM optimization algorithm and the mean squared error loss function to test the accuracy and performance of the algorithm. The latter is one of the best ways to evaluate the model, since it will use the square root of the error, making it easier for you to understand the issue with the algorithm.

define base model

```
def baseline_model():
```

create model

```
model = Sequential()

model.add(Dense(13, input_dim=13,
kernel_initializer='normal', activation='relu'))

model.add(Dense(1, kernel_initializer='normal'))
```

Compile model

```
model.compile(loss='mean_squared_error',
optimizer='adam')

return model
```

The Keras wrapper object for use in scikit-learn as a regression estimator is called KerasRegressor. We create an instance and pass it both the name of the function to create the neural network model and some parameters to pass along to the fit() function of the model later, such as the number of epochs and batch size. Both of these are set to sensible defaults.

We also initialize the random number generator with a constant random seed, a process we will repeat for each model evaluated in this tutorial. This is an attempt to ensure we compare models consistently.

```
1# fix random seed for reproducibility
2seed = 7
3numpy.random.seed(seed)
4# evaluate model with standardized data set
5estimator = KerasRegressor(build_fn=baseline_model,
  epochs=100,
  batch_size=5, verbose=0)
```

The final step is to evaluate this baseline model. We will use 10-fold cross-validation to evaluate the model.

```
1kfold = KFold(n_splits=10, random_state=seed)
2results = cross_val_score(estimator, X, Y, cv=kfold)
```

```
3print("Results: %.2f (%.2f) MSE" % (results.mean(),

results.std()))
```

Running this code gives us an estimate of the model's performance on the problem for unseen data. The result reports the mean squared error, including the average and standard deviation (average variance) across all ten folds of the cross-validation evaluation.

```
1Baseline: 31.64 (26.82) MSE
```

Modeling a Standardized Data Set

There is one important concern about the Boston house price data set; it's hard to work with these attributes since they are each measured on a different scale due to being used to measure numerous quantities. Therefore, you should prepare the data in advance if you want to use a neural network model. You can re-evaluate the model that we are using above by utilizing a standardized version of the Boston house price data set.

If you'd like to use the cross-validation technique to test the efficiency of the model using the standard data set, it's best to utilize the Pipeline framework found in scikit-learn. This will help to ensure that there is no leakage in the data during the cross-validation testing.

In the code below, we are trying to standardize the data set and then build a model and evaluate that model.

evaluate model with standardized data set

```
numpy.random.seed(seed)

estimators = []

estimators.append(('standardize', StandardScaler()))

estimators.append(('mlp',
KerasRegressor(build_fn=baseline_model,        epochs=50,
batch_size=5, verbose=0)))

pipeline = Pipeline(estimators)

kfold = KFold(n_splits=10, random_state=seed)

results = cross_val_score(pipeline, X, Y, cv=kfold)

print("Standardized: %.2f (%.2f) MSE" % (results.mean(),
results.std()))
```

When you run an example on this model, you can improve the performance of this model when compared to the baseline model. This can be done without having to standardize the data, thereby reducing the error.

```
Standardized: 29.54 (27.87) MSE
```

If you want to take it one step further, you can rescale the output variable by using a sigmoid or any other activation function and by normalizing it between the range 0 and 1. This will ensure that the output variables or predictions lie within the same range.

Tune the Network Topology

It's easy to optimize many of the concerns that are associated with the neural network model. This is one the biggest advantages of the structure of the neural network. This includes the number of neurons in every layer and the number of layers in the network.

In this section, we will look at two different network topologies that can be used to improve the performance or the accuracy of the model. The models we will be looking at include the deeper network topology and the wider network topology.

Evaluate a Deeper Network Topology

If you want to improve the performance or accuracy of a neural network, you should try to add more layers to it. This will allow the model to combine and extract some high order features that are not clear to the human eye.

In this section, we'll look at how the model will react when we add an additional hidden layer to it. It's simple to do this since the process is as easy as defining a function. This will help to create a new model that's deeper. However, this model is a copy of the baseline model that we've created in the sections above. All we're doing is inserting a new layer immediately after the first hidden layer, but this new layer will only have half the number of neurons as the first hidden one.

define the model

```
def larger_model():
# create model
    model = Sequential()
    model.add(Dense(13, input_dim=13,
    kernel_initializer='normal', activation='relu'))
    model.add(Dense(6, kernel_initializer='normal',
    activation='relu'))
    model.add(Dense(1, kernel_initializer='normal'))
# Compile model
    model.compile(loss='mean_squared_error',
    optimizer='adam')
    return model
```

The network topology will now look as follows: 13 inputs -> [13 -> 6] -> 1 output

This network topology can then be evaluated in the same way as the baseline neural network model. You can also use the standardization of the data set shown above if you want to improve the performance of the model.

```
numpy.random.seed(seed)

estimators = []

estimators.append(('standardize', StandardScaler()))

estimators.append(('mlp',
KerasRegressor(build_fn=larger_model, epochs=50,
batch_size=5, verbose=0)))

pipeline = Pipeline(estimators)

kfold = KFold(n_splits=10, random_state=seed)

results = cross_val_score(pipeline, X, Y, cv=kfold)

print("Larger: %.2f (%.2f) MSE" % (results.mean(),
results.std()))
```

When you run this model, you'll see that the performance has improved, since the error has decreased to 24,000 squared dollars from 28,000 squared dollars.

Larger: 22.83 (25.33) MSE

Evaluate a Wider Network Topology

You can also improve the representation capacity of the model using a wider network. In this section, we will look at how making a change to the number of neurons in the hidden layer will impact the performance of the algorithm. In this model, we will maintain the shallow network architecture but will double the number of neurons in one of the hidden layers. For this, all you need to do is define a function that will allow you to create a neural network model. In this function, the number of neurons has been increased to 20.

```
# define wider model

        def wider_model():

# create model

        model = Sequential()

        model.add(Dense(20, input_dim=13,
        kernel_initializer='normal', activation='relu'))

        model.add(Dense(1, kernel_initializer='normal'))

# Compile model

        model.compile(loss='mean_squared_error',
        optimizer='adam')

        return model
```

The network topology will now look like this: 13 inputs -> [20] -> 1 output

You can use the same method or scheme used above to evaluate the wider network.

```
numpy.random.seed(seed)

estimators = []

estimators.append(('standardize', StandardScaler()))

estimators.append(('mlp',
KerasRegressor(build_fn=wider_model, epochs=100,
batch_size=5, verbose=0)))

pipeline = Pipeline(estimators)

kfold = KFold(n_splits=10, random_state=seed)

results = cross_val_score(pipeline, X, Y, cv=kfold)

print("Wider: %.2f (%.2f) MSE" % (results.mean(),
results.std()))
```

You can only see a 21,000 squared dollars drop in the error value after you build this model, which is not a bad solution for this problem. The error value will be the following: Wider: 21.64 (23.75) MSE.

Most people do not understand that it's ideal to use a wider network, since it does outperform a deeper network on such a platform. It is for this reason that you should perform empirical tests while working on developing a neural network model.

Chapter Thirteen

How to Develop a Neural Network in Python Using Keras

————•◆•————

Now that you have the necessary libraries in Python, you can build your first neural network using Keras.

Load Data

If you want to use a machine-learning algorithm that only implements stochastic models to generate output, you must use a seed. This is to ensure that you can run the same code repeatedly and still generate a matching result. You should use this method if you want to compare the results from different models or algorithms for the same data or to debug some part of the code.

You can initialize a random number generator with any number as the seed. For example:

```
from keras.models import Sequential

from keras.layers import Dense

import numpy

numpy.random.seed(7)
```

The last statement in the code above allows you to fix a random seed that you can use to reproduce the results.

Now, you can load the data into Python. For the examples in this chapter, we will use a data set from the UCI Machine Learning Repository. The data set we'll be using is the Pima Indians onset of diabetes. This data set contains medical records of multiple patients for Pima India and provides information on whether or not they developed diabetes in five years.

This is a binary classification problem, since you are only checking whether the patient has developed diabetes, where the onset of diabetes is labeled 1 and no diabetes is labeled as 0. The input variables used in the data set are numerical, which means that you can use it when you work with neural networks that need numerical input and output values. This is an ideal example to use for your first neural network. Please download the data set from the following location:

https://raw.githubusercontent.com/jbrownlee/Datasets/master/pima-indians-diabetes.data.csv

Move the data set to the local working directory where you have saved the Python file, and save it with a file name. Now, you can load the file into Python using the function loadtxt(), which is a NumPy function. Go through the data set, and try to understand the different variables in the set.

The data set has one output variable in the last column and eight input variables. Once you load the data into Python, you can split the data into input and output variables.

dataset = numpy.loadtxt("file_name.csv", delimiter=",")

X = dataset[:,0:8]

Y = dataset[:,8]

In the first statement of the code above, you are loading the data set into Python. Remember to name the data set once you download it. The second and third statements of the code split the data into the input (X) and output (Y) variables. There are nine columns in the data set, and the range in the second line of the code, 0:8, will select the columns with their index between 0 and 7.

In the first part of this section, we defined the seed. Now, we will work on defining the neural network model.

Define the Model

You will use a sequence of layers when defining a model in Keras. In this section, you'll learn how to develop a sequential model and add layers to that model one at a time. You can stop adding layers to the model once you are happy with the topology of the network.

You'll first need to ensure that the input layer in your model has the correct number of inputs. You can specify this when you create the first layer using the argument input dim and set it to eight for each of the input variables. You may wonder how you'll know the number of layers and what their types are. This is a difficult question to answer, but you can use the trial and error method to understand the network structure better. You only need to worry about building a model that will capture the problem and understand if the network can solve the problem or not.

In the example in this section, we'll use a network structure that has three layers and is fully connected.

You can define the fully connected layers in Python using the Dense class. You can specify the number of neurons in each layer as the first argument, init (the initialization method) as the second argument, and use the activation argument to specify the activation function.

In the example below, we'll assign weights to the network using a small number generated from the uniform distribution. The weight is between the numbers 0 and 0.05 in the example below, since that's the default weight assigned to the neurons in Keras. An alternative would be to generate a random number from the normal, or Gaussian, distribution.

In this example, we will use the sigmoid function for the outer layer and the rectifier function for the first two layers of the network. Earlier, the tanh and sigmoid functions were used for all layers. Most engineers have moved from the tanh activation function to the rectifier activation function to enhance the performance of the network.

The sigmoid function is used on the output layer to ensure that the output is only between 0 and 1. The function makes it easy for the network to map the data into different classes with probabilities 0 and 1 using a threshold of 0.5.

```
model = Sequential()

model.add(Dense(12, input_dim=8, activation='relu'))

model.add(Dense(8, activation='relu'))

model.add(Dense(1, activation='sigmoid'))
```

In the model we have created above, the first layer has eight input variables and twelve neurons, the second layer (the hidden layer) has eight neurons, and the output layer has only one neuron to predict whether the patient has diabetes or not.

Compile the Model

Once you have defined the model, you can compile it. Python uses the libraries Theano and TensorFlow to do this because they have efficient numerical libraries. These libraries are at the backend, and they decide how the system should represent the network for training or making predictions. The backend will decide if the system should distribute the functions of the network evenly between the CPU and GPU or if it should only use the CPU or GPU.

When you want to compile the model, you should define some additional properties that are necessary to train the network. By this, we mean that you should let the network identify the weights or a set of weights it should use to predict the results for the problem. You should also specify the loss function that you will use to evaluate the calculated weights, the optimizer to search for different weights in the network, and any other metrics that you want to collect during the training.

In the example below, we use logarithmic loss, which is defined as "binary_crossentropy" in Keras for a binary classification problem. We will also use "adam", which is the gradient descent algorithm since it's an efficient default. Because we are solving a classification problem, we will report the accuracy of classification as the metric.

```
model.compile(loss='binary_crossentropy',
optimizer='adam', metrics=['accuracy'])
```

The code above is used to compile the model.

Fit the Model

Now that the model is defined and compiled, you can use it for computation. Enter some data to execute it. You can either fit or train your model by using the fit() function. When you train the network, the process will run for a specific number of iterations called epochs; you can specify the number of iterations using the nepochs statement. The model will run through the data set and assign weights to the different layers in the network. You can set the number of instances that the model can evaluate using the batch_size argument.

In the example below, we'll only run 150 iterations and use a batch size of 10. This means that we will only allow the model to define 10 instances. You can either increase or decrease the size once you have run the model a few times.

```
model.fit(X, Y, epochs=150, batch_size=10)
```

The code above fits the model.

Depending on what the model decides, the work will happen either on the CPU or GPU. For the example we are using, we do not require a GPU since the data set is not vast. If you want to run the code for a large data set, you can use GPU hardware that's available in the cloud.

Evaluate the Model

You have trained the neural network and let it run through the data set 150 times; now, you can evaluate how the neural network performs using the same data set. This will help you understand how well you have modeled it, but you will not gather information on how the model will perform on a new data set. In this example, we are using the same data set to train and evaluate the performance of your model, since it then makes it easier for you to understand how to test the model. You can split it into training and test data sets to train and evaluate your model.

You're able to evaluate the model using your training data set and the evaluate() function. Pass the same input and output that you used to train the model. The model will generate a prediction for every input and output pair and will also collect scores on any metrics that you have defined, such as average loss or accuracy.

You can use the following code to evaluate the model:

```
scores = model.evaluate(X, Y)

print("\n%s:     %.2f%%"  %  (model.metrics_names[1],
scores[1]*100))
```

Tie It All Together

Now that you know how to create a neural network in Keras, let us bring all the steps together and write the complete code. The sentences beginning with the '#' symbol represent the comments. These comments will help you understand what the statement in the code means.

```
# create your first network in Keras

from keras.models import Sequential
```

174

```python
from keras.layers import Dense

import numpy
# fix random seed to reproduce the results

numpy.random.seed(7)
# load the data set

dataset = numpy.loadtxt("file_name.csv", delimiter=",")
# split the data into input and output class variables

X = dataset[:,0:8]

Y = dataset[:,8]
# create the model

model = Sequential()

model.add(Dense(12, input_dim=8, activation='relu'))

model.add(Dense(8, activation='relu'))

model.add(Dense(1, activation='sigmoid'))
# compile the model

model.compile(loss='binary_crossentropy',
optimizer='adam', metrics=['accuracy'])
```

fit the model

```
model.fit(X, Y, epochs=150, batch_size=10)
```

evaluate the model

```
scores = model.evaluate(X, Y)
print("\n%s:    %.2f%%" % (model.metrics_names[1], scores[1]*100))
```

When you run this model, you should always read the message that you receive at the end of every iteration or epoch. This message provides information on the accuracy of the data and evaluates the trained model on the data set used for training. If you use a Theano backend on your CPU, this code will take 15 seconds to run. The output below is for the iteration number 145.

...

```
Epoch 145/150

768/768 [==============================] - 0s -
loss: 0.5105 - acc: 0.7396

Epoch 146/150

768/768 [==============================] - 0s -
loss: 0.4900 - acc: 0.7591

Epoch 147/150
```

768/768 [==============================] - 0s -
loss: 0.4939 - acc: 0.7565

Epoch 148/150

768/768 [==============================] - 0s -
loss: 0.4766 - acc: 0.7773

Epoch 149/150

768/768 [==============================] - 0s -
loss: 0.4883 - acc: 0.7591

Epoch 150/150

768/768 [==============================] - 0s -
loss: 0.4827 - acc: 0.7656

 32/768 [>.............................] - ETA: 0s

acc: 78.26%

If you use Jupyter notebook or IPython to run this program, you will receive an error since the output progress on these platforms are barred during training. You can turn off the output progress bars by making a change to the function verbose when you fit the model. You should also remember that the skill of your model will vary.

Neural networks are stochastic algorithms, which means that you can train a different model with a different skill using the same data and algorithm. This is not an error or a bug, but a feature of the neural network. You shouldn't worry if you don't receive the same output like the one above, although we did fix the same seed.

Make Predictions

Now that you have trained the model, you may wonder how you can use it to predict the output on new data sets. You can adapt the example above to generate predictions on the training data set.

It's easy to instruct the model to make predictions; all you need to do is use the function model.predict(). You can use the sigmoid function to activate the output layer to ensure that the results are only between 0 and 1, and you're able to convert the results into a binary prediction by using the rounding function on the data. You can use the following code to make predictions:

```
# create your first network in Keras

from keras.models import Sequential

from keras.layers import Dense

import numpy

# fix random seed to reproduce the results

numpy.random.seed(7)

# load the data set
```

```python
dataset = numpy.loadtxt("file_name.csv", delimiter=",")
# split the data into input and output class variables
X = dataset[:,0:8]
Y = dataset[:,8]
# create the model
model = Sequential()
model.add(Dense(12, input_dim=8, activation='relu'))
model.add(Dense(8, activation='relu'))
model.add(Dense(1, activation='sigmoid'))
# compile the model
model.compile(loss='binary_crossentropy',
optimizer='adam', metrics=['accuracy'])
# Fit the model
model.fit(X, Y, epochs=150, batch_size=10)
# evaluate the model
scores = model.evaluate(X, Y)
print("\n%s: %.2f%%" % (model.metrics_names[1],
scores[1]*100))
```

making predictions

```
predictions = model.predict(X)

rounded = [round(x[0]) for x in predictions]

print(rounded)
```

In the above example, we are rounding the predictions to obtain whole numbers as results.

When you run the complete program, you will receive an output for every input pattern. You can use these predictions in your application if necessary.

Chapter Fourteen

How to Evaluate the Performance of a Deep Learning Model

––––––––•◆•––––––––

You will need to make a lot of decisions when you design and configure the deep learning models. Most of the decisions you make should be resolved through the trial and error method. You should then evaluate the model on real data or test data. Therefore, it's important that you identify a robust way to evaluate the performance of a deep neural network. This chapter will provide you with some information on the different ways you can evaluate the model you're building using Keras.

Empirically Evaluate Network Configurations

There are many decisions that you need to make when you design and configure deep learning models. You can make most of these by copying a pre-existing model and making changes to the model depending on your requirement. The best technique is to design small segments of the model and evaluate the smaller segments using real data. If the model performs well, you can combine the small segments of it to develop the final model.

The decisions you need to make include the size of the network, the number of layers in the network and their types, activation function, the number of iterations or epochs, choice of the loss function, and optimization procedure.

You will often use deep learning models to solve problems where the input data set is large - that is, when it has at least a million instances. Therefore, you need to identify some criteria that will help you estimate the performance of different configurations of the network on unseen data.

Data Splitting

When you use large volumes of complex data, you need to give the deep neural network enough time to learn. Instead of using a large data set to train the data, you can split it into two sets: the training data set and the testing or validation data set.

Keras allows you to evaluate the deep learning algorithms using the following methods:

- Using a manual data set for verification

- Using an automatic data set for verification

Use an Automatic Data Set for Verification
You can use Keras to split the data set into a training and validation data set. You can then use this validation data set to evaluate how your model performs and validate the outputs after each epoch. You

can split the data including the validation split argument in the fit() function of the code. You're able to let Python know how much of the data you want to split into the validation data set. For example, you can tell Python to hold back at least 20 or 33% of the training data set into the validation data set.

The example in this section shows how you can use Keras to split the training data set into a validation data set. The data set used in the examples below is the same as the one we used in chapter six.

```
# neural network with an automatic validation set

        from keras.models import Sequential

        from keras.layers import Dense

        import numpy

# fix random seed to reproduce results

        numpy.random.seed(7)

# load pima indians data set

        dataset = numpy.loadtxt("file_name.csv", delimiter=",")

# split into input (X) and output (Y) variables

        X = dataset[:,0:8]

        Y = dataset[:,8]
```

create model

```
model = Sequential()

model.add(Dense(12, input_dim=8, activation='relu'))

model.add(Dense(8, activation='relu'))

model.add(Dense(1, activation='sigmoid'))
```

compile model

```
model.compile(loss='binary_crossentropy',
optimizer='adam', metrics=['accuracy'])
```

fit the model

```
model.fit(X,    Y,    validation_split=0.33,    epochs=150,
batch_size=10)
```

When you run the example above, you'll receive the output below for each iteration or epoch; this epoch will show the accuracy and loss on both the validation and training data sets.

```
Epoch 145/150

514/514 [==============================] - 0s -
loss: 0.5252 - acc: 0.7335 - val_loss: 0.5489 - val_acc: 0.7244
```

Use a Manual Data Set for Verification

Through Keras, you can manually specify the data set you want the model to use for validation during the training period. In the example below, we will use the train_test_split() function in the scikit library and separate the data into a training and validation data set. The model will use 67% of the data set for training and the remaining 33% for validation. You can specify the validation data set in the fit() function using the validation_data argument. This argument takes the tuple of both the input and output data sets.

neural network with manual validation set

```
from keras.models import Sequential

from keras.layers import Dense

from sklearn.model_selection import train_test_split

import numpy
```

fix random seed to reproduce results

```
seed = 7

numpy.random.seed(seed)
```

load the data set

```
dataset = numpy.loadtxt("file_name.csv", delimiter=",")
```

split into input (X) and output (Y) variables

```python
X = dataset[:,0:8]

Y = dataset[:,8]
```

split into 67% for train and 33% for validation

```python
X_train, X_test, y_train, y_test = train_test_split(X, Y, test_size=0.33, random_state=seed)
```

create model

```python
model = Sequential()

model.add(Dense(12, input_dim=8, activation='relu'))

model.add(Dense(8, activation='relu'))

model.add(Dense(1, activation='sigmoid'))
```

compile model

```python
model.compile(loss='binary_crossentropy', optimizer='adam', metrics=['accuracy'])
```

fit the model

```python
model.fit(X_train, y_train, validation_data=(X_test,y_test), epochs=150, batch_size=10)
```

Like the earlier example, you'll receive an output for every epoch which includes the accuracy and loss for every model for both the training and validation data sets.

Epoch 145/150

514/514 [==============================] - 0s - loss: 0.4847 - acc: 0.7704 - val_loss: 0.5668 - val_acc: 0.7323

Manual K-Fold Cross-Validation

One of the best ways to evaluate a deep learning model is by using the k-fold cross-validation method. This method provides the designer with an estimate of how the model performs on unseen data by splitting it into k subsets and then running the training data set through each of these subsets, aside from the one that it holds out. It then evaluates the model's performance on the data set that it has held out, and this process is repeated until every subset is held out of iteration at least once. The model calculates an average of the estimates and uses that as the performance measure. This method is not often utilized to evaluate a deep learning model since it is expensive. For instance, the k-cross-validation method is used for either five or ten folds. This means that five or ten models must be constructed and evaluated, which increases the time taken to evaluate the model. If you have a problem that is small, and you have enough resources to compute the number of models, this method will help you obtain a less biased estimate.

In the example below, we will use the StratifiedKFold class from the scikit library in Python to split the training data set into ten folds. The algorithm tries to maintain a balance between the number of instances in each class in every fold. In this example, we will create and evaluate the ten models and use the ten splits of data to collect the scores.

The algorithm prints the performance for each model and stores it. At the end of the cycle, the algorithm will calculate the average and the standard deviation of the model performance and print it in the output window after every run. This gives you a robust estimate of the performance of the model.

neural network for data set with ten-fold cross-validation

```
from keras.models import Sequential

from keras.layers import Dense

from sklearn.model_selection import StratifiedKFold

import numpy
```

fix random seed to reproduce the results

```
seed = 7

numpy.random.seed(seed)
```

load pima indians data set

```
dataset = numpy.loadtxt("file_name.csv", delimiter=",")
```

split into input (X) and output (Y) variables

```python
X = dataset[:,0:8]

Y = dataset[:,8]
```
define 10-fold cross-validation test harness
```python
kfold = StratifiedKFold(n_splits=10, shuffle=True,
random_state=seed)

cvscores = []

for train, test in kfold.split(X, Y):
```
 # create model
```python
model = Sequential()

model.add(Dense(12, input_dim=8, activation='relu'))

model.add(Dense(8, activation='relu'))

model.add(Dense(1, activation='sigmoid'))
```
compile model
```python
model.compile(loss='binary_crossentropy',
optimizer='adam', metrics=['accuracy'])
```
fit the model
```python
model.fit(X[train], Y[train], epochs=150, batch_size=10,
verbose=0)
```

evaluate the model

```
scores = model.evaluate(X[test], Y[test], verbose=0)

print("%s: %.2f%%" % (model.metrics_names[1],
scores[1]*100))

cvscores.append(scores[1] * 100)

print("%.2f%% (+/- %.2f%%)" % (numpy.mean(cvscores),
numpy.std(cvscores)))
```

You will receive the following output when you run the algorithm.

```
acc: 77.92%

acc: 68.83%

acc: 72.73%

acc: 64.94%

acc: 77.92%

acc: 35.06%

acc: 74.03%

acc: 68.83%

acc: 34.21%

acc: 72.37%

64.68% (+/- 15.50%)
```

Chapter Fifteen

How to Save and Load Deep Learning Models

———•◆•———

Since deep learning models take hours, days, weeks, and sometimes even months to train, it is important to know how you can save the model and load it off the disk whenever necessary. This chapter provides information on how you can save a Keras model to your disk and load it into Python when you need to make any predictions. With Keras, you do not have to worry about saving the architecture and model weights. All model weights are saved in the HDF5 format that is a grid format used to store multidimensional data. You can save the model structure using the following formats: JSON and YAML. In this chapter, we will take a look at the examples below:

- Save the model in the JSON format

- Save the model in the YAML format

The examples in this chapter will also demonstrate how you can save and load the model weights to the HDF5 format. We'll continue to use the data set that we did in the previous chapter for these examples.

You will first need to install h5py in Python:

sudo pip install h5py

Save Your Neural Network Model to JSON

JSON is a simple format that allows you to use a hierarchy to describe the data. Keras lets you save the file and later load it using the model_from_json() function. This will create a new model using the JSON specification or format. The weights that you use in the model are saved directly using the save_weights() function, and these are loaded once again into Python using the load_weights() function.

The weights from the model are saved directly using the function save_weights() and later loaded into Python using the load_weights() function. In the example below, you will load the model using the saved files and then create a new one. It is important that you compile the loaded model before you begin to use it. This is done to ensure that the predictions made use the efficient and appropriate computations from the Keras backend.

neural network for the data set Serialize to JSON and HDF5

```
from keras.models import Sequential

from keras.layers import Dense
```

```python
from keras.models import model_from_json

import numpy

import os
```
fix random seed to reproduce results
```python
numpy.random.seed(7)
```
load pima indians data set
```python
dataset = numpy.loadtxt("file_name.csv", delimiter=",")
```
split into input (X) and output (Y) variables
```python
X = dataset[:,0:8]

Y = dataset[:,8]
```
create model
```python
model = Sequential()

model.add(Dense(12, input_dim=8,
kernel_initializer='uniform', activation='relu'))

model.add(Dense(8, kernel_initializer='uniform',
activation='relu'))

model.add(Dense(1, kernel_initializer='uniform',
activation='sigmoid'))
```

```python
# compile model
model.compile(loss='binary_crossentropy',
optimizer='adam', metrics=['accuracy'])
# fit the model
model.fit(X, Y, epochs=150, batch_size=10, verbose=0)
# evaluate the model
scores = model.evaluate(X, Y, verbose=0)
print("%s:    %.2f%%"    %    (model.metrics_names[1],
scores[1]*100))
# serialize model to JSON
model_json = model.to_json()
with open("model.json", "w") as json_file:
json_file.write(model_json)
# serialize weights to HDF5
model.save_weights("model.h5")
print("Saved model to disk")
# load json and create model
json_file = open('model.json', 'r')
```

```
loaded_model_json = json_file.read()

json_file.close()

loaded_model = model_from_json(loaded_model_json)
```
load weights into new model
```
loaded_model.load_weights("model.h5")

print("Loaded model from disk")
```
 # evaluate loaded model on test data
```
loaded_model.compile(loss='binary_crossentropy',
optimizer='rmsprop', metrics=['accuracy'])

score = loaded_model.evaluate(X, Y, verbose=0)

print("%s: %.2f%%" % (loaded_model.metrics_names[1],
score[1]*100))
```

When you run the example, you will obtain the following output:

acc: 78.78%

Saved model to disk

Loaded model from disk

acc: 78.78%

The format of the model in JSON looks as follows:

```
{

"keras_version":"2.0.2",

"backend":"theano",

"config":[

{

"config":{

"dtype":"float32",

"bias_regularizer":null,

"activation":"relu",

"bias_constraint":null,

"use_bias":true,

"bias_initializer":{

"config":{


},

"class_name":"Zeros"

},
```

"kernel_regularizer":null,

"activity_regularizer":null,

"kernel_constraint":null,

"trainable":true,

"name":"dense_1",

"kernel_initializer":{

"config":{

"maxval":0.05,

"minval":-0.05,

"seed":null

},

"class_name":"RandomUniform"

},

"batch_input_shape":[

null,

8

],

"units":12

},

"class_name":"Dense"

},

{

"config":{

"kernel_regularizer":null,

"bias_regularizer":null,

"activation":"relu",

"bias_constraint":null,

"use_bias":true,

"bias_initializer":{

"config":{

},

"class_name":"Zeros"

},

"activity_regularizer":null,

"kernel_constraint":null,

"trainable":true,

"name":"dense_2",

"kernel_initializer":{

"config":{

"maxval":0.05,

"minval":-0.05,

"seed":null

},

"class_name":"RandomUniform"

},

"units":8

},

"class_name":"Dense"

},

{

"config":{

"kernel_regularizer":null,

"bias_regularizer":null,

"activation":"sigmoid",

"bias_constraint":null,

"use_bias":true,

"bias_initializer":{

"config":{

},

"class_name":"Zeros"

},

"activity_regularizer":null,

"kernel_constraint":null,

"trainable":true,

"name":"dense_3",

"kernel_initializer":{

```
"config":{

"maxval":0.05,

"minval":-0.05,

"seed":null

},

"class_name":"RandomUniform"

},

"units":1

},

"class_name":"Dense"

}

],

"class_name":"Sequential"

}
```

Save Your Neural Network Model to YAML

The example in this section is the same as the one above, except we will use the YAML format to specify the model. The model described below uses YAML, saves the model to the file named neural_yaml, and loads the new model using the function model_from_yaml(). The weights are handled in the same way as the example above in the HDF5 format as model.h5.

neural network for the Pima Indians Data Set to serialize to YAML and HDF5

```
from keras.models import Sequential

from keras.layers import Dense

from keras.models import model_from_yaml

import numpy

import os
```
fix random seed to reproduce results
```
seed = 7

numpy.random.seed(seed)
```
load pima indians data set
```
dataset = numpy.loadtxt("file_name.csv", delimiter=",")
```
split into input (X) and output (Y) variables
```
X = dataset[:,0:8]

Y = dataset[:,8]
```

```python
# create model
    model = Sequential()

    model.add(Dense(12, input_dim=8,
    kernel_initializer='uniform', activation='relu'))

    model.add(Dense(8, kernel_initializer='uniform',
    activation='relu'))

    model.add(Dense(1, kernel_initializer='uniform',
    activation='sigmoid'))
# compile model
    model.compile(loss='binary_crossentropy',
    optimizer='adam', metrics=['accuracy'])
# fit the model
    model.fit(X, Y, epochs=150, batch_size=10, verbose=0)
# evaluate the model
    scores = model.evaluate(X, Y, verbose=0)

    print("%s: %.2f%%" % (model.metrics_names[1],
    scores[1]*100))
# serialize model to YAML
    model_yaml = model.to_yaml()
```

```python
    with open("model.yaml", "w") as yaml_file:

        yaml_file.write(model_yaml)

# serialize weights to HDF5

        model.save_weights("model.h5")

        print("Saved model to disk")

 # load YAML to create the model

        yaml_file = open('model.yaml', 'r')

        loaded_model_yaml = yaml_file.read()

        yaml_file.close()

        loaded_model = model_from_yaml(loaded_model_yaml)

# load weights into the new model

        loaded_model.load_weights("model.h5")

        print("Loaded model from disk")

 # evaluate the model using test data

        loaded_model.compile(loss='binary_crossentropy',
        optimizer='rmsprop', metrics=['accuracy'])

        score = loaded_model.evaluate(X, Y, verbose=0)
```

```
print("%s: %.2f%%" % (loaded_model.metrics_names[1],
score[1]*100))
```

When you run the program above, you will receive the following output:

acc: 78.78%

Saved model to disk

Loaded model from disk

acc: 78.78%

The model that you described in the YAML format will look like this:

```
backend: theano

class_name: Sequential

config:

- class_name: Dense

config:

activation: relu

activity_regularizer: null

batch_input_shape: !!python/tuple [null, 8]

bias_constraint: null
```

bias_initializer:

class_name: Zeros

config: {}

bias_regularizer: null

dtype: float32

kernel_constraint: null

kernel_initializer:

class_name: RandomUniform

config: {maxval: 0.05, minval: -0.05, seed: null}

kernel_regularizer: null

name: dense_1

trainable: true

units: 12

use_bias: true

class_name: Dense

config:

activation: relu

activity_regularizer: null

bias_constraint: null

bias_initializer:

class_name: Zeros

config: {}

bias_regularizer: null

kernel_constraint: null

kernel_initializer:

class_name: RandomUniform

config: {maxval: 0.05, minval: -0.05, seed: null}

kernel_regularizer: null

name: dense_2

trainable: true

units: 8

use_bias: true

class_name: Dense

config:

activation: sigmoid

activity_regularizer: null

bias_constraint: null

bias_initializer:

class_name: Zeros

config: {}

bias_regularizer: null

kernel_constraint: null

kernel_initializer:

class_name: RandomUniform

config: {maxval: 0.05, minval: -0.05, seed: null}

kernel_regularizer: null

name: dense_3

trainable: true

units: 1

use_bias: true

keras_version: 2.0.2

Chapter Sixteen

Reducing Dropouts in Deep Learning Models

———————•◆•———————

O ne of the most powerful yet simplest techniques you can use to regularize a neural network and deep learning is the dropout. In this chapter, you gather information regarding what the dropout regularization technique is and how you can apply it to your deep learning models in Python using Keras.

Dropout Regularization for Neural Networks

Srivastava and his team proposed the use of dropouts to regularize neural networks. They explained the concept of dropouts and how they help to regularize neural networks in the paper *Dropout: A Simple Way to Prevent Neural Networks from Overfitting*.

Dropout is a technique where the model ignores some neurons in every iteration during the training period. These neurons are "dropped out" at random, so they do not contribute to obtaining the results. Their contribution is not taken into account on the forward pass, and any updates made during the iteration are not pushed back toward these neurons.

As the neural network learns, every neuron is assigned a weight; some neurons in the network will be assigned an additional weight to represent a special feature in the training data set. The neighboring neurons will rely on this special weight, and if this weight is too high, it can result in a sensitive model that's specialized to the training data. The phenomenon where many neurons rely on one neuron in the network is known as co-adaptation.

If neurons are dropped out of the network at random during training, other ones will need to step up and handle the problem. They should learn to make predictions, even if one neuron is missing. This ensures that the network learns to make multiple independent internal representations of the data set.

The effect of this is that the neurons in the network will become less sensitive to a change in the specific weights of other neurons. This will help you develop a model that can make better predictions. These models will not overfit the training data, which will reduce the effect of co-adaptation.

Regularizing Dropouts in Keras

You can easily implement dropouts by randomly selecting which notes should be dropped-out given a specific probability in each epoch or weight cycle. This is how you can implement dropouts in Keras. It's important to remember that dropouts can only be used when you are training the model and not when you want to evaluate the model.

We will now look at different ways to use Dropout in Keras. The examples use the Sonar data set, which is taken from the UCI Machine Learning repository. Like the examples used above, it provides a binary classification problem. The model needs to differentiate between mock-mines and rocks from the sonar chirp returns in the data. This is a good training data set to use since the input values have the same scale and are numerical.

The data set has a single output value and 60 input values. You must standardize these input values before you use the data set in the network. The neural network model has one input layer, an output layer, and two hidden layers. The first hidden layer has 60 units and the second has 30 units. We train the model with a low momentum and learning rate using the stochastic gradient descent.

Once you download the data, move it to the working directly and give the file a name. In the example below, we will evaluate the model using the scikit-learn method and a ten-fold cross-validation. This will help you identify the differences in the results. The following code will develop the neural network model.

baseline model on the sonar data set

    import numpy

```python
from pandas import read_csv

from keras.models import Sequential

from keras.layers import Dense

from keras.layers import Dropout

from keras.wrappers.scikit_learn import KerasClassifier

from keras.constraints import maxnorm

from keras.optimizers import SGD

from sklearn.model_selection import cross_val_score

from sklearn.preprocessing import LabelEncoder

from sklearn.model_selection import StratifiedKFold

from sklearn.preprocessing import StandardScaler

from sklearn.pipeline import Pipeline
# fix random seed for reproducibility
seed = 7

numpy.random.seed(seed)
# load data set
dataframe = read_csv("file_name.csv", header=None)
```

```python
    dataset = dataframe.values
# split into input (X) and output (Y) variables
    X = dataset[:,0:60].astype(float)
    Y = dataset[:,60]
# encode class values as integers
    encoder = LabelEncoder()
    encoder.fit(Y)
    encoded_Y = encoder.transform(Y)
# baseline
    def create_baseline():
# create model
    model = Sequential()
    model.add(Dense(60, input_dim=60,
    kernel_initializer='normal', activation='relu'))
    model.add(Dense(30, kernel_initializer='normal',
    activation='relu'))
    model.add(Dense(1, kernel_initializer='normal',
    activation='sigmoid'))
```

```python
# compile model
    sgd = SGD(lr=0.01, momentum=0.8, decay=0.0,
    nesterov=False)

    model.compile(loss='binary_crossentropy', optimizer=sgd,
    metrics=['accuracy'])

    return model

    numpy.random.seed(seed)

    estimators = []

    estimators.append(('standardize', StandardScaler()))

    estimators.append(('mlp',
    KerasClassifier(build_fn=create_baseline, epochs=300,
    batch_size=16, verbose=0)))

    pipeline = Pipeline(estimators)

    kfold = StratifiedKFold(n_splits=10, shuffle=True,
    random_state=seed)

    results = cross_val_score(pipeline, X, encoded_Y,
    cv=kfold)

    print("Baseline: %.2f%% (%.2f%%)" %
    (results.mean()*100, results.std()*100))
```

The code will generate results with an 86% estimated classification accuracy.

Using Dropout on Visible Layers

You can apply dropouts to the input neurons in the visible layer. In the example below, we have included a dropout layer between the visible layer and the first hidden one. The rate is set to 20%, which means that one in five inputs will be excluded from every update cycle. The input will be selected at random. Additionally, we have imposed a constraint on the weights in every hidden layer. This ensures that the maximum weights in the layers do not exceed three. We do this by including the kernel_contraint argument in the dense class when you build the model. The momentum is increased to 0.9, and the learning rate is increased by one. The paper mentioned in the first section of the book recommends that you increase the learning rate when you want to use dropouts in your model.

Continuing from the example above, the code includes an input dropout for the same network.

dropout in the input layer with weight constraint

        def create_model():

create model

        model = Sequential()

        model.add(Dropout(0.2, input_shape=(60,)))

```python
model.add(Dense(60, kernel_initializer='normal',
activation='relu', kernel_constraint=maxnorm(3)))

model.add(Dense(30, kernel_initializer='normal',
activation='relu', kernel_constraint=maxnorm(3)))

model.add(Dense(1, kernel_initializer='normal',
activation='sigmoid'))
```

Compile model

```python
sgd    =    SGD(lr=0.1,    momentum=0.9,    decay=0.0,
nesterov=False)

model.compile(loss='binary_crossentropy',    optimizer=sgd,
metrics=['accuracy'])

return model


numpy.random.seed(7)

estimators = []

estimators.append(('standardize', StandardScaler()))

estimators.append(('mlp',
KerasClassifier(build_fn=create_model, epochs=300,
batch_size=16, verbose=0)))
```

```
pipeline = Pipeline(estimators)

kfold = StratifiedKFold(n_splits=10, shuffle=True,
random_state=seed)

results = cross_val_score(pipeline, X, encoded_Y,
cv=kfold)

print("Visible: %.2f%% (%.2f%%)" % (results.mean()*100,
results.std()*100))
```

When you run the example above, you will notice that the classification accuracy has reduced in at least one test run. You will receive the following output when you run the code:

Visible: 83.52% (7.68%)

Using Dropout on Hidden Layers

You can also apply dropouts to the hidden layers and neurons in the model. The example below displays how you can apply a dropout between two hidden layers and the output and the final hidden layer. The dropout rate used is 20%, and a constraint is placed on the weights used in those layers.

```
def create_model():

# create model

    model = Sequential()
```

```python
        model.add(Dense(60, input_dim=60,
        kernel_initializer='normal', activation='relu',
        kernel_constraint=maxnorm(3)))

        model.add(Dropout(0.2))

        model.add(Dense(30, kernel_initializer='normal',
        activation='relu', kernel_constraint=maxnorm(3)))

        model.add(Dropout(0.2))

        model.add(Dense(1, kernel_initializer='normal',
        activation='sigmoid'))
# compile model
        sgd = SGD(lr=0.1, momentum=0.9, decay=0.0,
        nesterov=False)

        model.compile(loss='binary_crossentropy', optimizer=sgd,
        metrics=['accuracy'])

        return model

        numpy.random.seed(7)

        estimators = []

        estimators.append(('standardize', StandardScaler()))
```

```
estimators.append(('mlp',
KerasClassifier(build_fn=create_model, epochs=300,
batch_size=16, verbose=0)))

pipeline = Pipeline(estimators)

kfold = StratifiedKFold(n_splits=10, shuffle=True,
random_state=seed)

results = cross_val_score(pipeline, X, encoded_Y,
cv=kfold)

print("Hidden: %.2f%% (%.2f%%)" % (results.mean()*100,
results.std()*100))
```

The output for the above code is,

Hidden: 83.59% (7.31%)

You will find that using dropouts for the problem and the chosen network did not improve the performance of the model; the performance was worse than the benchmark. It is possible that you may need to increase the number of epochs during the training stage. Alternatively, you may need to fine-tune the learning rate in the code.

Tips for Using Dropout

The paper mentioned above provides information on the various machine learning problems. They also provide information on what you should consider when you use dropouts in your model.

- It is better to use a small dropout value - anywhere between 20-40% of the neurons. It is best to use 20% as the starting point. If you use a very small or very big value of probability, the network will not learn enough.

- If you want to include dropouts in your model, you should use a large model since you will get better performance this way. Dropouts help the model learn how to represent the data without the use of some neurons in the layers.

- You should use dropouts on hidden and visible units.

- To obtain good results, it's best to apply dropout at each layer in the network.

- You can use a large learning rate with large momentum and decay. Increase the learning rate in the model by a factor of 100, and use a momentum value of 0.99 or 0.9.

- Maintain the size of the weights in the network. If you have a large learning rate, it can result in a very large weight. When you impose or maintain the size of the weight, it will improve the results of the model.

Conclusion

———◆———

Thank you for deciding to choose this book.

Over the course of the book, you hopefully have learned more about neural networks and deep learning and about how to build a deep neural network in Python using Keras. We hope that the examples in the book were easy to follow and that you continue to use them as a base when you want to build your own deep neural network. If you do not know how to develop a deep learning model or are unsure of how to build the model, you can use pre-existing code and tweak them to help you obtain the desired output.

I hope you've been able to build a basic deep learning model using the information presented in the book.

References

What Is Deep Learning? | How It Works, Techniques &
    Applications. (2019). Retrieved from
    https://in.mathworks.com/discovery/deep-learning.html

Brownlee, J. (2019). What is Deep Learning?. Retrieved from
    https://machinelearningmastery.com/what-is-deep-learning/

Crawford, C. (2019). An introduction to deep learning. Retrieved
    from https://blog.algorithmia.com/introduction-to-deep-
    learning/

Deep Learning in Python. (2019). Retrieved from
    https://www.datacamp.com/courses/deep-learning-in-python

Top 15 Deep Learning applications that will rule the world in 2018
    and beyond. (2019). Retrieved from
    https://medium.com/@vratulmittal/top-15-deep-learning-
    applications-that-will-rule-the-world-in-2018-and-beyond-
    7c6130c43b01

Brownlee, J. (2019). Develop Your First Neural Network in Python
    With Keras Step-By-Step. Retrieved from
    https://machinelearningmastery.com/tutorial-first-neural-
    network-python-keras/

Brownlee, J. (2019). Evaluate the Performance Of Deep Learning Models in Keras. Retrieved from https://machinelearningmastery.com/evaluate-performance-deep-learning-models-keras/

Brownlee, J. (2019). 8 Inspirational Applications of Deep Learning. Retrieved from https://machinelearningmastery.com/inspirational-applications-deep-learning/

Recurrent Neural Networks and LSTM. (2019). Retrieved from https://towardsdatascience.com/recurrent-neural-networks-and-lstm-4b601dd822a5

Nielsen, M. (2019). Neural Networks and Deep Learning. Retrieved from http://neuralnetworksanddeeplearning.com/

A Beginner's Guide to Generative Adversarial Networks (GANs). (2019). Retrieved from https://skymind.ai/wiki/generative-adversarial-network-gan

Brownlee, J. (2019). Regression Tutorial with the Keras Deep Learning Library in Python. Retrieved from https://machinelearningmastery.com/regression-tutorial-keras-deep-learning-library-python/

Deep Reinforcement Learning | DeepMind. (2019). Retrieved from https://deepmind.com/blog/deep-reinforcement-learning/

Learning, D., & Them?, F. (2019). Fundamentals of Deep Learning - Activation Functions and their use. Retrieved from https://www.analyticsvidhya.com/blog/2017/10/fundamentals-deep-learning-activation-functions-when-to-use-them/

Rosebrock, A. (2019). My Top 9 Favorite Python Deep Learning Libraries - PyImageSearch. Retrieved from https://www.pyimage search.com/2016/06/27/my-top-9-favorite-python-deep-learning-libraries/

CS231n Convolutional Neural Networks for Visual Recognition. (2019). Retrieved from http://cs231n.github.io/convolutional-networks/

Nielsen, M. (2019). Neural Networks and Deep Learning. Retrieved from http://neuralnetworksanddeeplearning.com/chap1.html

Brownlee, J. (2019). Save and Load Your Keras Deep Learning Models. Retrieved from https://machinelearningmastery.com/save-load-keras-deep-learning-models/

DEEP LEARNING
WITH PYTHON

A Comprehensive Guide
Beyond The Basics

Travis Booth

Introduction

———◆———

s far as buzz words go, deep learning is so hot right now, it's
sizzling. With computing hardware advancing in leaps and
bounds, and with many thousands of terabytes of data, more
companies than ever before, not to mention the organizations
involved in research, are building more and more intelligent
machines using deep learning. These machines can do many
thousands of different tasks and they help us mere humans to make
much better and more informed decisions.

Now is the time for me to say, welcome to the second book in my
series on Deep Learning with Python. While the first book was aimed
at novices and complete beginners, this one takes things a step
further.

The first book covered the absolute basics of deep learning and
machine learning and now we are going to delve deeper; we start
with linear regression and logistic regression, both very important
subjects for anyone wishing to go into the field of deep learning.
Next we move onto different types of deep neural networks –
artificial, recurrent, and convolutional – going in-depth on each one
with practical Python coding examples. Then we will take a look at
Natural Language Processing before moving onto deep learning

using PyTorch. Lastly, we will look at LSTM and deep multi-task learning.

Don't just read this guide; work with it. Follow the examples and try the code for yourself. Seeing is believing and you will learn far more by doing than by just reading and don't be afraid to go over something more than once if you don't understand it.

I want to wish you luck in your deep learning journey and this guide will provide you with many of the tools you need to start learning how to solve deep learning problems.

Ready?

Then let's dive right in.

Part 1

Deep Learning Prerequisites

————————◆————————

There can be no doubt that artificial intelligence is growing faster than we could ever have believed. Millions of miles have been clocked up on self-drive cars already; AlphaGo from Google Deepmind has already beaten the Go world champion (and that is game that requires intuition), and IBM Watson is already making far better diagnoses on patients than a whole army of doctors put together.

But as AI continues to advance, it needs to solve problems that are more complex. The only way to do that is through deep learning and that is why it plays a central role in artificial intelligence.

One of the best open-source libraries is TensorFlow, a library that we use with data flow graphs to solve numerical computations. The nodes in the data flow graphs each represent a mathematical operation and the edges of the graph each represent a multi-dimensional data array, known as a tensor, that is communicated between the operations. Because the architecture is so flexible, computation can be deployed to one or more GPUs or CPUs in a mobile device, a desktop or a server using just one API.

TensorFlow was developed originally by a bunch of Google engineers and researchers who were working in the Google Machine Intelligence organization on the Brain Team. It was originally meant to be for conducting research on deep neural networks and machine learning but it is general enough that it can easily be used in many other domains too. In fact, TensorFlow is used by some of the biggest companies in the world, including, of course, Google, Twitter, Dropbox, Airbnb, Uber, IBM, eBay, Snapchat, Intel, Qualcomm and SAP.

In this first part we are going to look at two subjects that are very important to get to grips with for deep learning – linear regression and logistic regression.

Linear Regression in Python

Powerful computers, vast amounts of data and artificial intelligence. That is the world we live in now and this is really just the start. Machine learning and data science are the driving forces behind the development of autonomous vehicles, image recognition, medical advances, decisions made in the energy and financial sectors, the fast growth of the social networks and much, much more. One of the most important parts of this is linear regression.

Linear regression is a fundamental technique in machine learning and statistics. Whether you want to get involved in machine learning, statistics or scientific computing, you are going to need to know what linear regression is and how to use it. This is your starting point, the subject you should learn first before moving onto more complex subjects.

By the end of this section on linear regression, you will have learned:

- What it is

- What we use it for

- How it works

- How we implement it, step by step, in Python

What is Regression?

Perhaps one of the most important of all the machine learning and statistics fields, regression analysis is used for searching for relationships between different variables. For example, let's say that you run an observation on a number of employees from one company. You want to see if the salary they are paid is dependent on certain features, such as education level, experience, the role they work in, the city they work from and so on.

A regression problem, this is where the data that relates to each individual employee represents a single observation. There is a presumption that the independent features are the city, the education, experience, role etc., while the salary is the dependent feature.

In a similar way, you could try establishing if there were a mathematical dependence on house prices by looking at the area the house is in, how many bedrooms it is, the size of the garden, how close it is to the city center, and so on.

In general, with regression analysis, a point of interest is considered together with a number of different observations. Each of those observations will have at least two features and, if we stick with the assumption that one or more of the features are dependent on the other features, you can attempt to establish some kind of relationship between them.

In basic terms, you must find some function that maps some variables or features to other variables or features in a sufficient manner.

- **Dependent features -** known as the dependent responses, outputs or variable

- **Independent features** – known as the independent predictors, inputs or variables

Normally, a regression problem will have a single unbounded, continuous independent variable. However, the inputs may be discrete or continuous, or they may even be categorical data, for example, brand, nationality, gender, etc.

Common practice dictates that the outputs are denoted with y and the inputs denoted with x. If you have at least two independent variables, they would be represented as a vector of

$$x = (x1, \ldots, x_r)$$

with r indicating the number of the inputs.

When is Regression Needed?

Typically, regression is required when you need to answer if and how a point of interest influences another or how multiple variables are related to one another. For example, you could use regression for determining if gender or experience impact salary and how they do.

Regression can also be used for forecasting responses using a new predictor set. For example, you could attempt to predict how much electricity one household will consume within the next 60 minutes, given the time of day, the outside temperature and how many people reside in the household.

In fact, regression has a good many uses these days in many different fields, including social science, computer science, economy, and so on. As each day passes it becomes more important, especially as the amount of data available rises, and as we become more aware of the practical value of that data.

Linear Regression

Of all the regression techniques, linear regression is one of the most important and is definitely one of the most used. It is also very simple compared to other regression methods and one of the biggest advantages to using it is the ease with which results can be interpreted.

Problem Formulation

Let's say that we have an independent variable y and we also have a set of independent variables

$$x = (x1, \ldots, x_r)$$

We know from before that r indicates the number of predictors.

To implement linear regression on this problem, we will assume that there is a linear relationship between

y

and

$$x: y = \beta_0 + \beta_1 x_1 + \cdots + \beta_r x_r + \varepsilon.$$

That equation above is known as the regression equation where the regression coefficients are $\beta_0, \beta_1, \ldots, \beta_r$ and the random error is ε.

We use linear regression to calculate what the estimators are of those coefficients or, in simple terms, the predicted weights, denoted using

b_0, b_1, ..., b_r. These are used for defining the estimated regression function

$$f(\mathbf{x}) = b_0 + b_1 x_1 + \cdots + b_r x_r.$$

This function should, in theory, sufficiently capture any dependencies that exist between the inputs and the output.

The predicted or estimated response, which is $f(x_i)$, for each individual observation of

$$i = 1, \ldots, n,$$

should really be as near to the actual response of

$$y_i$$

that corresponds to it.

The differences of

$$y_i - f(x_i)$$

for each of the observations of

$$i = 1, \ldots, n,$$

are known as the residuals.

Regression is all about working out what the best predicted weights are, i.e. the weights that correspond to the smallest residuals.

Getting the best weights usually requires you to minimize the SSR, or 'sum of squared residuals for all of the observations of

$$i = 1, \ldots, n: \text{SSR} = \Sigma_i(y_i - f(\mathbf{x}_i))^2$$

We call this approach the 'method of ordinary least squares'.

Regression Performance
The variation of the actual responses of

$$y_i, i = 1, \ldots, n,$$

Happens in part because of the dependence on the predictors of x. However, we also have to take into account an extra output variance.

The denotation of R^2 is the coefficient of determination and this informs us how much of the variation in y may be explained away by the dependence that x will use the specified regression model. The larger R^2 is indicative of a much better fit and it means that the model can explain the output variation much better with other outputs.

And the value of

$$R^2 = 1$$

is correspondent to

$$\text{SSR} = 0$$

which is the perfect fit because the values of both the actual and the predicted responses completely fit one another.

Simple Linear Regression

Simple linear regression, otherwise called single-variate regression, is the simplest linear regression case, having one independent variable of

$$x = y.$$

When it comes to implementing simple linear regression, you would normally start with a specified set of x-y pairs, which are the input-output pairs. These are the observations. For example, let's say that we have an observation with an input of

$$x = 5$$

and the actual output response of

$$y = 5$$

the next would be

$$x = 15$$

and

$$y = 20$$

and so on.

Now, the equation for the estimated regression function is

$$f(x) = b_0 + b_1 x$$

Your job is to work out what the optimal values are of the predicted weights of b_0 and b_1, which minimize the SSR, and work out what the estimated regression function is. b_0, also known as the intercept, has a value that indicates the point at which the regression line (estimated) will cross the y axis. This is value for the estimated response of

$$f(x)$$

for

$$x = 0$$

The b_1 value is used for determining what the estimated regression line slope is.

Predicted responses are specific points on the line that corresponds to specific input values. For example, for an input of

$$x = 5$$

the predicted response would be something like

$$f(5) = 8.33$$

The residuals may be calculated for

$$i = 1, \ldots, n$$

as

$$y_i - f(\mathbf{x}_i) = y_i - b_0 - b_1 x_i$$

When linear regression is implemented, what you are doing is attempting to minimize the distances between the intercept and the predicted responses.

Multiple Linear Regression

Multiple linear regression is otherwise known as multivariate linear regression and this is a case where there are at least two independent variables. If there are only two independents, the estimated regression function would be

$$f(x_1, x_2) = b_0 + b_1 x_1 + b_2 x_2$$

It is representative of a regression plane in a 3D space. With regression, the goal is to work out what the values of the weights of b_0, b_1, and b_2 are in such a way that the plane is as near to the actual responses as possible and provide the minimal SSR.

When you have more than the two independents, it is similar but in a more general manner. With an estimated regression function of

$$(x_1, \ldots, x_r) = b_0 + b_1 x_1 + \cdots + b_r x_r,$$

we have weights of

$$r + 1$$

that need to be determined when we have an input number of r.

Polynomial Regression

Polynomial regression could be seen as a linear regression but in a more generalized way. The polynomial dependence between the inputs and outputs is assumed and, as a consequence, we also assume the estimated regression function.

In short, as well as the linear terms such as $b1x1$, the regression function of f may also have some non-linear terms like $b_2x_1^2$, $b_3x_1^3$, or $b_4x_1x_2$, $b_5x_1^2x_2$, and so on. The very simplest polynomial regression example would have a single independent variable and the regression function (estimated) would be a polynomial of degree

$$2: f(x) = b_0 + b_1x + b_2x^2.$$

Remember, we need b_0, b_1, and b_2 calculated and this minimizes SSR – these are what you call your unknowns. Now, keeping all this in mind, we can compare the regression function from earlier with the function of

$$f(x_1, x_2) = b_0 + b_1x_1 + b_2x_2$$

that was used for the linear regression.

Both are quite similar in the way they look and both are linear functions of the b_0, b_1, and b_2 unknowns. And this is why the polynomial regression problem can be solved as a linear problem using the term of

$$x^2$$

as an input variable.

Where the two variables, together with the polynomial of degree 2, are concerned, the regression function will take this format:

$$f(x_1, x_2) = b_0 + b_1x_1 + b_2x_2 + b_3x_1^2 + b_4x_1x_2 + b_5x_2^2.$$

We use the exact same procedure to solve this as we did with the previous regression case. The linear aggression is applied for these five inputs:

$$x_1, x_2, x_1^2, x_1x_2, \text{ and } x_2^2$$

and the result of the regression will be the values of the six weights that minimize the SSR:

$$b_0, b_1, b_2, b_3, b_4, \text{ and } b_5.$$

There are problems that are more general but this should be sufficient to show you the point of it.

Underfitting and Overfitting

One of the most important questions that could arise when polynomial regression is being implemented is related to which polynomial regression function optimal degree is chosen.

There isn't a straightforward way of doing this; it will all depend on the specific case. However, there are two problems you should be aware of that can follow this degree of choice and those problems are known as underfitting and overfitting and all I will do here is a give you a brief overview of what they are.

- **Underfitting** – this happens when the dependencies in the data cannot be captured accurately and this is normally one of the consequences of the simplicity of the model. Often, a low R^2 will be yielded having known data and bad capabilities for generalization when new data is applied to it.

- **Overfitting** – this happens when both dependencies among random and data fluctuations are learned by the model. In basic terms, the model will learn the existing data a bit too well. Complex models tend to have a lot of terms or features and these are prone to overfitting. When these models are applied to known data, they tend to yield a high R^2 but very often, they are not good at generalizing and, when used with newer data they will yield a much lower R^2.

Implementation of Linear Regression

Time to get practical and implement linear regression in Python. All you need to do is apply the correct packages along with the relevant classes and functions.

Linear Regression – Python Packages

The most basic and important scientific package in Python is NumPy. This package allows for multiple operations, mostly high-performance, on both single-dimensional and multi-dimensional arrays, alongside offering a large number of mathematical routines. And, even better, it is an open-source package.

One of the most widely used packages for both machine and deep learning is scikit-learn. This is built on NumPy and a few other different packages, providing you with the means to preprocess data, reduce dimensionality, implement regression, clustering, classification and much more. And like NumPy, it is an open-source package.

If your functionality requirements for implementing linear regression go above what scikit-learn is capable of, you can also use a package called statsmodels. This is incredibly powerful and is used for carrying out tests, estimating statistical models, and a whole lot more besides.

Using scikit-learn for Simple Linear Regression

We'll begin with simple linear regression, one of the easiest and simplest of cases to start with. When you implement linear regression, there are five steps to follow:

1. Import all the packages and their classes that you need

2. Provide the relevant data for working with and, eventually, so the transformations needed

3. Create your regression model and fit it with the data you have

243

4. Check the model fitting results so you know whether you have a satisfactory model or not

5. Apply that model for the predictions

These are pretty general, fundamental steps from almost all regression implementations and approaches. Let's go through them one at a time and see how it's done.

Step 1: Import the Packages and Classes

This is the very first step and you need to import the package called numpy along with the class called LinearRegression; this class is found in sklearn.linear_model:

Python

import numpy as np

from sklearn.linear_model import LinearRegression

With these you have the functionalities needed for implementing linear regression.

NumPy has a fundamental data type; this is the array type and it is called numpy.ndarray. For the rest of this section, I will use the term "array" when I need to reference an instance of the numpy.ndarray type, just for the sake of simplicity.

We will use the sklearn.linear_model.LinearRegression class for doing both linear and polynomial regression and to make the predictions.

Step 2: Provide the Data

The next step is to define the data that we want to work with. The inputs, which are the regressors and x, and the output, which is the predictor and y, should really be arrays (an instance of numpy.ndarray class), or they should be similar objects. The easiest way of providing the data to be used for regression is this:

x = np.array([5, 15, 25, 35, 45, 55]).reshape((-1, 1))

y = np.array([5, 20, 14, 32, 22, 38])

Here, we have two arrays. They are the input of x and the output of y. It is important that .reshape() is called on x because the array must be two-dimensional. More precisely, it should have a single column but as many rows as are required and that is what the (-1, 1) argument for .reshape() is specifying.

x and y now look like this:

>>>

>>> print(x)

[[5]

[15]

[25]

[35]

[45]

[55]]

>>> print(y)

[5 20 14 32 22 38]

As is clear, there are two dimensions to x, with x.shape being (6,) and y is just one dimension with y.shape being (6,).

Step 3: Creating the Model and Fitting it

Next, we are going to create the linear regression model and use the existing data to fit it. We'll start with an instance of the LinearRegression class which we will use for representing the regression model:

model = LinearRegression()

Using this statement, we have created an instance of the LinearRegression class as a variable model. The LinearRegression class can be given a number of optional parameters, such as:

- **fit_intercept** – this is a Boolean and, by default, it is True. This determines whether the intercept of b_0 should be calculated as True or whether it should be considered as being equal to zero, which makes it False.

- **normalize** – another Boolean, this time False by default. This one will determine whether the input variables should be normalized, making them True or not, making them False.

- **copy_X** – a final Boolean which is True by default. This determines if we need to copy the input variables, thus making it True, or overwrite them, making it False.

- **n_jobs** – this one is an integer or, by default None. It is used to represent how many jobs are used in parallel computation – None tends to indicate one job and -1 indicates all processors are to be used.

In our example, we will use the default values for each of the parameters.

Now it's time to start using this model so, the first thing to do is call .fit() on model, like this:

model.fit(x, y)

Using .fit(), we can calculate what the optimal values are of the weights b_0 and b_1, and the arguments are the existing input of x and output of y. In basic terms, this means that .fit() will fit our model.

247

The return value is self and this is the variable model. This is why the last two statements may be replaced with just one:

model = LinearRegression().fit(x, y)

This does exactly the same as the last two statements but in a shorter, more succinct manner.

Step 4: Get the Results

Once the model has been fitted, we can get the results to make sure the model works as we want and to interpret it.

The coefficient of determination, which is R^2, can be obtained by calling .score() on model, like this:

>>>

>>> r_sq = model.score(x, y)

>>> print('coefficient of determination:', r_sq)

coefficient of determination: 0.715875613747954

When .score() is applied, the arguments become the predictor of x and the regressor of y, with R^2 being the return value.

model has two attributes - .intercept_, which is representing the coefficient of b_0, and .coef_, which is representing b_1:

>>>

```
>>> print('intercept:', model.intercept_)
```

intercept: 5.633333333333329

```
>>> print('slope:', model.coef_)
```

slope: [0.54]

The above code shows how we get b_0 and b_1.. Note that .intercept_ is a scaler and .coef_ is an array.

The value, $b_0 = 5.63$, is showing you that, when x is zero, the model is predicting a response of 5.63. The value, $b_1 = 0.54$, indicates a rise of 0.54 in the predicted response when x gets increased by 1.

Note that y may also be provided as a two-dimensional array and, in that case, the result would be similar, looking something like this:

```
>>>
```

```
>>> new_model = LinearRegression().fit(x, y.reshape((-1, 1)))
```

```
>>> print('intercept:', new_model.intercept_)
```

intercept: [5.63333333]

```
>>> print('slope:', new_model.coef_)
```

slope: [[0.54]]

This example is much like the last one but, this time, .intercept is a one-dimensional array, having just one element of b_0 and .coef becomes a two-dimensional array with just one element of b_1.

Step 5: Predicting the Response

When you have a model that you are satisfied with, it can be used for making predictions on new or existing data. To get a predicted response, you would use .predict():

>>>

>>> y_pred = model.predict(x)

>>> print('predicted response:', y_pred, sep='\n')

The predicted response is:

[8.33333333 13.73333333 19.13333333 24.53333333
29.93333333 35.33333333]

When .predict() is applied, the regressor must be passed as the argument and the predicted response that corresponds to it retrieved/ The following way of predicting a response is almost identical:

>>>

>>> y_pred = model.intercept_ + model.coef_ * x

>>> print('predicted response:', y_pred, sep='\n')

The predicted response is:

[[8.33333333]

[13.73333333]

[19.13333333]

[24.53333333]

[29.93333333]

[35.33333333]]

In this example, each element of x is multiplied with model.coef_, and model.intercept_ is added to the product.

The output is a little different from the last example but only as far as dimensions go. We now have a two-dimensional array for the predicted response whereas, previously, it was just a one-dimension array.

If the number of dimensions for x is reduced to one, both of the above approaches would give you the same result. This is done by using either x.flatten(), x.reshape(-), or x.ravel() in place of x when it is multiplied with model.coef_.

In practical terms, we often use regression models with forecasts, meaning that fitted models can be used for calculating what the outputs are based on other, newer inputs:

```
>>>

>>> x_new = np.arange(5).reshape((-1, 1))

>>> print(x_new)

[[0]

 [1]

 [2]

 [3]

 [4]]

>>> y_new = model.predict(x_new)

>>> print(y_new)

[5.63333333    6.17333333    6.71333333    7.25333333
 7.79333333]
```

In this one, we apply .predict() to the new regressor called x_new and get a response of y_new. Conveniently, we have used arrange(), found in NumPy, in this example to generate the array that has elements inclusively from 0 to 5 (exclusively), meaning the elements are 0,1, 2, 3, 4.

Using scikit-learn for Multiple Linear Regression

Multiple linear regression can be implemented using the same steps as for simple linear regression.

Steps 1 and 2: Import Your Classes and Packages and Provide the Data

First, as before, import the numpy package and the sklearn.linear_model.LinearRegression. Then provide the inputs and the outputs (known ones):

import numpy as np

from sklearn.linear_model import LinearRegression

```
x = [[0, 1], [5, 1], [15, 2], [25, 5], [35, 11], [45, 15], [55, 34],
[60, 35]]

y = [4, 5, 20, 14, 32, 22, 38, 43]

x, y = np.array(x), np.array(y)
```

This is a very easy way of defining the input of x and the output of y; x and y can now be printed to see what they look like:

```
>>>

>>> print(x)

[[ 0  1]

 [ 5  1]
```

[15 2]

[25 5]

[35 11]

[45 15]

[55 34]

[60 35]]

>>> print(y)

[4 5 20 14 32 22 38 43]

With multiple linear regression, y is a one-dimensional array and is a two-dimensional array that has a minimum of two columns. We are using one of the simplest multiple linear regression examples with x having two columns exactly.

Step 3: Create Your Model and Fit it

Next, we create our regression model. It will be created as a LinearRegression instance and we use .fit() to fit the model:

model = LinearRegression().fit(x, y)

This statement will result in the variable model referencing the object that has the LinearRegression type; it is representing the regression model that has been fitted with the existing data.

Step 4: Get the Results

We can use the same method for obtaining the model properties as we did with the simple linear regression:

>>>

>>> r_sq = model.score(x, y)

>>> print('coefficient of determination:', r_sq)

coefficient of determination: 0.8615939258756776

>>> print('intercept:', model.intercept_)

intercept: 5.52257927519819

>>> print('slope:', model.coef_)

slope: [0.44706965 0.25502548]

We use .score() to get the value of R^2 and we use .intercept_ and .coef_ to get the values for the regression coefficient estimators. Once again, .intercept_ has the b_0 bias and .coef is now an array with, respectively, b_1 and b_2.

The intercept in our example is around 5.52, which is the value that the predicted response gives when

x1 = x2 = 0

Increasing x1 by 1 will provide a rise of 0.45 in the predicted response and, by the same token, when x2 is increased by 1, we get an increase of 0.26 in the response.

Step 5: Predict the Response

Predictions for multiple linear regression work the same way as they do for simple linear regression:

>>>

>>> y_pred = model.predict(x)

>>> print('predicted response:', y_pred, sep='\n')

The predicted response is:

[5.77760476 8.012953   12.73867497 17.9744479
23.97529728 29.4660957

38.78227633 41.27265006]

We use .predict() to get the predicted response, which is much the same as this:

>>>

>>> y_pred = model.intercept_ + np.sum(model.coef_ * x, axis=1)

>>> print('predicted response:', y_pred, sep='\n')

The predicted response is:

[5.77760476   8.012953   12.73867497   17.9744479
23.97529728 29.4660957

38.78227633 41.27265006]

The output values can be predicted through multiplication of each of the input columns with the correct weights, sum the results and then add the intercept to that sum.

The model can also be applied to new data:

```
>>>

>>> x_new = np.arange(10).reshape((-1, 2))

>>> print(x_new)

[[0 1]

 [2 3]

 [4 5]

 [6 7]

 [8 9]]

>>> y_new = model.predict(x_new)

>>> print(y_new)
```

[5.77760476   7.18179502   8.58598528   9.99017554
11.3943658]

That prediction uses the linear regression model.

Using scikit-learn for Polynomial Regression

Lastly, using scikit-learn to implement polynomial regression is also much the same as linear regression with just one additional step – the array of inputs must be transformed so it can include terms that are non-linear, like x^2.

Step 1: Import the Packages and Classes

As well as importing both numpy and sklearn.linear_model.LinearRegression, you also need another class from sklearn.preprocessing, called PolynomialFeatures:

import numpy as np

from sklearn.linear_model import LinearRegression

from sklearn.preprocessing import PolynomialFeatures

With this, you have all you need to do polynomial regression using scikit-learn.

Step 2: Provide the Data

With this step, we are defining the input and the output; this is the same as we did with linear regression:

x = np.array([5, 15, 25, 35, 45, 55]).reshape((-1, 1))

y = np.array([15, 11, 2, 8, 25, 32])

The input and the output are now in a format that is suitable to work with. Keep in mind that the reason we use .reshape() is that the input has to be a two-dimensional array.

Step 3: Transform the Input Data

This is the additional step that must be done for polynomial regression to be implemented. As you saw a while back, x^2 must be included, and possibly other terms too, as extra features when we implement polynomial regression. It is for this reason that the input array called x needs to be transformed so it has the extra column/s containing the x^2 values and, later, other features.

The input array could be transformed in a number of ways, such as insert(), which is found in numpy. However, we're going to use a very convenient way, the class we imported earlier called PolynomialFeatures.

First, we need an instance of the class created:

transformer = PolynomialFeatures(degree=2, include_bias=False)

The variable called transformer is referring to a PolynomialFeatures instance which we will use for transforming the input of x.

There are several other parameters, all optional, that can be given to PolynomialFeatures:

- **degree** – this is an integer of 2 by default. It is representing the polynomial regression function degree.

- **interaction_only** – this is a Boolean with a default of False. It is used to decide whether we should include interaction features only, resulting in True or all the features, resulting in False.

- **include_bias** – also a Boolean that has a default of True. This is used for deciding whether the bias, or intercept, a column of ones is included, resulting in true, or whether it is excluded, resulting in False.

In our example, we use the default values for all the parameters but don't be afraid to experiment, play around with the degree of function.

Before the transformer is applied it needs to be fitted with .fit():

transformer.fit(x)

When the transformer has been fitted, it is now ready for creating a new input that is modified. To do that, .transform() is applied:

x_ = transformer.transform(x)

That takes care of transforming the input array, using .transform().
The input array is the argument and the modified array is returned.

fit.transform() could also be used for replacing the last three
statements with a single one:

x_ = PolynomialFeatures(degree=2,
include_bias=False).fit_transform(x)

That takes care of both fitting the input array and transforming it in
a single statement using fit.transform(). And the statement can also
take the input array and it does pretty much what .fit() and .transform
do when called in that particular order. The modified array will be
returned too.

The new input array looks like this:

```
>>>

>>> print(x_)

[[  5.   25.]

 [ 15.  225.]

 [ 25.  625.]

 [ 35. 1225.]

 [ 45. 2025.]
```

[55. 3025.]]

There are two columns in the input array; one contains the original inputs and the other has the squares of those inputs.

Step 4: Creating Your Model and Fitting it

Again, this is much the same as it was with linear regression. The model is created and fitted like this:

model = LinearRegression().fit(x_, y)

Our regression model has been created, fitted and is ready to be used.

Do keep in mind that we use array_x, a modified input, as the initial argument for .fit() and not x, which was the original input.

Step 5: Get the Results

The model properties can be obtained in the same way as we did with linear regression:

>>>

>>> r_sq = model.score(x_, y)

>>> print('coefficient of determination:', r_sq)

coefficient of determination: 0.8908516262498564

>>> print('intercept:', model.intercept_)

intercept: 21.372321428571425

>>> print('coefficients:', model.coef_)

coefficients: [-1.32357143 0.02839286]

Again, R^2 is returned by .score(). The first argument is x_, which is the modified input and not the original input of x. And the weight values are associated to .intercept_, which represents b_0, and .coef_ is referencing the array containing, respectively, b_1 and b_2.

A similar result could be obtained using different arguments for transformation and regression:

x_ = PolynomialFeatures(degree=2,
include_bias=True).fit_transform(x)

If PolynomialFeatures were called with its default parameter of include_bias=True, or if that parameter were just left out, the new input array of x_ is obtained with an extra column on the left that contains just ones and corresponds to the intercept. In this scenario, the modified input array would look like this:

>>>

>>> print(x_)

[[1.000e+00 5.000e+00 2.500e+01]

[1.000e+00 1.500e+01 2.250e+02]

[1.000e+00 2.500e+01 6.250e+02]

[1.000e+00 3.500e+01 1.225e+03]

[1.000e+00 4.500e+01 2.025e+03]

[1.000e+00 5.500e+01 3.025e+03]]

The first column in x_ has once while the second has the x values and the third has the squares of x. The intercept has been included in the left column containing ones and it doesn't need to be included again when the new instance of LinearRegression is created. As such, fit_intercept=False can be provided. The next statement looks like this:

model = LinearRegression(fit_intercept=False).fit(x_ , y)

Again, the variable model will correspond to the array_ input and, as such, x_ is the first argument and not x.

Using this approach, we get these results, much like we did with the first one:

```
>>>

>>> r_sq = model.score(x_, y)

>>> print('coefficient of determination:', r_sq)

coefficient of determination: 0.8908516262498565
```

```
>>> print('intercept:', model.intercept_)
```

intercept: 0.0

```
>>> print('coefficients:', model.coef_)
```

coefficients: [21.37232143 -1.32357143 0.02839286]

Now you can see that .intercept_ is actually zero but .coef_ has a first element of b_0 while everything else remains as it was.

Step 6: Predicting the Response

If all you want is the predicted response, you can use .predict() so long as you keep in mind that x_ should be used instead of x:

```
>>>
```

```
>>> y_pred = model.predict(x_)
```

```
>>> print('predicted response:', y_pred, sep='\n')
```

The predicted response is:

[15.46428571 7.90714286 6.02857143 9.82857143
19.30714286 34.46428571]

It should be clear that the prediction works in pretty much the same way as it did with linear regression so long as you remember to use the modified input and not the original.

The same procedure can be applied if you have multiple input variables; most things will stay the same but you will have an input array that has two or more columns.

Take a look at this example:

Step 1: Import the Packages

```
import numpy as np

from sklearn.linear_model import LinearRegression

from sklearn.preprocessing import PolynomialFeatures
```

Step 2a: Provide the Data

```
x = [[0, 1], [5, 1], [15, 2], [25, 5], [35, 11], [45, 15], [55, 34], [60, 35]]

y = [4, 5, 20, 14, 32, 22, 38, 43]

x, y = np.array(x), np.array(y)
```

Step 3: Transform the Input Data

```
x_ = PolynomialFeatures(degree=2, include_bias=False).fit_transform(x)
```

Step 4: Create and Fit the Model

```
model = LinearRegression().fit(x_, y)
```

Step 5: Get the Results

```
r_sq = model.score(x_, y)

intercept, coefficients = model.intercept_, model.coef_
```

Step 6: Make the Prediction

```
y_pred = model.predict(x_)
```

If you use this example, you should see these results and predictions:

```
>>>

>>> print('coefficient of determination:', r_sq)

coefficient of determination: 0.9453701449127822

>>> print('intercept:', intercept)

intercept: 0.8430556452395734

>>> print('coefficients:', coefficients, sep='\n')

coefficients:

[ 2.44828275   0.16160353  -0.15259677   0.47928683 -
0.4641851 ]

>>> print('predicted response:', y_pred, sep='\n')
```

predicted response:

[0.54047408   11.36340283   16.07809622   15.79139

29.73858619 23.50834636

39.05631386 41.92339046]

Here, we have no less than six regression coefficients and that includes the intercept, as you can see from our estimated regression function:

$$f(x_1, x_2) = b_0 + b_1x_1 + b_2x_2 + b_3x_1^2 + b_4x_1x_2 + b_5x_2^2.$$

You should also see that, when we use polynomial regression, the coefficient of determination is much higher than it is with linear regression when used with an identical problem. You might think, to start with, that a much larger R^2 is a great result and well it might be. However, when you think in terms of real-world situations, complex models and an R^2 that is very near 1 could also indicate overfitting. To ensure your model is performing as it should be, test it with new data, i.e. observations that you have not already used for training the model.

Using statsmodels for Advanced Linear Regression

scikit-learn isn't the only package that we can use for linear regression. If you want to go more advanced then scikit-learn won't provide what you need but the statsmodels package will and the procedure really isn't much different from scikit-learn.

Step 1: Import the Packages

First off, we need to do a few imports. You will need numpy and you will also need statsmodels.api:

import numpy as np

import statsmodels.api as sm

Those are the two packages needed for advanced linear regression.

Step 2: Provide the Data and Transform the Inputs

The inputs and outputs must be provided now and this is done in pretty much the same way as we did it with scikit-learn:

x = [[0, 1], [5, 1], [15, 2], [25, 5], [35, 11], [45, 15], [55, 34], [60, 35]]

y = [4, 5, 20, 14, 32, 22, 38, 43]

x, y = np.array(x), np.array(y)

Although the input array and output array have been created, we have more to do. The column of ones must be added to the inputs if we are to have statsmodels calculate the intercept of b_0 because it won't take b_0 into account as a default. This is done with a single function call:

x = sm.add_constant(x)

That is all you need to do to provide x with the column of ones, using add_constant(). The input array of x is taken as an argument and a new array is returned; the new array has the column of ones at the start. Here you can see what x and y now look like:

```
>>>

>>> print(x)

[[ 1.  0.  1.]

 [ 1.  5.  1.]

 [ 1. 15.  2.]

 [ 1. 25.  5.]

 [ 1. 35. 11.]

 [ 1. 45. 15.]

 [ 1. 55. 34.]

 [ 1. 60. 35.]]

>>> print(y)

[ 4  5 20 14 32 22 38 43]
```

As you can see, our modified input x now has three columns – the first is the column of ones, which corresponds to b_0 and replaces the intercept; the second and third both contain the original features.

Step 3: Create and Fit the Model

An instance of the statsmodels.regression.linear_model.OLS is the regression model that is based on ordinary least squares and you get one like this:

model = sm.OLS(y, x)

Be careful – note that the output is the first argument and that is followed by the input. Once the class has been created, .fit() can be applied to it:

results = model.fit()

When you call .fit(), you get the variable results and this is a statsmodels.regression.linear_model.RegressionResultsWrapper class instance. The object contains a whole heap of information about our regression model.

Step 4: Get the Results

The variable results are referring to the object that has all that detailed info about the model and, while it is beyond the scope of this guide to delve into them, we can look at how you can extract them.

To obtain a tale containing the linear regression results, simply call .summary():

>>>

```
>>> print(results.summary())
```

OLS Regression Results

==

Dep. Variable:	y	R-squared:	0.862
Model:	OLS	Adj. R-squared:	0.806
Method:	Least Squares	F-statistic:	15.56
Date:	Sun, 17 Feb 2019	Prob (F-statistic):	0.00713
Time	19:15:07	Log-Likelihood:	-24.316
No. Observations:	8	AIC:	54.63
Df Residuals:	5	BIC:	54.87
Df Model:	2		
Covariance Type:	nonrobust		

==

	coef	std err	t	P>|t|	[0.025	0.975]
const	5.5226	4.431	1.246	0.268	-5.867	16.912
x1	0.4471	0.285	1.567	0.178	-0.286	1.180

x2	0.2550	0.453		0.563	0.598	-0.910		1.420

===

Omnibus:	0.561	Durbin-Watson:	3.268
Prob(Omnibus):	0.755	Jarque-Bera (JB):	0.534
Skew:	0.380	Prob(JB):	0.766
Kurtosis:	1.987	Cond. No.	80.1

===

Warnings:

[1] Standard Errors assume that the covariance matrix of the errors is correctly specified.

This is an incredibly complex table and it contains a large number of statistical values that go with linear regression, and that includes R^2, b_0, b_1, and b_2.

Any value from that table can be extracted; have a look at this example:

>>>

>>> print('coefficient of determination:', results.rsquared)

coefficient of determination: 0.8615939258756777

```
>>> print('adjusted coefficient of determination:',
results.rsquared_adj)

adjusted coefficient of determination: 0.8062314962259488

>>> print('regression coefficients:', results.params)

regression coefficients: [5.52257928 0.44706965
0.25502548]
```

That is how the linear regression results are obtained:

- **.rsquared** – this has R in it.

- **.rsquared_adj** – this is used to represent the adjusted R^2 which is a corrected version of R^2 based on how many input features there are.

- **.params** – this is referencing the array that has, respectively, b_0, b_1, and b_2.

Also note that the results are exactly the same as the results we obtained using scikit-learn on an identical problem.

Step 5: Predict the Response

The predicted response for the input values that we used to create our model can be obtained using either .predict() or .fittedvalues with an argument of the input array:

```
>>>
```

```
>>> print('predicted response:', results.fittedvalues, sep='\n')
```

predicted response:

```
[  5.77760476    8.012953       12.73867497  17.9744479
23.97529728 29.4660957
```

```
 38.78227633 41.27265006]
```

```
>>> print('predicted response:', results.predict(x), sep='\n')
```

The predicted response is:

```
[  5.77760476    8.012953       12.73867497  17.9744479
23.97529728 29.4660957
```

```
 38.78227633 41.27265006]
```

This predicted response is for the known inputs. If you wanted predictions using new regressors, .predict() can also be applied with an argument of new data:

```
>>>
```

```
>>> x_new = sm.add_constant(np.arange(10).reshape((-1, 2)))
```

```
>>> print(x_new)
```

```
[[1. 0. 1.]
```

```
 [1. 2. 3.]
```

[1. 4. 5.]

[1. 6. 7.]

[1. 8. 9.]]

>>> y_new = results.predict(x_new)

>>> print(y_new)

[5.77760476   7.18179502   8.58598528   9.99017554
11.3943658]

Note that these predicted results are identical as those we get using scikit-learn with the same problem.

Beyond Linear Regression

Linear regression will not always be the most appropriate approach, particularly where we have highly complex models that are not linear. Thankfully, we do have some more regression techniques more suited for when linear regression simply doesn't work as it should. Some of those techniques include decision trees, support vector machines, neural networks and random forest, some of which will be discussed in this guide.

There are also a number of Python libraries that you can use for regression with those techniques and most are free, open-source libraries. That is one of the biggest reasons why Python is one of the most used computer programming languages for machine learning and deep learning.

The scikit-learn package provides us with what we need to use these other regression techniques in ways similar to what you have already observed. In it, you will find classes that go with decision trees, support vector machines, random forest and many more, using the methods called .predict(), .fit(), .score(), and more.

You are now aware of linear regression, what it is, how it works and how it can be implemented using Python and a number of open-source libraries, namely NumPy, statsmodels, and scikit-learn.

NumPy is used for array handling and linear regression is implemented using the following:

- **scikit-learn** – if you are not looking for results that are highly detailed and you want an approach that is consistent with many other regression techniques.

- **statsmodels** - if you are looking for the model parameters that are more advanced statistically

Both of these are well worth taking the time to learn and looking into further than we have explored here.

When you perform linear regression in Python, these steps are the ones to follow for success:

1. Import the classes and packages required

2. Provide the data that is going to be worked with and, at some point, do the relevant transformations

3. Create your regression model and fit it (train it) on the existing data

4. Check the model fitting results to determine whether the model is satisfactory or not

5. Apply that model for the predictions

Next we look at another important subject to learn for deep learning – logistical regression.

Logistical Regression in Python

One of the most important parts of machine learning, deep learning and data mining is the classification techniques. Almost 70% of Data Science problems fall into the category of classification problems and there are plenty of these problems available. However, the logistics regression is one of the most common and most useful of all regression methods for solving one particular classification problem – the binary classification problem.

Multinomial classification is another classification category which is used for handling issues where the target variable contains multiple classes. An example of that is the IRIS dataset, one of the most famous of all the multiple class classifications.

We can use logistic regression for a number of classification problems, including the spam detection problem. Other examples include diabetes prediction, predicting whether specific products will be purchased by a customer or whether they go to a competitor, or whether users are likely to click on a specific ad link or not.

It is one of the most common and easiest of the two-class machine learning algorithms. It is the simplest to implement and is commonly used as a baseline for many binary classification problems. The fundamental concepts of logistic regression are also incredibly constructive as far as deep learning goes. It both describes and estimates what the relationship is between one dependent and two or more independent variables.

In this section, you will learn:

- What logistic regression is

- Logistic vs linear regression

- Ordinary Least Square Method vs Maximum Likelihood Estimation

- How logistic regression works

- Using scikit-learn for model building

- Using confusion matrix for model evaluation

- The pros and cons of logistic regression

Logistic Regression

Logistic regression is one of the statistical methods used for the prediction of binary classes. The target variable (outcome) is dichotomous which means that there can only be two possible classes For example, we can use logistic regression for problems surrounding cancer detection because it is used for computing the probability that an event will occur.

Logistic regression is a special linear regression case with a categorical target variable. The dependent variable is a log of odds and logistic regression will predict what the probability is of a binary event that uses a logit function occurring.

The linear regression equation is:

$$y = \beta 0 + \beta 1 x 1 + \beta 2 x 2 + \ldots + \beta n X n$$

In this equation, y is a dependent variable and the explanatory variables are x1, x2, … and Xn.

The sigmoid function is:

$$p = 1/1 + e^{-y}$$

Applying the Sigmoid function on linear regression looks like this:

$$p = 1/1 + e^{-\beta0 + \beta1x1 + \beta2x2 + \ldots + \beta nXn}$$

The properties of logistic regression are:

- The dependent variable always follows the Bernoulli Distribution

- Maximum likelihood is used for estimation

- Calculation of No R Square Model fitness is done using Concordance, KS-Statistics

Logistic Vs Linear Regression

With linear regression, we get a continuous output whereas logistic regression gives us a constant output. As an example of continuous, think about house prices and stock prices. Examples of discrete output would be cancer prediction, predicting if a customer will go to a competitor, and so on. We estimate linear regression using OLS (Ordinary Least Square) while MLE (Maximum Likelihood Estimation) is used for estimating logistic regression.

Least Square Method Vs Maximum Likelihood Estimation

Where OLS is a method for distance-minimizing approximation, MLE is a method of maximizing likelihood. The MLE function will determine which parameters are best for producing the observed data. From the point of view of statistics, MLE will set the variance and the mean as the parameters needed to determine which parametric values are needed for any specific model. We can use this parameter set to predict what data is required for a normal distribution.

Conversely, to compute OLS estimates, we fit a regression line on specified data points with the least square error (minimum sum of squared deviations). Both can be used for determining what a linear regression model's parameters are. MLE will assume a function of joint probability mass while OLS can minimize distance without needing any stochastic assumptions.

The Sigmoid Function

The sigmoid function is also known as a logistic function and it provides an S curve. This curve can take on any number that has a real value and map it to any value between 0 and 1. Should the curve head to positive infinity, the y prediction will be 1 whereas if the curve goes to negative infinity, the y prediction will be 0. If the sigmoid function produces an output that is higher than 0.5, the outcome could be classified as either 1 or as YES. If we had an output of 0.75, we could say, in probability terms, that a patient has a 75% chance of getting cancer.

Types of Logistic Regression

There are three main types of logistic regression:

- **Binary Logistic Regression** – this is where the target variable has just two outcomes possible, i.e. cancer/no cancer, spam/not spam, etc.

- **Multinomial Logistic Regression** – this is where the target variable has at least three nominal categories, such as the prediction of a wine type.

- **Ordinal Logistic Regression** – this is where the target variable has at least three ordinal categories, such as product or restaurant ratings from 1 through 5.

Using scikit-learn for Model Building

To demonstrate this, we can build a model that predicts diabetes and we do this with a logistic regression classifier. First we need to load the dataset. This is the Pima Indian Diabetes dataset and we load it using the read CSV function in pandas.

The data can be downloaded from https://data.world/uci/pima-indians-diabetes

Load the data like this:

#import pandas

```
import pandas as pd

col_names = ['pregnant', 'glucose', 'bp', 'skin', 'insulin', 'bmi',
'pedigree', 'age', 'label']
```

load dataset

```
pima = pd.read_csv("pima-indians-diabetes.csv",
header=None, names=col_names)
```

pima.head()

Feature Selection

For this, the given columns need to be divided up into two variables types – dependent, which is the target variable, or independent which are the feature variables.

feature_cols = ['pregnant', 'insulin', 'bmi', 'age','glucose','bp','pedigree']

X = pima[feature_cols] # Features

y = pima.label # Target variable

Split the Data

In order to properly understand model performance, one of the best strategies is to divide your dataset into two – a training set and a test set. We can do this using a function called train_test_split(). It requires three parameters of target, features and test_set size and random_state can also be used for the random selection of records.

split X and y into training and testing sets

from sklearn.cross_validation import train_test_split

X_train,X_test,y_train,y_test=train_test_split(X,y,test_size=0.25,random_state=0)

/home/admin/.local/lib/python3.5/site-packages/sklearn/cross_validation.py:41:

The dataset is divided into two with a ratio of 75:25 which means that we use 75% of the data to train the model and 25% to test it.

Development of the Model and Prediction

First, the logistic regression model needs to be imported and a logistic regression classifier created and this is done using the function called LogisticRegression(). Then, we use fit() for fitting the model on the training set and use predict() for performing the prediction on the test data set.

import the class

    from sklearn.linear_model import LogisticRegression

instantiate the model (using the default parameters)

    logreg = LogisticRegression()

fit the model with data

    logreg.fit(X_train,y_train)

#

    y_pred=logreg.predict(X_test)

Using Confusion Matrix for Model Evaluation

A confusion matrix is a table used for the performance evaluation of classification models and for visualizing the performance of a given algorithm. The basis of a confusion matrix is that class-wise

285

summing up is done for the number of correct predictions and incorrect predictions.

import the metrics class

from sklearn import metrics

cnf_matrix = metrics.confusion_matrix(y_test, y_pred)

cnf_matrix

array([[119, 11],

[26, 36]])

When you input this, a graph will show up. Note that the confusion matrix is in the same format as the array object. The matrix has a dimension of 2*2 and this is because we have a binary classification model. There are two classes here, 0 and 1, and the diagonal values are representing the accurate predictions while the inaccurate predictions are represented by the non-diagonal elements. The output shows us that both 36 and 119 are actual predictions while 11 and 26 and inaccurate.

Using Heatmap to Visualize a Confusion Matrix

Using seaborn and matplotlib, we can visualize our model results as a confusion matrix. We'll do this with Heatmap:

import required modules

```python
import numpy as np

import matplotlib.pyplot as plt

import seaborn as sns

%matplotlib inline

class_names=[0,1] # name  of classes

fig, ax = plt.subplots()

tick_marks = np.arange(len(class_names))

plt.xticks(tick_marks, class_names)

plt.yticks(tick_marks, class_names)
# create heatmap

sns.heatmap(pd.DataFrame(cnf_matrix),          annot=True,
cmap="YlGnBu" ,fmt='g')

ax.xaxis.set_label_position("top")

plt.tight_layout()

plt.title('Confusion matrix', y=1.1)

plt.ylabel('Actual label')

plt.xlabel('Predicted label')
```

Text(0.5,257.44,'Predicted label')

Evaluation Metrics of the Confusion Matrix

We can use a number of evaluation metrics for evaluating our model, like precision, accuracy, and recall:

```
print("Accuracy:",metrics.accuracy_score(y_test, y_pred))

print("Precision:",metrics.precision_score(y_test, y_pred))

print("Recall:",metrics.recall_score(y_test, y_pred))

Accuracy: 0.8072916666666666

Precision: 0.7659574468085106

Recall: 0.5806451612903226
```

The classification rate comes out as 80% and this is generally considered to be a good rate of accuracy.

- **Precision -** this is all about, as you would expect, being precise. In terms of the model, we want to know how accurate it is. So, when a prediction is made by our model, we want to know how often a correct prediction is made. In our case, our logistic regression model predicted that 76% of patients will get diabetes.

- **Recall** – if patients in the test data set have got diabetes and our logistic regression model can produce accurate predictions to the tune of 58%.

ROC Curve

The ROC, or Receiver Operating Characteristic, curve is a plot showing the true positive against the false positive rate. Basically, it shows up the tradeoff that exists between specificity and sensitivity:

```
y_pred_proba = logreg.predict_proba(X_test)[::,1]

fpr, tpr, _ = metrics.roc_curve(y_test, y_pred_proba)

auc = metrics.roc_auc_score(y_test, y_pred_proba)

plt.plot(fpr,tpr,label="data 1, auc="+str(auc))

plt.legend(loc=4)

plt.show()
```

The AUC score is 0.86; a score of 1 is representative of the perfect classifier while 0.5 is indicative of a very poor classifier.

Pros and Cons of Logistic Regression

Everything has its good and bad sides and logistic regression is no different.

Advantages

Logistic regression is highly efficient and incredibly straightforward. This means we don't need to use tons of computational power, it is very simple to implement and it is easy to interpret. It is used by data scientists and data analysts a lot and there is no need for feature scaling. Lastly, the use of logistic regression provides us with a probability score for the purpose of observation.

Disadvantages

Now to the downsides. Logistic regression cannot handle cases where there are many categorical variables or features and it is prone to overfitting. We cannot use this type of regression to solve non-linear problems, hence we need to transform non-linear features first. Logistic regression really doesn't work too well with independent variables that have no correlation to the target variable and those that are correlated or similar to one another.

That completes our look at the basics needed for deep learning. In the next section, we turn our attention to deep neural networks, or DNNs.

Part 2

Deep Neural Networks

━━━━━━━◆━━━━━━━

Before we can even begin to look into DNNs, or deep neural networks, you need to have a decent understanding of what artificial neural networks (ANNs) are and how they work.

Artificial Neural Networks

An artificial neural network takes its inspiration from the biological neural network. An ANN can observe examples and can learn how to do things, how to perform tasks. There isn't any need to program an ANN with any rules; it will simply look at images, for example, those with a dog and those without, and learn how to identify even more images by itself.

A network like this is made up of artificial neurons which are basically a series of nodes connected together. These nodes are modeled on the neurons in our own brains and each node has the capability to send a signal to another one. That neuron will process what it receives and then send signals out to more nodes. In this way, we input, we have output and we have those hidden layers.

Some of the more common examples of ANNs are speech recognition, computer vision, social network filtering, machine translation, game playing, medical diagnoses and more.

In this section we are going to build our very own ANN using NumPy in Python. We will build it from the ground up and use it for classifying image from the dataset called Fruits360, which you can download from https://data.mendeley.com/datasets/rp73yg93n8/1.

This dataset contains 60 separate fruit classes including kiwi, apple, peach, lemon, cherry, etc. but to make things easier for now we are going to work on just four classes – apple Braeburn, lemon Meyer, mango, raspberry. Each of the classes contains approximately 490 training images and 160 test images with each image being 100 x 100 pixels.

Extracting Features

We begin by selecting the features that we want to ensure the highest accuracy in the classification. If you were to look at the images for each of our four classes, you would see that they are all very different in color and this is why it makes sense for us to use the color features.

If we use RGB for image representation, all three of the channels (red, blue, green) will be used in the calculation – the RGB color space doesn't separate the color information from any other information type. For this reason, it is far better that we use a different color space, one like HSV (hue, saturation, value) that will

292

isolate the information into just one channel – in this case, it would be the hue channel. This remains as 100 x 100 for the channel size and if we applied this whole channel to our ANN, we would have an input layer of a massive 10,000 neurons. We need to reduce how much data we are using so we use the histogram for channel representation. This will indicate the number of possible values using 360 bins; this results in far less overlap among the classes than if we used RGB, For example, take the apple histogram vs the mango – the apple has bins ranging from 0 to 10 while mango goes from 90 to 110. We can cut down on classification ambiguity and increase prediction accuracy quite easily.

The code below will use the four images selected and calculate our histogram for the hue channel:

```
import numpy

import skimage.io, skimage.color

import matplotlib.pyplot


raspberry    =    skimage.io.imread(fname="raspberry.jpg",
as_grey=False)

apple    =    skimage.io.imread(fname="apple.jpg",
as_grey=False)
```

```python
mango       =       skimage.io.imread(fname="mango.jpg",
as_grey=False)

lemon       =       skimage.io.imread(fname="lemon.jpg",
as_grey=False)


apple_hsv = skimage.color.rgb2hsv(rgb=apple)

mango_hsv = skimage.color.rgb2hsv(rgb=mango)

raspberry_hsv = skimage.color.rgb2hsv(rgb=raspberry)

lemon_hsv = skimage.color.rgb2hsv(rgb=lemon)


fruits = ["apple", "raspberry", "mango", "lemon"]

hsv_fruits_data = [apple_hsv, raspberry_hsv, mango_hsv,
lemon_hsv]

idx = 0

for hsv_fruit_data in hsv_fruits_data:

fruit = fruits[idx]

hist = numpy.histogram(a=hsv_fruit_data[:, :, 0], bins=360)
```

```
matplotlib.pyplot.bar(left=numpy.arange(360),
height=hist[0])

matplotlib.pyplot.savefig(fruit+"-hue-histogram.jpg",
bbox_inches="tight")

matplotlib.pyplot.close("all")

idx = idx + 1
```

Feature extraction from each image is done by looping through every image in each of our four image classes and you can see how that is done in our next code example. First, in the four classes, there are 1,962 images; we extracted a feature vector length of 360 from each of the images and created an array of zeros in NumPy. This was saved in a variable called dataset_features. For a class label to be stored for each image, we use another NumPy array we call outputs. The class labels are:

- Apple – 0

- Lemon – 1

- Mange – 2

- Raspberry – 3

Our code will expect to run in a root directory which contains four folders. Each folder is named as per the fruits that are in the list called fruits. The code will loop through every image in every folder, extracting the histogram (hue) from them; it then assigns a class label to each image and saves the features it extracted, along with the labels, using a library called pickle. You could also use NumPy if you preferred for this:

```
import numpy

import skimage.io, skimage.color, skimage.feature

import os

import pickle


fruits = ["apple", "raspberry", "mango", "lemon"]

#492+490+490+490=1,962


dataset_features = numpy.zeros(shape=(1962, 360))

outputs = numpy.zeros(shape=(1962))

idx = 0

class_label = 0


for fruit_dir in fruits:

    curr_dir = os.path.join(os.path.sep, fruit_dir)

    all_imgs = os.listdir(os.getcwd()+curr_dir)
```

```
for img_file in all_imgs:

    fruit_data                                                    =
skimage.io.imread(fname=os.getcwd()+curr_dir+img_file,
as_grey=False)

    fruit_data_hsv = skimage.color.rgb2hsv(rgb=fruit_data)

    hist    =    numpy.histogram(a=fruit_data_hsv[:,    :,    0],
bins=360)

    dataset_features[idx, :] = hist[0]

    outputs[idx] = class_label

    idx = idx + 1

class_label = class_label + 1


with open("dataset_features.pkl", "wb") as f:

    pickle.dump("dataset_features.pkl", f)


with open("outputs.pkl", "wb") as f:

    pickle.dump(outputs, f)
```

Right now, each of our images is represented with a 360 element feature vector. These elements are filtered so that only the relevant elements are kept for differentiation between the classes. That reduces the vector length to 102 and this ensures the training is much faster. The variable called dataset_features will have a shape of 1962 x 102.

Our training features are ready so it is time to use NumPy for implementing our ANN.

Implementing the ANN

The target ANN structure will have an output layer that has 102 inputs. It will also have two hidden layers, one with 150 neurons and one with 60 neurons, along with an output layer that has four outputs, one for each of the fruit classes.

We use matrix multiplication to multiply the input vectors at any layer by the weight matrix that connects it to the next layer – this gives us the output vector. This vector will then be multiplied again by the weight matrix that connects it to the next layer and this process will carry on until it gets to the output layer.

So, keeping in mind this is matrix multiplication, our input vector, which is 1 x 102 size, will be multiplied by the first hidden layer's weight matrix, size 102 x 150. The shape of the output array will be 1 x 150. This output becomes the input for the next hidden layer and is, in turn, multiplied by the weight matrix with a size of 150 x 60, giving a result of 1 x 60. Lastly, this output will be multiplied by the weight matrix that is in between the output layer with a size of 60 x 4 and the second hidden layer. The final output is 1 x 4. Each of the elements in a vector like this is referencing one output class and the input sample is given a label as per the class that has the highest score.

Here's the code that will implement all this:

```
import numpy

import pickle


def sigmoid(inpt):

  return 1.0 / (1 + numpy.exp(-1 * inpt))


f = open("dataset_features.pkl", "rb")

data_inputs2 = pickle.load(f)

f.close()


features_STDs = numpy.std(a=data_inputs2, axis=0)

data_inputs = data_inputs2[:, features_STDs > 50]


f = open("outputs.pkl", "rb")

data_outputs = pickle.load(f)

f.close()
```

```python
HL1_neurons = 150

input_HL1_weights = numpy.random.uniform(low=-0.1,
high=0.1,

    size=(data_inputs.shape[1], HL1_neurons))


HL2_neurons = 60

HL1_HL2_weights = numpy.random.uniform(low=-0.1,
high=0.1,

    size=(HL1_neurons, HL2_neurons))


output_neurons = 4

HL2_output_weights = numpy.random.uniform(low=-0.1,
high=0.1,

    size=(HL2_neurons, output_neurons))


H1_outputs = numpy.matmul(a=data_inputs[0, :],
b=input_HL1_weights)

H1_outputs = sigmoid(H1_outputs)

H2_outputs = numpy.matmul(a=H1_outputs,
b=HL1_HL2_weights)

H2_outputs = sigmoid(H2_outputs)
```

```
out_otuputs = numpy.matmul(a=H2_outputs,
b=HL2_output_weights)


predicted_label = numpy.where(out_otuputs ==
numpy.max(out_otuputs))[0][0]
print("Predicted class : ", predicted_label)
```

Once the features that were saved earlier have been read, along with their corresponding output labels and the features have been filtered, we can define the weight matrix for each layer. These matrices are provided with random values from -0.1 to 0.1. For example, take the variable called input_HL1_weights – this contains the weight matrix between the first hidden layer and the input layer. The size of this is determined using the number of the elements (features) and the number of the neuron present in the first hidden layer.

Once the weight matrices have been created, we move on to applying the matrix multiplications. For example, in the variable called H1_outputs, there is the output from the multiplication of a specified sample and the weight matrix that is between the first hidden layer and the input layer.

Normally, we would apply an activation function to each hidden layer's outputs, thus creating a relationship between the inputs and outputs that is non-linear. For example, we would apply the matrix multiplication outputs to the sigmoid activation function.

Once the outputs from the output layer have been generated, we can move onto prediction. The label for the predicted class is saved in the variable called predicted_label and this is repeated for every input sample. For all the samples, this is the complete code:

```python
import numpy

import pickle


def sigmoid(inpt):
    return 1.0 / (1 + numpy.exp(-1 * inpt))


def relu(inpt):
    result = inpt
    result[inpt < 0] = 0
    return result


def update_weights(weights, learning_rate):
    new_weights = weights - learning_rate * weights
    return new_weights
```

```python
def train_network(num_iterations, weights, data_inputs,
data_outputs, learning_rate, activation="relu"):

for iteration in range(num_iterations):

print("Iteration ", iteration)

for sample_idx in range(data_inputs.shape[0]):

r1 = data_inputs[sample_idx, :]

for idx in range(len(weights) - 1):

curr_weights = weights[idx]

r1 = numpy.matmul(a=r1, b=curr_weights)

if activation == "relu":

r1 = relu(r1)

elif activation == "sigmoid":

r1 = sigmoid(r1)

curr_weights = weights[-1]

r1 = numpy.matmul(a=r1, b=curr_weights)

predicted_label = numpy.where(r1 == numpy.max(r1))[0][0]

desired_label = data_outputs[sample_idx]

if predicted_label != desired_label:

weights = update_weights(weights,

learning_rate=0.001)
```

```python
    return weights

def predict_outputs(weights, data_inputs, activation="relu"):
    predictions = numpy.zeros(shape=(data_inputs.shape[0]))
    for sample_idx in range(data_inputs.shape[0]):
        r1 = data_inputs[sample_idx, :]
        for curr_weights in weights:
            r1 = numpy.matmul(a=r1, b=curr_weights)
            if activation == "relu":
                r1 = relu(r1)
            elif activation == "sigmoid":
                r1 = sigmoid(r1)
        predicted_label = numpy.where(r1 == numpy.max(r1))[0][0]
        predictions[sample_idx] = predicted_label
    return predictions

f = open("dataset_features.pkl", "rb")
data_inputs2 = pickle.load(f)
f.close()
```

```python
features_STDs = numpy.std(a=data_inputs2, axis=0)

data_inputs = data_inputs2[:, features_STDs > 50]


f = open("outputs.pkl", "rb")

data_outputs = pickle.load(f)

f.close()


HL1_neurons = 150

input_HL1_weights = numpy.random.uniform(low=-0.1, high=0.1,

size=(data_inputs.shape[1], HL1_neurons))


HL2_neurons = 60

HL1_HL2_weights = numpy.random.uniform(low=-0.1, high=0.1,

size=(HL1_neurons, HL2_neurons))


output_neurons = 4

HL2_output_weights = numpy.random.uniform(low=-0.1, high=0.1,
```

```
size=(HL2_neurons, output_neurons))


weights = numpy.array([input_HL1_weights,

  HL1_HL2_weights,

  HL2_output_weights])


weights = train_network(num_iterations=10,

weights=weights,

data_inputs=data_inputs,

data_outputs=data_outputs,

learning_rate=0.01,

activation="relu")


predictions = predict_outputs(weights, data_inputs)

num_flase = numpy.where(predictions != data_outputs)[0]

print("num_flase ", num_flase.size)
```

The variables named weights will hold the weights from across the whole network. Dynamic specification of the network structure is based on each weight matrix size. For example, if the variable called inout_HL1_weights had a size of 102 x 80, it would easy to work out that the first hidden layer contained 80 neurons.

The core function is called train_network because it loops through every sample to train the network. For each individual sample, the function accepts the training iteration number, the feature, the output labels, the weights, the learning rate and, finally, the activation function, which will be either ReLU or sigmoid. The ReLU function is a threshold function – for as long as it is zero, it will return the same function, otherwise zero is returned.

If a false prediction were made by the network for any given sample, the function called update_weights is used to update the weights rather than using an optimization algorithm. Each weight is updated as per the learning rate and the accuracy will never go over 45%. If you want far higher accuracy you would need to use an optimization algorithm, such as the gradient descent technique that you can find in the scikit-learn library (ANN implementation).

That gives you an overview of the artificial neural network, time to get back to our deep neural networks.

Deep Neural Networks

Back to our deep neural networks; these are really nothing more than an ANN with several layers in between the input and output layers. Networks like this look through several layers, calculating what the probability is for each output. And a DNN can model a complex relationship that isn't linear.

DNN Structure

DNNs are normally feedforward networks, which means that the input layer data will flow onto the output layer with no loopback. A network like this with one hidden layer is called a shallow feedforward neural network. However, in a deep neural network, you could have, for example, 1000 or more hidden layers. Whatever the number, to be considered as a DNN, it must have more than two.

DNNs create maps showing virtual neurons and then assigns a weight randomly to the connection between each neuron. The weights are multiplied with the inputs and the return is an output of somewhere between 0 and 1. If a DNN cannot find a pattern, it will adjust the weights using an algorithm.

Different Types of DNN with Python

In broad terms, Python deep neural networks can be classified into two categories and we'll discuss them now.

RNNs – Recurrent Neural Networks

RNNs are a type of ANN with the node connections forming a graph directed along a specified sequence. RNNs can make use of their own internal memory or state for processing the input sequences. As such, an RNN can be used for several different tasks, such as speech recognition, and connected handwriting recognition (unsegmented). There are two main types of RNN:

- **Infinite Impulse RNN** – a directed cyclic graph that cannot be unrolled

- **Finite Impulse RNN** – a directed acyclic graph that can be replaced by a strict feedforward network.

A simple RNN is just a neuron network where the neurons are stored in layers. Each node in each layer will connect directly and one-directional with each node in the next layer. Data may flow in any direction in an RNN and we can use LSTM (Long Short-Term Memory); RNNs can be used in many different applications including language modeling.

Before we look at how to implement them, let's take a deeper look. At its highest level, an RNN can process sequences – this could be sentences, daily stock prices, sensor measurements, and so on – one individual element at a time, all the while retaining the state or memory of what came before in that sequence.

The 'Recurrent' in Recurrent Neural Network indicates that the current time step output will become the input to the next one. At each sequence element, the model will consider both the current input and everything it can remember about the elements that came before, known as state or memory.

This memory is how the network can learn the long-term dependencies in sequences that mean the whole context can be considered when a prediction is made. RNNs are designed in a way that they can mimic human behavior for sequence processing- when a human forms a response, they will consider everything, for example instead of individual words, we would take an entire sentence into account. Look at the following sentence:

"For the first 15 minutes, while the band was warming up, the concert was very boring but then things got exciting."

For a machine learning model that looks at each work individually and unconnected to all the others, this would likely be considered as a negative sentence. However, an RNN would be able to see the words, "but" and "exciting" and would see that the sentence is actually a positive one. This is because it reads the whole sequence and that is what provides the context needed to process the meaning – recurrent neural networks have this concept encoded into them.

A layer consisting of memory cells lies at the heart of every RNN. The LSTM is the 'cell of the moment', a cell that maintains both cell state and a carry which ensures that the signal (a gradient containing the information), isn't lost while the sequence is being processed. We will be spending more time on the LSTM shortly but, for now, the LSTM considers three things at every time step – current word, carry and cell state.

LSTMs have three gates and weight vectors:

- **Forget gate** – this discards any information that is irrelevant

- **Input gate** – this handles current input

- **Output gate** – this produces the predictions at each of the time steps.

Each cell element function will be decided by the weights or parameters that were learned in the training phase. Each cell part could be labeled if you wanted but it really isn't necessary; don't forget that the RNN will retain a memory of the whole sequence so that previous information cannot be lost.

Problem Formulation

When it comes to training an RNN so it writes text, we have a choice of methods. For this example, training the RNN to write patent abstracts, we are going to train it as a 'many-to-one' mapper. In other words, a sequence of words is input and the model is trained to predict the next word in the sequence. The words are mapped, first to integers and then vectors and this is done with an embedding matrix – it could be a pre-trained one or a trainable one. Lastly, they go to the LSTM layer.

For writing a new patent, we begin by passing a sequence of words in. Next, a prediction for the next word is made, the input sequence is updated, another prediction made, and a new word added to our starting sequence. This continues as many times as needed for the number of words we want to be generated.

The approach steps are outlined below:

1. The abstracts are converted from a list of strings to a list of integers, which is the sequence

2. The feature and the labels are created from the sequence

3. The LSTM model is built using Embeddings, LSTM and Dense layers

4. Pre-trained embeddings are loaded in

5. The model is trained to predict the next word in the given sequence

6. The starting sequence is passed on so the predictions can be made

Bear in mind that this is just a single formulation of our problem. We could also go down the route of using a character-level model or we could make a prediction for every word in the sequence. Like most things in both machine and deep learning, there is always more than one answer. In practice though, the approach outlined above works well.

Preparing the Data

A neural network may have very powerful capabilities for representation but the most important thing is getting a dataset that is clean and high quality. You can download the raw data for the project from http://www.patentsview.org/querydev/ - simply type in your search term of 'neural network' and download the patent abstracts that result from this (there should be around 3500.

Patent Abstract Data

We'll begin with lists of strings for the patent abstracts and the main step for preparing the data for the model are:

1. Delete all punctuation and then split the strings into lists containing individual words

2. Convert each individual work into an integer

We can do both with the Keas Tokenizer class which, by default, will remove the punctuation, place all words into lowercase and then convert each one to an integer sequence. First, a tokenizer is fit on a string list and then it converts that list to a list of integers. We can see this demonstrated below:

Abstracts is a list of strings

abstracts[100] [:300]

Create Tokenizer object

tokenizer = Tokenizer(num_words=None'

filters=' ! "#$%&()*+, ; <=>?@[\\]^_'{|}~\t\n',

lower = True, split = ' ')

Train the tokenizer to the texts

```
tokenizer.fit_on_texts(abstracts)
```

\# Convert list of strings into list of lists of integers

```
sequencers = tokenizer.texts_to_sequences(abstracts)

sequences [100] [:15]

[1, 88, 71, 130, 11, 60, 4, 2, 29, 10, 586, 4, 583, 30,129]
```

The output that results from the first cell will show us the origianl abstract while that from the second will show us the tokenized sequence. An integer now represents each abstract.

The idx_word attribute from the tokenizer that was trained can be used to work out what those integers mean:

\# Mapping of indexes to words

```
idx_word = tokenizer.index_word

' ' .join(idx_word[w] for w in sequences [100] [:40]
```

Look close enough and you will see that the punctuation has been removed and all the words are now in lower case, thanks to the tokenizer. If we carried on with these settings, the RNN isn't going to learn proper English so we need to adjust things. We can change the Tokenizer filter so it doesn't remove the punctuation.

\# Do not remove the punctuation or uppercase the words

```
tokenizer = Tokenizer(num_words=None,
```

filters='#$%&()*+-<=>@[\\]^_`{|}~\t\n',

lower = False, split = ' ')

When pre-trained embeddings are used, the uppercase would need to be removed simply because the embeddings do not contain any lowercase letters.

Features and Labels

The last step will convert every abstract into an integer sequence so the next step is to create a problem to train the network with. That problem is a supervised machine learning problem and, while there are a number of ways to set an RNN task up to generate text, we will use this one:

'Provide a sequence of words to the network and then train it so it predicts the next one'.

One parameter is the number of words and, for our example, we are going to use 50. So we provide the network with 50 words and then train it so it predicts word 51. You could also train the network so it predicts the next word at each given point in a sequence, use individual characters to train it or have it predict each of the input words instead of one prediction for the whole sequence.

The implementation we are using isn't necessarily the best one because there is no best solution, but it does work well.

It is a relatively simple task to create features and labels and for each of the abstracts, we create several sets. The first 50 words are used as features and the 51st word is the label. Next the 2nd to 51st words are used as features and we predict the 52nd, and so on. Doing it this way gives us a lot of training data and this is really useful because network performance is directly proportional to how much data it sees while it is being trained.

Implementation of the feature and label creation can be seen below. The features will have a shape of 296866, 50, meaning there are nearly 300,000 sequences and each one has 50 tokens. In RNN language, every sequence will have 50 timesteps and each one has one feature.

The labels could be left as integers but neural networks are far more effective at training on one-hot encoded labels. We can use numpy to one-hot encode our labels quickly like this:

Number of words in the vocabulary

num_words = len(word_idx) + 1

Empty array to hold the labels

label_array = np.zeros((len(features), num_words), dtype = mp.int8)

One hot encode labels

for example_index, word_index in enumerate (labels):

label_array[example_index, word_index] = 1

label_array.shape

(29866, 11755)

label_array[100]

array([0, 0, 0, ..., 0, 0, 0], dtype=int8)

Finding the word that corresponds to a given row in label_array requires the following to be used:

Find word corresponding to the encoding

idx_word[np.argmax(label_array[100])]

'of'

Once we have formatted the labels and features correctly, we need to split them down into two sets – a training set and a validation set. A very important point to keep in mind is that the features and labels should be shuffled simultaneously so that we don't have the same abstracts ending up in the same set.

Building an RNN

This is where Keras comes in, one of the very best Python libraries that lets you use just a couple of easy Python code lines to build high-end models. There may be faster or more flexible models but, when it comes to ease of use and development time, Keras wins hands down.

We will use the Keras Sequential API to build our RNN from the ground up, one layer at a time. The layers we will use are:

- **Embedding Layer** – this will map each of the input words to a vector that is 100-dimensional. The embedding layer can make use of weights that are pre-trained and these are supplied in the parameter (weights). If we don't require the embeddings to be updated, we set training to False.

- **Masking Layer** – this masks any of the words that don't have the pre-trained embedding, represented as zeros. You should not use this layer for training the embeddings.

- **LSTM Cell Layer** – this should have dropout which will eliminate overfitting. Because we have just one of these layers, the sequences will not be returned. If you use more than one LSTM layer, ensure that the sequences are returned.

- **Dense Layer** – fully connected and with ReLU activation, thus giving the network extra representational capacity.

- **Dropout Layer** – this prevents overfitting

- **Dense Layer** – this one is a connected output layer and produces the probability for each word in the vocabulary. This is done with SoftMax activation.

The Adam optimizer is used to compile the model and the categorical_crossentropy loss is used for training it. Throughout the training, the network is going to adjust the trainable weights (parameters) to attempt minimization of log loss. Backpropagation is used to calculate the parameter gradients and the optimizer used to update them. Because it is Keras we using, we don't have to waste any time worrying about what's going on behind the scenes; all we have to is correctly set the network up.

LSTM Network Layout.

If the embeddings are not updated, we have far fewer parameters with which to train our network. The LSTM layer input is (None, 50, 100) and this means that, for each of the batches, there are 50 timesteps in each sequence and each timestep has 100 features (following embedding). LSTM layer input will always have the shape of (batch_size, timesteps, features).

Pre-Trained Embeddings

Once we have built the network, it still needs to be supplied with the pre-trained embeddings. You can find loads of these embeddings online, all trained on different bodies of text. We're going to use embeddings from an algorithm called GloVe, which stands for Global Vectors for Word Representation; they come from Stanford, are trained on Wikipedia and we will use the 100-dimension embeddings.

You can download them from

https://nlp.stanford.edu/projects/glove/

Although these pre-trained embeddings have 400,000 words in them, some of the words in our vocabulary have been included. When we use embeddings to represent these words, each will have 100-dimensional vectors of zeros. We can overcome this by training embeddings ourselves or by setting the trainable parameter for the embedding layer to True and by eliminating the Masking layer.

The pre-trained embeddings can be quickly loaded and an embedding matrix made with this code, that assigns each of the words in the vocabulary with a 100-dimensional vector. The vector is all zeros if the word doesn't have pre-trained embedding:

word_lookup['neural'][:10]

array([9.6690e-02, -1.5132e-02, -6.6492e-01, 1.4422e-04, 5.1057e-02,

-8.5086e-01, -6.1281e-01, -4.1836e-01, 2.0780e-01, 3.9385-01])

The cosine similarity can be used for exploring the embeddings; this finds those words that are the nearest to a specified query word within the embedding space:

Query: neural

Word: neural	Cosine Similarity:	1.0
Word: neuronal	Cosine Similarity:	0.6841
Word: cortical	Cosine Similarity:	0.676
Word: plasticity	Cosine Similarity:	0.6625
Word: pathways	Cosine Similarity:	0.6534
Word: neurons	Cosine Similarity:	0.6485
Word: sensory	Cosine Similarity:	0.6391
Word: cognitive	Cosine Similarity:	0.6125
Word: brain	Cosine Similarity:	0.6082
Word: physiological	Cosine Similarity	0.6022

Representations may only apply to one specific task because the embeddings have to be learned. When we use the pre-trained embeddings, it is with the hope that they were trained on a task that is near to what ours is. If, for example, the embeddings had been trained on Twitter tweets, they probably wouldn't work too well but because Wikipedia was used, they should work pretty well for most language processing.

Training Our Model

Now that our training data and validation data are ready, our network is built and our embeddings loaded, it is nearly time for the model to learn the task of writing the patent abstracts. However, best practice states that, when you are training a neural network, you use Keras callbacks of Early Stopping and Model Checkpoint:

- **Early Stopping** – this will stop the training when the validation loss stops decreasing

- **Model Checkpoint** – this will save the best model, using validation loss measurements, on disk

By using Early Stopping, we are ensuring that the model doesn't overfit to the training data and we don't waste any time on training for additional epochs that simply won't result in performance improvements. With Model Checkpoint, we have access to the very best model and, should the training get stopped many epochs in, we would not lose all the work.

Next, we can use this code to train the model and, once finished, the best saved model can be loaded back in and evaluated on the validation data for the last time:

```
from keras import load_model# Load in the model and
evaluate on validation data
model = load_model('../models/model.h5')
model.evaluate(X_valid, y_valid)
```

Overall, using the pre-trained embeddings, the model gave us a 23.9% validation accuracy. That isn't bad when you consider how difficult it would be for a human to predict the next word in a patent abstract!

What is important to remember here is that an RNN does not have any concepts surrounding the understanding of language. Effectively, it is a sophisticated machine that can recognize patterns. What it is doing is making a prediction based on how elements are ordered in a sequence and, if you wanted to get properly philosophical about things, it would be easy to argue that a human is nothing more than a pattern recognition machine and an RNN is acting as if it is a human machine.

RNN use goes way beyond generating text; we can use them for captioning images, machine translation, even identifying authorship. What we have discussed here is not going to put any humans out of work but, given more training data and a much larger model, it isn't inconceivable that a neural network could come up with new, even more reasonable abstracts.

It is all too easy to get stuck into the theory of a complex technique but a much better way of learning it is to simply get stuck in and start building. The theory isn't going anywhere and you can always go back to it. Most of us will never get as far as designing a neural network, let alone building one, but learning how to use them effectively is well worth it. What that means is, put the books away, get the computer out and start building.

In the next part, we turn to the Convolutional Neural Network.

CNN – Convolutional Neural Network

Otherwise known as ConvNet, a CNN is another type of ANN, this time, a deep, feedforward one. It tends to be used for applications like computer vision, analysis of visual imagery, NLP (Natural Language Processing), ASR (Automatic Speech Recognition) acoustic modeling, Recommender systems and more. CNN's use multilayer perceptrons to ensure the minimum amount of preprocessing and, in networks like this, the connection pattern that runs between the neurons mimics the organization of the visual cortex in animals.

The CNN has undoubtedly been one of the more influential points in the computer vision field. These networks tend to perform far better than standard computer vision and the results they produce are state-of-the-art. The CNN has also proven itself as being very successful in multiple real-life applications and studies, such as:

- Object detection, image classification, face recognition, and segmentation

- Self-drive cars that make use of vision systems based on a CNN

- Crystal structure classification using a CNN

To get a good understanding of all this success we need to go back in time a few years, to 2012. It was then that Alex Krizhevsky won the 2012 ImageNet Competition using a convolutional neural network, bringing classification error down to 15% from 26%. This competition, formally known as ILSVRC (ImageNet Large Scale Visual Recognition Challenge) started in 2010 and runs yearly. Research teams enter the competition to test our their algorithms on a provided data set and the idea is to find the highest accuracy over a number of recognition tasks.

It was at this time that neural networks finally regained their prominence, part of what is known as the 'third wave of neural networks'. Wave one was from the 1940s to the 1960s and wave two was from the 1970s to the 1980s. This time, the world was ready for them.

So, with a CNN you are going to be working with a feedforward network that takes its inspiration from the biological visual cortex. What does this mean though?

An image is fed to the network as an input. Multiple convolutions take place, followed by subsampling, a layer that is fully connected and lastly, we get an output. What, exactly, are these concepts?

- **Convolutional layer** – this layer computes the neuron output. These neurons are connected to receptive fields or local regions within the input and each computes a dot product on between each of their weights and a receptive field in the input volume that the neuron is connected to. Each of these computation results in feature map extraction from the input image. In basic terms, let's say that you have an image, represented by a matrix of values of 5 x 5. We take a matrix of 3 x 3 and slide it around our image. At each of the matrix positions, the values of the 3 x 3 window are multiplied by the values from the image the window is covering. The result is a single number and this number is representative of every value in the image window. This layer is used for filtering – as the window passes over the image, we can check to see if there are any patterns in each section. The filters make this possible as they are multiplied by the values the convolution outputs.

- **Subsampling** – the idea of this is to obtain an input representation. This is done by dimension reduction which also helps to reduce the chance of overfitting. Max pooling is one technique used in subsampling, involving selection of the highest value from a given region, dependent on size. In other words, with max-pooling we take the biggest value from the image window the kernel is covering at the time. You could, for example, have a size 2 x 2 max-pooling layer that gets the highest pixel value from a region of 2 x 2. In that way the max-pooling layer works much like a convolutional layer with two differences – we apply the function the kernel, and the image window is non-linear.

- **Fully connected layer** – the idea here is that the high-level features the convolutional layers learn are flattened and all the features are combined. The flattened output gets passed to the output layer and a SoftMax classifier or sigmoid used for predicting the label of the input class.

The Fashion-MNIST Data Set

Before you jump into downloading this, let's see what you will work with. The Fashion-MNIST dataset contains 70,000 grayscale images, each 28 x 8, each of a fashion product in 10 categories; each category contains 7,000 images. There are 60,000 images in the training dataset and 10,000 in the test dataset.

Loading the Data

In Keras, you will find a library named datasets. We use this library for loading datasets built-in to Keras, such as the Fashion-MNIST dataset. The data is downloaded from the server and provides a significant boost to processing time because the data doesn't need to be downloaded to your computer first. You will find the training images, along with the labels, stored in variables called train_X and train_Y, while the test images and labels are in test_X and test_Y.

from keras.datasets import fashion_mnist

```
(train_X,train_Y), (test_X,test_Y) =
fashion_mnist.load_data()
```

Using TensorFlow backend.

That was easy enough, wasn't it!

Now we are ready to begin the data analysis, before processing and then modeling the data.

Data Analysis

The next step is to analyze what the dataset images look like. You already know the image dimension but it is worth taking the time to programmatically analyze it – you may have to resize the images and scale the image pixels again:

```
import numpy as np

from keras.utils import to_categorical

import matplotlib.pyplot as plt

%matplotlib inline


print('Training data shape : ', train_X.shape, train_Y.shape)


print('Testing data shape : ', test_X.shape, test_Y.shape)
```

('Training data shape : ', (60000, 28, 28), (60000,))

('Testing data shape : ', (10000, 28, 28), (10000,))

From this, it is possible to see that our training data has a 60000 x 28 x 28 shape. This is because there are 60,000 images for training and each one is 28 x 28. In the same way, the test data has a 10000 x 28 x 28 shape for the same reasons.

Find unique numbers from the training labels

```
classes = np.unique(train_Y)

nClasses = len(classes)

print('Total number of outputs : ', nClasses)

print('Output classes : ', classes)
```

('Total number of outputs : ', 10)

('Output classes : ', array([0, 1, 2, 3, 4, 5, 6, 7, 8, 9], dtype=uint8))

And we have ten output classes, 0 through 9.

More importantly, don't forget to look at the images in the dataset:

```
plt.figure(figsize=[5,5])
```

Display first image in training data

    plt.subplot(121)

    plt.imshow(train_X[0,:,:], cmap='gray')

    plt.title("Ground Truth : {}".format(train_Y[0]))

Display first image in testing data

    plt.subplot(122)

    plt.imshow(test_X[0,:,:], cmap='gray')

    plt.title("Ground Truth : {}".format(test_Y[0]))

    Text(0.5,1,u'Ground Truth : 9')

These two plots produce an output that looks much like an ankle boot and a class label of 9 is assigned to the class. Other products will have their own labels while products similar to this one will have the same label. By this token, all of the 7,000 images in the ankle boot class will be labeled with the same class label – 9.

Data Preprocessing

If you followed the above practically, you will see the plot that results from the above. Note that the images are all grayscale and all have pixel values of somewhere between 0 and 255, with a dimension of

28 x 28. Because of this, the data must be preprocessed before it can be fed to the model.

The first step is to convert each train image of 28 x 28 ad each test image of 28x 28 into a size 28 x 28 x 1 matrix. This is then fed to the network:

train_X = train_X.reshape(-1, 28,28, 1)

test_X = test_X.reshape(-1, 28,28, 1)

train_X.shape, test_X.shape

((60000, 28, 28, 1), (10000, 28, 28, 1))

We now have our data in a format of int8 so before it can be fed to our network, it must be converted to float32 type. The pixel values in the range 0 to 1 (inclusive) also need to be rescaled:

train_X = train_X.astype('float32')

test_X = test_X.astype('float32')

train_X = train_X / 255.

test_X = test_X / 255.

Next, the class labels need to be converted to a one-hot encoding vector.   In this the categorical data is converted to a vector of numbers. Why do we do this? Simply because machine learning algorithms can't work directly with categorical data. A Boolean column is generated for each class or category; just one column can take the value of 1 for each of the samples, hence the reason it is called one-hot encoding.

For our statement, we will have a row vector for the one-hot encoding; there will be a 1 10 dimension for each of the images. What is important is that our vector will contain zeros all the way, except for the class being represented, which is a 1. The ankle boot image, for example, the one we plotted earlier, is labeled 9 so for every image in the ankle boot class, the vector will be [0 0 0 0 0 0 0 0 1 0].

Time to do the conversion

Change labels from categorical to one-hot encoding

train_Y_one_hot = to_categorical(train_Y)

test_Y_one_hot = to_categorical(test_Y)

Display change for category label with one-hot encoding

print('Original label:', train_Y[0])

print('After conversion to one-hot:', train_Y_one_hot[0])

('Original label:', 9)

('After conversion to one-hot:', array([0., 0., 0., 0., 0., 0., 0., 0., 0., 1.]))

/

Is that clear enough for you? Note that train_Y_one_hot can also be printed and this displays a 60000 x 10 matrix where each of the rows is depicting individual image one-hot encoding

Right, the last step is the most important of all. With any data-specific task like machine learning, the data must be correctly partitioned. In order for good generalization from the model, the training data needs to be split into two – training and validation. In our case, the model is going to be trained on 80% of the data and validated on 20% of the rest of the training data. This results in a reduction in overfitting because the model is being validated on data it didn't see in training and this helps to give test performance a boost.

```
from sklearn.model_selection import train_test_split

train_X,valid_X,train_label,valid_label =
train_test_split(train_X, train_Y_one_hot, test_size=0.2,
random_state=13)
```

For the final time, we can check the training and validation set shape:

```
train_X.shape,valid_X.shape,train_label.shape,valid_label.shape
```

((48000, 28, 28, 1), (12000, 28, 28, 1), (48000, 10), (12000, 10))

The Network

Okay, we have images that are 28 x 28 in size. The image matrix is converted to an array, it is rescaled to between 0 and 1, reshaped to 28 x 28 x 1 and this is then fed to the network as an input.

Three convolutional layers are required:

- **Layer 1 -** this has filters of 32-3 x 3

- **Layer 2** – this has filters of 64-3 x 3

- **Layer 3** – this has filters of 128-3 x 3

On top of this we have three max-pooling layers, each one 2 x 2 in size.

Modeling the Data

The first thing we need to do is import the modules we need for training our model:

```
import keras

from keras.models import Sequential,Input,Model

from keras.layers import Dense, Dropout, Flatten

from keras.layers import Conv2D, MaxPooling2D
```

from keras.layers.normalization import BatchNormalization

from keras.layers.advanced_activations import LeakyReLU

A batch size of 64 is used although, depending on the memory, it is better to use a higher size of 128 or 256. We'll stick with 64 for this example but the higher the batch size, the better the learning parameters and the more accurate the predictions. Our network is going to be trained for 20 epochs:

batch_size = 64

epochs = 20

num_classes = 10

The Architecture of the Neural Network

With Keras, it is possible to add layers one at a time to stack them up and that is what we are going to do. We use Conv2D() to add the first convolutional layer – this function is used because it is images that we are working with. Next, we add the Leaky ReLU activation function; this enables the network to learn the non-linear decision boundary. Because we are working with 10 classes, that boundary is required because the classes are not separable linearly.

The most important part is adding the Leaky ReLUs. These will try to fix the issue of the ReLUs (Rectified Linear Units) that are dying. The ReLU activation function gets using a good deal these neural network architectures and, crucially in convolutional networks. It is in these that they have proven to be highly effective, more so than the logistic sigmoid function which is also used a lot. The ReLU function provides the capability for activation thresholding at zero. However, in the training part, it is possible for ReLU units to die, usually when a big gradient goes through one of the ReLU neurons. This causes the weights to update in a way that means the neuron cannot activate, ever again, on any data point. When this happens, the gradient going through the unit will always be zero from that point forward. We can use Leaky ReLUs to try and fix this; instead of zero, the function has a small negative slope.

Next, we use MaxPooling2D() to add the max pooling layer and so on. The final, Dense layer has a SoftMax activation function that has 10 units and this is a requirement for classification problems with multiple classes.

```
fashion_model = Sequential()

fashion_model.add(Conv2D(32, kernel_size=(3,
3),activation='linear',input_shape =(28,28,1),padding='same'))

fashion_model.add(LeakyReLU(alpha=0.1))

fashion_model.add(MaxPooling2D((2, 2),padding='same'))

fashion_model.add(Conv2D(64, (3, 3),
activation='linear',padding='same'))

fashion_model.add(LeakyReLU(alpha=0.1))
```

```
fashion_model.add(MaxPooling2D(pool_size=(2,
2),padding='same'))

fashion_model.add(Conv2D(128, (3, 3),
activation='linear',padding='same'))

fashion_model.add(LeakyReLU(alpha=0.1))

fashion_model.add(MaxPooling2D(pool_size=(2,
2),padding='same'))

fashion_model.add(Flatten())

fashion_model.add(Dense(128, activation='linear'))

fashion_model.add(LeakyReLU(alpha=0.1))

fashion_model.add(Dense(num_classes, activation='softmax'))
```

Compiling the Model

Once we have created our model, we can use the Adam optimizer to compile it. The Adam optimizer is one of the most used of all the optimization algorithms. In addition, we also need to specify what the loss type is; this is categorical cross entropy, always used for multiple class classification but the binary cross entropy can also be used as the loss function. Last but not least, the metrics are specified as the accuracy we will be analyzing during training.

fashion_model.compile(loss=keras.losses.categorical_crosse ntropy,

optimizer=keras.optimizers.Adam(),metrics=['accuracy'])

We can visualize these layers using the summary function. This shows us some weights and biases in each of the layers and the total number of parameters in the model:

fashion_model.summary()

Layer (type)	Output Shape	Param #
conv2d_51 (Conv2D)	(None, 28, 28, 32)	320
leaky_re_lu_57 (LeakyReLU)	(None, 28, 28, 32)	0
max_pooling2d_49 (MaxPooling	(None, 14, 14, 32)	0
conv2d_52 (Conv2D)	(None, 14, 14, 64)	18496

leaky_re_lu_58 (LeakyReLU)	(None, 14, 14, 64)	0
max_pooling2d_50 (MaxPooling	(None, 7, 7, 64)	0
conv2d_53 (Conv2D)	(None, 7, 7, 128)	73856
leaky_re_lu_59 (LeakyReLU)	(None, 7, 7, 128)	0
max_pooling2d_51 (MaxPooling	(None, 4, 4, 128)	0
flatten_17 (Flatten)	(None, 2048)	0
dense_33 (Dense)	(None, 128)	262272
leaky_re_lu_60 (LeakyReLU)	(None, 128)	0
dense_34 (Dense)	(None, 10)	1290

===

Total params: 356,234

Trainable params: 356,234

Non-trainable params: 0

Training the Model

At last, it's training time and we will use the fit() function from Keras for this. The model is going to train for 20 epochs and the fit() function returns an object of history type. We store this result in fashion_train so that, later, we can use it again to plot the accuracy plot and the loss function plots in between the training and the validation; this will help you to visually see the performance of your model:

```
fashion_train = fashion_model.fit(train_X, train_label,
batch_size=batch_size,epochs=epochs,verbose=1,validation
_data=(valid_X, valid_label))
```

Train on 48000 samples, validate on 12000 samples

Epoch 1/20

48000/48000 [==============================] - 60s
1ms/step - loss: 0.4661 - acc: 0.8311 - val_loss: 0.3320 - val_acc: 0.8809

Epoch 2/20

48000/48000 [==============================] - 60s 1ms/step - loss: 0.2874 - acc: 0.8951 - val_loss: 0.2781 - val_acc: 0.8963

Epoch 3/20

48000/48000 [==============================] - 60s 1ms/step - loss: 0.2420 - acc: 0.9111 - val_loss: 0.2501 - val_acc: 0.9077

Epoch 4/20

48000/48000 [==============================] - 59s 1ms/step - loss: 0.2088 - acc: 0.9226 - val_loss: 0.2369 - val_acc: 0.9147

Epoch 5/20

48000/48000 [==============================] - 59s 1ms/step - loss: 0.1838 - acc: 0.9324 - val_loss: 0.2602 - val_acc: 0.9070

Epoch 6/20

48000/48000 [==============================] - 59s 1ms/step - loss: 0.1605 - acc: 0.9396 - val_loss: 0.2264 - val_acc: 0.9193

Epoch 7/20

48000/48000 [==============================] - 59s
1ms/step - loss: 0.1356 - acc: 0.9488 - val_loss: 0.2566 - val_acc:
0.9180

Epoch 8/20

48000/48000 [==============================] - 59s
1ms/step - loss: 0.1186 - acc: 0.9553 - val_loss: 0.2556 - val_acc:
0.9149

Epoch 9/20

48000/48000 [==============================] - 59s
1ms/step - loss: 0.0985 - acc: 0.9634 - val_loss: 0.2681 - val_acc:
0.9204

Epoch 10/20

48000/48000 [==============================] - 59s
1ms/step - loss: 0.0873 - acc: 0.9670 - val_loss: 0.2712 - val_acc:
0.9221

Epoch 11/20

48000/48000 [==============================] - 59s
1ms/step - loss: 0.0739 - acc: 0.9721 - val_loss: 0.2757 - val_acc:
0.9202

Epoch 12/20

48000/48000 [==============================] - 60s 1ms/step - loss: 0.0628 - acc: 0.9767 - val_loss: 0.3126 - val_acc: 0.9132

Epoch 13/20

48000/48000 [==============================] - 61s 1ms/step - loss: 0.0569 - acc: 0.9789 - val_loss: 0.3556 - val_acc: 0.9081

Epoch 14/20

48000/48000 [==============================] - 60s 1ms/step - loss: 0.0452 - acc: 0.9833 - val_loss: 0.3441 - val_acc: 0.9189

Epoch 15/20

48000/48000 [==============================] - 60s 1ms/step - loss: 0.0421 - acc: 0.9847 - val_loss: 0.3400 - val_acc: 0.9165

Epoch 16/20

48000/48000 [==============================] - 60s 1ms/step - loss: 0.0379 - acc: 0.9861 - val_loss: 0.3876 - val_acc: 0.9195

Epoch 17/20

48000/48000 [==============================] - 60s 1ms/step - loss: 0.0405 - acc: 0.9855 - val_loss: 0.4112 - val_acc: 0.9164

Epoch 18/20

48000/48000 [==============================] - 60s 1ms/step - loss: 0.0285 - acc: 0.9897 - val_loss: 0.4150 - val_acc: 0.9181

Epoch 19/20

48000/48000 [==============================] - 61s 1ms/step - loss: 0.0322 - acc: 0.9877 - val_loss: 0.4584 - val_acc: 0.9196

Epoch 20/20

48000/48000 [==============================] - 61s 1ms/step - loss: 0.0262 - acc: 0.9906 - val_loss: 0.4396 - val_acc: 0.9205

At last, your model is trained. You used the fashion-MNIST dataset and trained for 20 epochs. By looking at the accuracy and the loss, we can happily say that our model did an excellent job. The accuracy after 20 epochs was 99% with a low training loss.

However, there is a bit of a problem here. Our model looks like it is overfitting because we see a validation accuracy of 92% and a validation loss of 0.4396. Overfitting tells us that, while the network did a great job of memorizing the data, there is no guarantee that it will work all that well on unseen data – that explains the difference between training accuracy and validation accuracy.

This needs to be handled and, in the rest of this section, we will look at giving our network a Dropout layer but retaining all other layers as they are – this will ensure much better performance from the model. First, we need to do a performance evaluation of our model on the test data set before you can finalize your conclusions.

Test Set Model Evaluation

```
test_eval = fashion_model.evaluate(test_X, test_Y_one_hot, verbose=0)

print('Test loss:', test_eval[0])

print('Test accuracy:', test_eval[1])

('Test loss:', 0.46366268818555401)

('Test accuracy:', 0.91839999999999999)
```

This looks pretty impressive. As it turns out, our classifier is doing a much better job than, let's say, an SVM classifier. The model is also performing very well compared to some of the deep learning models that the fashion-MNIST dataset creators tested.

Just how good are these results though? You did see your model overfitting, after all.

We can put the evaluation into some perspective and plot those accuracy and loss plots from between the training data and the validation data:

```
accuracy = fashion_train.history['acc']

val_accuracy = fashion_train.history['val_acc']

loss = fashion_train.history['loss']

val_loss = fashion_train.history['val_loss']

epochs = range(len(accuracy))

plt.plot(epochs, accuracy, 'bo', label='Training accuracy')

plt.plot(epochs, val_accuracy, 'b', label='Validation accuracy')

plt.title('Training and validation accuracy')

plt.legend()

plt.figure()

plt.plot(epochs, loss, 'bo', label='Training loss')

plt.plot(epochs, val_loss, 'b', label='Validation loss')
```

```
plt.title('Training and validation loss')

plt.legend()

plt.show()
```

From the two plots that result from this, it can be seen that, after 4 or 5 epochs, the validation accuracy started to stagnate and we rarely saw an increase after that. At the start, we had linear increases with loss but then it slowed right down.

One sure sign of overfitting is the validation loss; in much the same way as the validation accuracy, it decreases linearly but, when we got to the fourth or fifth epochs, it started increasing. This tells us that the model attempted, and succeeded, to memorize the data.

Keeping this in mind, now is a good time to look at adding a dropout layer to see if we can reduce the overfitting.

Adding Dropout to the Network

While it is possible to add a dropout layer, it will only overcome overfitting to a certain extent. What dropout does is it turns a fraction of neurons off randomly throughout training and this cuts down on the training set dependency to a small amount. A hyperparameter is used to determine how many fractions you want turned off and this can be tuned as you need it. In this way, the network cannot memorize the data because it won't have all the neurons active all the time inactive neurons are not able to learn.

So, here we go – we'll create our network again, compile and train it again but, this time, will add dropout. Then we will run it again for 20 epochs with a batch of size 64:

```
batch_size = 64

epochs = 20

num_classes = 10

fashion_model = Sequential()

fashion_model.add(Conv2D(32, kernel_size=(3, 3),activation='linear',padding='same',input_shape=(28,28,1)))

fashion_model.add(LeakyReLU(alpha=0.1))

fashion_model.add(MaxPooling2D((2, 2),padding='same'))

fashion_model.add(Dropout(0.25))

fashion_model.add(Conv2D(64, (3, 3), activation='linear',padding='same'))

fashion_model.add(LeakyReLU(alpha=0.1))

fashion_model.add(MaxPooling2D(pool_size=(2, 2),padding='same'))

fashion_model.add(Dropout(0.25))
```

```
fashion_model.add(Conv2D(128, (3, 3),
activation='linear',padding='same'))

fashion_model.add(LeakyReLU(alpha=0.1))

fashion_model.add(MaxPooling2D(pool_size=(2,
2),padding='same'))

fashion_model.add(Dropout(0.4))

fashion_model.add(Flatten())

fashion_model.add(Dense(128, activation='linear'))

fashion_model.add(LeakyReLU(alpha=0.1))

fashion_model.add(Dropout(0.3))

fashion_model.add(Dense(num_classes,
activation='softmax'))

fashion_model.summary()
```

Layer (type)	Output Shape	Param #
conv2d_54 (Conv2D)	(None, 28, 28, 32)	320

leaky_re_lu_61 (LeakyReLU)	(None, 28, 28, 32)	0
max_pooling2d_52 (MaxPooling	(None, 14, 14, 32)	0
dropout_29 (Dropout)	(None, 14, 14, 32)	0
conv2d_55 (Conv2D)	(None, 14, 14, 64)	18496
leaky_re_lu_62 (LeakyReLU)	(None, 14, 14, 64)	0
max_pooling2d_53 (MaxPooling	(None, 7, 7, 64)	0
dropout_30 (Dropout)	(None, 7, 7, 64)	0
conv2d_56 (Conv2D)	(None, 7, 7, 128)	73856
leaky_re_lu_63 (LeakyReLU)	(None, 7, 7, 128)	0

max_pooling2d_54 (MaxPooling	(None, 4, 4, 128)	0
dropout_31 (Dropout)	(None, 4, 4, 128)	0
flatten_18 (Flatten)	(None, 2048)	0
dense_35 (Dense)	(None, 128)	262272
leaky_re_lu_64 (LeakyReLU)	(None, 128)	0
dropout_32 (Dropout)	(None, 128)	0
dense_36 (Dense)	(None, 10)	1290

===

Total params: 356,234

Trainable params: 356,234

Non-trainable params: 0

```
fashion_model.compile(loss=keras.losses.categorical_crosse
ntropy,
optimizer=keras.optimizers.Adam(),metrics=['accuracy'])

fashion_train_dropout        =        fashion_model.fit(train_X,
train_label,
batch_size=batch_size,epochs=epochs,verbose=1,validation
_data=(valid_X, valid_label))
```

Train on 48000 samples, validate on 12000 samples

Epoch 1/20

48000/48000 [==============================] - 66s
1ms/step - loss: 0.5954 - acc: 0.7789 - val_loss: 0.3788 - val_acc:
0.8586

Epoch 2/20

48000/48000 [==============================] - 64s
1ms/step - loss: 0.3797 - acc: 0.8591 - val_loss: 0.3150 - val_acc:
0.8832

Epoch 3/20

48000/48000 [==============================] - 64s 1ms/step - loss: 0.3302 - acc: 0.8787 - val_loss: 0.2836 - val_acc: 0.8961

Epoch 4/20

48000/48000 [==============================] - 64s 1ms/step - loss: 0.3034 - acc: 0.8868 - val_loss: 0.2663 - val_acc: 0.9002

Epoch 5/20

48000/48000 [==============================] - 64s 1ms/step - loss: 0.2843 - acc: 0.8936 - val_loss: 0.2481 - val_acc: 0.9083

Epoch 6/20

48000/48000 [==============================] - 64s 1ms/step - loss: 0.2699 - acc: 0.9002 - val_loss: 0.2469 - val_acc: 0.9032

Epoch 7/20

48000/48000 [==============================] - 65s 1ms/step - loss: 0.2561 - acc: 0.9049 - val_loss: 0.2422 - val_acc: 0.9095

Epoch 8/20

48000/48000 [==============================] - 65s 1ms/step - loss: 0.2503 - acc: 0.9068 - val_loss: 0.2429 - val_acc: 0.9098

Epoch 9/20

48000/48000 [==============================] - 65s 1ms/step - loss: 0.2437 - acc: 0.9096 - val_loss: 0.2230 - val_acc: 0.9173

Epoch 10/20

48000/48000 [==============================] - 65s 1ms/step - loss: 0.2307 - acc: 0.9126 - val_loss: 0.2170 - val_acc: 0.9187

Epoch 11/20

48000/48000 [==============================] - 65s 1ms/step - loss: 0.2307 - acc: 0.9135 - val_loss: 0.2265 - val_acc: 0.9193

Epoch 12/20

48000/48000 [==============================] - 65s 1ms/step - loss: 0.2229 - acc: 0.9160 - val_loss: 0.2136 - val_acc: 0.9229

Epoch 13/20

48000/48000 [==============================] - 65s
1ms/step - loss: 0.2202 - acc: 0.9162 - val_loss: 0.2173 - val_acc:
0.9187

Epoch 14/20

48000/48000 [==============================] - 64s
1ms/step - loss: 0.2161 - acc: 0.9188 - val_loss: 0.2142 - val_acc:
0.9211

Epoch 15/20

48000/48000 [==============================] - 65s
1ms/step - loss: 0.2119 - acc: 0.9196 - val_loss: 0.2133 - val_acc:
0.9233

Epoch 16/20

48000/48000 [==============================] - 65s
1ms/step - loss: 0.2073 - acc: 0.9222 - val_loss: 0.2159 - val_acc:
0.9213

Epoch 17/20

48000/48000 [==============================] - 65s
1ms/step - loss: 0.2050 - acc: 0.9231 - val_loss: 0.2123 - val_acc:
0.9233

Epoch 18/20

48000/48000 [==============================] - 64s 1ms/step - loss: 0.2016 - acc: 0.9238 - val_loss: 0.2191 - val_acc: 0.9235

Epoch 19/20

48000/48000 [==============================] - 65s 1ms/step - loss: 0.2001 - acc: 0.9244 - val_loss: 0.2110 - val_acc: 0.9258

Epoch 20/20

48000/48000 [==============================] - 64s 1ms/step - loss: 0.1972 - acc: 0.9255 - val_loss: 0.2092 - val_acc: 0.9269

Save the model so it can be loaded directly and you won't have to train it again. If you want, later you will be able to load it and make modifications to the architecture if needed. Alternatively, you could use this saved model for training again. Always save your model and its weights; it will save you a lot of time in the future. You can, if you want, also save it after each epoch. This way, if there is a problem and the training stops, you won't have to start right from the beginning again.

fashion_model.save("fashion_model_dropout.h5py")

Test Set Model Evaluation

Lastly, we can evaluate our new model for performance:

```
test_eval = fashion_model.evaluate(test_X, test_Y_one_hot,
verbose=1)
```

```
10000/10000 [==============================] - 5s
461us/step
```

```
print('Test loss:', test_eval[0])
```

```
print('Test accuracy:', test_eval[1])
```

```
('Test loss:', 0.21460009642243386)
```

```
('Test accuracy:', 0.92300000000000004)
```

And, as you can see, by adding dropout, the model has worked. The test accuracy didn't show a significant improvement but the test loss showed a significant decrease.

And now, for the last time, we can plot those accuracy and loss plots:

```
accuracy = fashion_train_dropout.history['acc']

val_accuracy = fashion_train_dropout.history['val_acc']

loss = fashion_train_dropout.history['loss']

val_loss = fashion_train_dropout.history['val_loss']

epochs = range(len(accuracy))

plt.plot(epochs, accuracy, 'bo', label='Training accuracy')
```

```
plt.plot(epochs, val_accuracy, 'b', label='Validation accuracy')

plt.title('Training and validation accuracy')

plt.legend()

plt.figure()

plt.plot(epochs, loss, 'bo', label='Training loss')

plt.plot(epochs, val_loss, 'b', label='Validation loss')

plt.title('Training and validation loss')

plt.legend()

plt.show()
```

At last you can see that we have synchronization between the validation loss/accuracy and the training loss/accuracy. Even though the validation loss/accuracy is not linear, it does indicate that there is no overfitting – the loss is showing a decrease rather than an increase and there is little gap between the accuracy for training and validation.

In that way, it is possible to say that the generalization capability of our model improved quite a bit.

Predicting Labels

```
predicted_classes = fashion_model.predict(test_X)
```

Because our predictions are floating point values, we can't compare predicted and true test labels. So, the output needs to be rounded off and this converts floats to integers. Then we use np.argmax() for selecting the highest value index number from a row.

For example, let's say that, for one test image we have a prediction of 0 1 0 0 0 0 0 0 0 0; the output class label should be 1,

```
predicted_classes =
np.argmax(np.round(predicted_classes),axis=1)

predicted_classes.shape, test_Y.shape

((10000,), (10000,))

correct = np.where(predicted_classes==test_Y)[0]

print "Found %d correct labels" % len(correct)

for i, correct in enumerate(correct[:9]):

plt.subplot(3,3,i+1)

plt.imshow(test_X[correct].reshape(28,28), cmap='gray',
interpolation='none')

plt.title("Predicted {}, Class
{}".format(predicted_classes[correct], test_Y[correct]))

plt.tight_layout()
```

Found 9188 correct labels

```
incorrect = np.where(predicted_classes!=test_Y)[0]

print "Found %d incorrect labels" % len(incorrect)

for i, incorrect in enumerate(incorrect[:9]):

plt.subplot(3,3,i+1)

plt.imshow(test_X[incorrect].reshape(28,28), cmap='gray',
interpolation='none')

plt.title("Predicted {}, Class
{}".format(predicted_classes[incorrect], test_Y[incorrect]))

plt.tight_layout()
```

Found 812 incorrect labels

It isn't possible to be sure why the model cannot classify the images correctly just by looking at a small sample of images. It does seem as though a range of similar patterns on multiple classes can have an effect on a classifier, even with a strong architecture lie a CNN.

Classification Reports

These can help us to work out more detail about the misclassified classes because you can see which class the model performed badly on:

```
from sklearn.metrics import classification_report

target_names = ["Class {}".format(i) for i in
range(num_classes)]

print(classification_report(test_Y, predicted_classes,
target_names=target_names))
```

	precision	recall	f1-score	support
Class 0	0.77	0.90	0.83	1000
Class 1	0.99	0.98	0.99	1000
Class 2	0.88	0.88	0.88	1000
Class 3	0.94	0.92	0.93	1000
Class 4	0.88	0.87	0.88	1000
Class 5	0.99	0.98	0.98	1000
Class 6	0.82	0.72	0.77	1000
Class 7	0.94	0.99	0.97	1000
Class 8	0.99	0.98	0.99	1000
Class 9	0.98	0.96	0.97	1000
avg / total	0.92	0.92	0.92	10000

As you can see, class 6 is where our classifier underperforms, both for precision and for recall. For classes 0 and 2, there is a lack of precision and for class 4, we have a slight lack of recall and precision.

Challenges Faced By Deep Neural Networks

DNNs face two main challenges:

Overfitting

Because there are added abstraction layers in a DNN, rare dependencies can be modeled in the training data. Fighting this can be done by:

- Using regularization methods such as unit pruning, sparsity, or weight decay

- Using dropout regularization when training to omit units randomly from hidden layers

- Use rotation and cropping methods for data augmentation; this enlarges the small training sets

Computation Time

When you sweep through the size, the learning rate, and the initial weights, which is the parameter space, it could lead to a requirement for more time and computational resources. Again, fighting this involves:

- Performing batching; this computes the gradient to several training examples simultaneously

- Using many-core architectures – these have capabilities for large processing and are also suitable for both vector and matrix computations

Deep Belief Networks

Before we sign off from part 2 of this guide, there is one more subject to briefly touch on – deep belief networks. A DBN is a kind of neural network that has several layers containing hidden units or latent variables. A network like this will observe the connections between the layers and not the connections between the units in the layers.

If a DBN is trained without supervision on an example set, it can be allowed to probabilistically learn to reconstruct the input. The layers can be called feature detectors and, once this is done, the model can be trained with supervision for classification.

In the next part, we move on to examine the Natural Language Processing (NLP).

Part 3

Natural Language Processing

--------•◆•--------

A large amount of today's data is not structured and includes things like your browsing history, comments on social media, customer feedback and so on. If you are in a position where you have a load of textual data that needs analyzing and don't know where to start, the best place is with natural language processing in Python.

The idea of this section is to allow you to understand NLP and use Python to analyze textual data with NLP. The first thing you will learn is tokenizing your data down to small chunks, before we look at normalizing words into their root forms and then getting rid of noise so your documents are ready for more analysis.

The very best way to learn about anything is to do so let's get started on Natural Language Processing.

Prerequisites

We're going to use the nltk library from Python for all the NLP operations on our text. Installing the library is as simple as opening a terminal and using the pip command:

pip install nltk==3.4

Checking the nltk version in your system is nothing more than importing the library into your Python interpreter:

import nltk

print(nltk.__version__)

There may be a need to download other resources throughout this section for the purpose of performing some actions in nltk. Don't worry; as and when you need them I will tell you. If you don't want to wait and you don't want to download these resources individually, use the following command to get them all now:

python -m nltk.downloader all

Step 1: Convert Text into Tokens

Computer systems are not able to garner any meaning from natural language by themselves; they need a little help. The first step in NLP is converting the text to tokens; these are combinations of continuous characters that have a meaning. How you break a sentence into tokens is entirely up to you but one of the easiest methods is to use the whitespace in a sentence to split it down into individual words.

The NLTK library contains a function called word_tokenize that we use to convert strings into tokens. However, for this you are going to need the punkt resource. If you didn't download it earlier, input this command into your terminal now:

```
nltk.download('punkt')
```

Now we can import word_tokenize so we can use it:

```
from nltk.tokenize import word_tokenize

print(word_tokenize("Hello, this is a great hotel."))
```

And the output of this will be:

['Hello', ',', 'this', 'is', 'a', great, 'hotel', '.']

Note that word_tokenize won't just split the string as per the white space; it will also separate each bit of punctuation into a token too.

Step 2: Converting Words to their Root Forms

When you process natural language, you will find that some words have several grammatical forms. For example, 'go', 'gone', and 'going' are all forms of the verb 'to go'.

While your specific project may expect that some words are retained in all their grammatical forms, we can look at a way of converting those grammatical forms into the base or root form of the word. We can do this using any one of two techniques.

The first is known as 'stemming'. This is a simple algorithm that takes affixes away from a word. While there are a few stemming algorithms in NLTK, we'll be using one called the Porter algorithm.

First, PorterStemmer is imported and then the stemmer is initialized to the stemmer variable. Lastly, the .stem() method is used to find the root or base form of the word:

```
from nltk.stem.porter import PorterStemmer

stemmer = PorterStemmer()

print(stemmer.stem("going"))
```

This code output is

```
go
```

If you were to run this stemmer for any other form of go, you would find that the same base form would be returned. If you were to try it using the word 'constitutes', you would get a result that is not intuitive:

```
print(stemmer.stem("constitutes"))
```

The output here is

```
constitut
```

We can solve these issues by using an approach that is a bit more complex, finding base forms in given contexts. This process is called 'lemmatization' and it will normalize a word based on the text vocabulary and context. Using NLTK, we can use the class called WordNetLemmatizer to lemmatize the sentences.

First, the wordnet resource needs to be downloaded from the NLTK downloader so open your terminal and run this command:

```
nltk.download('wordnet')
```

Next, import WordNetLemmatizer and then initialize it:

```
from nltk.stem.wordnet import WordNetLemmatizer

lem = WordNetLemmatizer()
```

Using the lemmatize approach requires the use of the .lemmatize() method. This method takes two arguments – context and word. In this example, 'v' is being used for the context so let's go into a bit deeper after we see the output from the .lemmatize() method:

```
print(lem.lemmatize('constitutes', 'v'))
```

Note that this method has converted the word, 'constitutes' correctly into its root form of 'constitute'. You will probably also have spotted that the lemmatization approach takes a longer time to complete than stemming and that is because we are using a more complex algorithm.

Now we can look at determining the second method argument programmatically. In NLTK, there is a function called pos_tag which helps us to determine the context of words in sentences. First, download a resource called averaged_perceptron_tagger from the NLTK downloader:

nltk.download('averaged_perceptron_tagger')

Then the pos_tag function is imported and runs on a sentence:

from nltk.tag import pos_tag

sample = "Hello, this is a great hotel."

print(pos_tag(word_tokenize(sample)))

Note that we get a list of pairs as the output, each one with a token and a corresponding tag, signifying the token context in the text. As an aside, a punctuation tag is the punctuation mark itself.

You will notice that the output is a list of pairs. Each pair consists of a token and its tag, which signifies the context of a token in the overall text. Notice that the tag for a punctuation mark is itself.

[('Hello', 'NNP'),

(',', ','),

('this', 'DT'),

('is', 'VBZ'),

('a', 'DT'),

('great', 'JJ'),

('hotel', 'NN'),

('.', '.')]

So, how is the context for each token decoded? All nouns have tags starting with 'N' and verb tags start with 'V' and this information can be used in the next argument for the .lemmatize() method:

```
def lemmatize_tokens(sentence):

lemmatizer = WordNetLemmatizer()

lemmatized_tokens = []

for word, tag in pos_tag(sentence):

if tag.startswith('NN'):

pos = 'n'

elif tag.startswith('VB'):

pos = 'v'

else:

pos = 'a'

lemmatized_tokens.append(lemmatizer.lemmatize(word, pos))

return lemmatized_tokens
```

```
sample = "Legal authority constitute all magistrates."

print(lemmatize_tokens(word_tokenize(sample)))
```

This code will output:

```
['Legal', 'authority', 'constitute', 'all', 'magistrate', '.']
```

And this is expected because 'constitute' and 'magistrates' have both been converted to their root forms.

Step 3: Data Cleaning

In the third step, we need to clean the data and get rid of everything that has no meaning in the context of the analysis. In broad terms, we will look at getting rid of the stop words and the punctuation from the analysis. Taking the punctuation out of the equation is easy. The string library contains a punctuation object which has all the English punctuation makes in it:

```
import string

print(string.punctuation)
```

This code will output this:

```
'!"#$%&\'()*+,-./:;<=>?@[\\]^_`{|}~'
```

To get rid of the punctuation from your tokens, all you need to do is run:

```
for token in tokens:
```

```
if token in string.punctuation:

# Do something
```

Next, we look at the stop words. These are the common words in any language, such as 'a', 'I', 'the' and so on. These don't really add anything to text in terms of analysis so we can get rid of them. First, you need to use the NTLK downloader to get the stop words resource:

```
nltk.download('stopwords')
```

Now import it and use the method called .words() with an argument of 'english'. This is a list containing 179 different stop words from the English language.

```
from nltk.corpus import stopwords

stop_words = stopwords.words('english')
```

The lemmatization example can be combined with all the concepts we discussed here to come up with a function called clean_data(). And, before doing a comparison to see if the word is part of the list, we convert it into lowercase – in this way, a stop word is still captured if it happens at the beginning of a sentence and starts with an uppercase letter:

```
def clean_data(tokens, stop_words = ()):

cleaned_tokens = []
```

```python
for token, tag in pos_tag(tokens):

    if tag.startswith("NN"):

        pos = 'n'

    elif tag.startswith('VB'):

        pos = 'v'

    else:

        pos = 'a'


    lemmatizer = WordNetLemmatizer()

    token = lemmatizer.lemmatize(token, pos)


    if token not in string.punctuation and token.lower() not in stop_words:

        cleaned_tokens.append(token)

return cleaned_tokens

sample = "The quick brown fox jumps over the lazy dog."

stop_words = stopwords.words('english')
```

```
clean_data(word_tokenize(sample), stop_words)
```

The output will be:

```
['quick', 'brown', 'fox', 'jump', 'lazy', 'dog']
```

All the stop words and the punctuation have been removed.

Word Frequency Distribution

Those are the basic techniques used for cleaning in NLP so now we can look at finding word frequency in the text. We are going to use text from a fairy tale called 'The Mouse, The Bird and the Sausage' and the text is stored in a string called text.

First, the text is tokenized and then cleaned using the clean_data function that we defined earlier.

```
tokens = word_tokenize(text)

cleaned_tokens = clean_data(tokens, stop_words = stop_words)
```

The class called FreqDist from NLTK can be used for finding frequency distribution. The class is initialized using the tokens as the argument. Next, the method called .most_common() is used to see which terms occur most frequently. What we are going to look for is the top ten terms:

```
from nltk import FreqDist
```

```python
freq_dist = FreqDist(cleaned_tokens)

freq_dist.most_common(10)
```

Those top ten terms form the fairy tale are:

```python
python [('bird', 15), ('sausage', 11), ('mouse', 8), ('wood', 7),
('time', 6), ('long', 5), ('make', 5), ('fly', 4), ('fetch', 4), ('water',
4)]
```

And it shouldn't surprise you that the top three terms are the main fairy tale characters.

In this section, you learned about natural language processing using Python; you learned how text is converted to tokens, words are converted into their root forms, and lastly, how to clean text to get rid of anything that isn't required. We may have only looked at the simplest of NLP tasks, there are a good many more techniques that you can explore.

Part 4

Deep Learning with PyTorch

———•◆•———

In this penultimate part of my hands-on deep learning guide, we're going to look at how to use the PyTorch framework for deep learning. PyTorch was released by Facebook with full integrations for Azure Machine Learning, AWS and Google Cloud. By now, you should already be familiar with NumPy, scikit-learn, SciPy and Pandas; if not, go back over the previous guide and this guide up to this point until you are familiar with them because they are important packages for deep learning with PyTorch.

Introduction to PyTorch

PyTorch is a machine learning package for Python that is based on Torch. In turn, Torch is an open-source package based on Lua, which is a programming language. There are two fundamental features in PyTorch:

- Tensor computation, such as NumPy, with a very strong GPU acceleration

- Automatic differentiation to build neural networks and train them

There are a couple of reasons why PyTorch stands out above other deep learning libraries in Python:

1. In many other libraries, such as TensorFlow, a computational graph must first be defined before the model can be run but, with PyTorch, that graph can be defined dynamically.

2. PyTorch is one of the best packages for deep learning research, providing maximum speed and flexibility.

PyTorch Tensors

PyTorch tensors are much like the arrays in NumPy but with an extra feature – they can run on a GPU. This is crucial because it significantly speeds up numerical computations and this can help increase neural network speeds by more than 50 times. To use PyTorch, you need to install it by going to https://PyTorch.org/ or, if you use Conda, just type in this command:

conda install PyTorch torchvision -c PyTorch

For a PyTorch tensor to be defined, you need to start with the torch package which must be imported. Two types of tensor can be defined in PyTorch – CPU and GPU. We're going to focus on the CPU machine but I will touch on GPUs briefly too. First, the import:

import torch

In PyTorch, torch.FloatTensor is the default tensor type. This is a float tensor and you can use it to get a tensor out of a Python list:

torch.FloatTensor([[20, 30, 40], [90, 60, 70]])

On a GPU machine you would define it like this:

torch.cuda.FloatTensor([[20, 30, 40], [90, 60, 70]])

And you can use PyTorch tensors for math computations like subtraction and addition:

x = torch.FloatTensor([25])

y = torch.FloatTensor([30])

x + y

Lastly, matrices can be defined and matrix operations performed. This is how a matrix is defined and transposed:

matrix = torch.randn(4, 5)

matrix

matrix.t()

PyTorch Autograd
There is a technique in PyTorch called automatic differentiation, used for the numerical evaluation of functions. Automatic differentiation does backward pass computations in a neural network and, in the training networks, the weights are initialized randomly to a number near to but not quite zero. A backward pass is a process of

adjusting the weights right to left while a forward pass adjusts left to right.

The Python library that supports this is called torch.autograd with a central class called torch.Tensor. if you want all operations tracked, you need to set .requires_grad to True while computation of all gradients requires that you call the .backward() method. The tensor gradient is accumulated in the attribute called .grad.

If you want a tensor detached from the computation history, the function called .detach() needs to be called. This also stops tracking on future tensor computations. Another way you can do this is to wrap the code with torch.no_grad().

Both the Function and the Tensor classes are interconnected, enabling an acyclic graph to be built. This graph will encode the entire computation history. The Function responsible for creating the tensor is referenced by the .grad_fn attribute for the tensor. If you want derivatives computed, .backward() needs to be called on the tensor.

If a tensor has just one element, there is no need for parameters to be specified for the backward() function but, if there are two or more elements, you need to specify which gradient is to be used – it must be a tensor that has a matching shape.

We are going to create two tensors net, one that has requires_grad set as True and another with requires_grad set as False. Then these tensors will be used for addition operations and sum operations. After that, the gradient for one tensor will be computed:

```
a = torch.tensor([3.0, 2.0], requires_grad=True)

b = torch.tensor([4.0, 7.0])

ab_sum = a + b

ab_sum

ab_res = (ab_sum*8).sum()

ab_res.backward()

ab_res

a.grad
```

If you call .grad on b, nothing will be returned; this is because requires_grad has not been set to True.

The PyTorch nn Module

The PyTorch nn module is used to help build neural networks and it is dependent on autograd for model definition and differentiation. The first step is to define the procedure needed to train the neural network:

The neural network is defined with parameters that are learnable. These parameters are called weights

A dataset of inputs is iterated over

1. The input is processed through the network

2. The predicted results are compared to the actual values and the error is measured

3. The gradients are propagated back to the parameters for the network

4. A simple update rule is used to update the network weights:

weight = weight—learning_rate * gradient

A two-layer neural network is now created using the nn package:

N, D_in, H, D_out = 64, 1000, 100, 10

x = torch.randn(N, D_in)

y = torch.randn(N, D_out)

model = torch.nn.Sequential(

torch.nn.Linear(D_in, H),

torch.nn.ReLU(),

torch.nn.Linear(H, D_out),

)

loss_fn = torch.nn.MSELoss()

learning_rate = 1e-4

Let's look at some of these parameters:

- N – the batch size. This is the number of observations that take place before the weights are updated

- D_in – this the input dimension

- H – the hidden dimension

- D_out – the output dimension

- torch.randn – defining a matrix that has a given set of dimensions

- torch.nn.Sequential – initializes a stack of layers (linear)

- torch.nn.Linear – applies a linear transformation to the data that is incoming

- torch.nn.ReLU – applies an element-wise ReLU function

- torch.nn.MSELoss – used for creating criteria for the measurement of mean squared error or MSE between n elements in x (input) and y (target).

PyTorch optim Package

The next package we use is the optim package and this is for defining an optimizer for updating the weights. This package is an abstraction of a standard optimization algorithm and brings in implementation of the more common ones, like Adam, RMSProp, and AdaGrad. We will be using the Adam optimizer.

The first argument to be provided is the tensors that the optimizer is going to update. The forward pass will compute y (predicted) and to do this, x is passed to the model. Then the loss is computed and printed.

Before the backward pass can be run, all the gradients need to be zeroed for the variables that the optimizer updates. We do this because, when .backward() is used, gradients are not overwritten by default. After that, the step function is called on the optimizer and the parameters are updated:

```
optimizer      =      torch.optim.Adam(model.parameters(),
lr=learning_rate)

for t in range(500):

y_pred = model(x)

loss = loss_fn(y_pred, y)

print(t, loss.item())

optimizer.zero_grad()

loss.backward()

optimizer.step()
```

Custom PyTorch nn Modules

On occasion, you will want to build custom modules and this will require the nn.Module to be subclassed. Then a forward must be defined to receive the input tensors and to produce the output tensors. Below you can see how a two-layer network is implemented using nn.Module, creating the neural network using torch.nn.Module. We also put Adam to one side and use a stochastic gradient descent optimizer instead:

```python
import torch

class TwoLayerNet(torch.nn.Module):

def __init__(self, D_in, H, D_out):

super(TwoLayerNet, self).__init__()

self.linear1 = torch.nn.Linear(D_in, H)

self.linear2 = torch.nn.Linear(H, D_out)


def forward(self, x):

h_relu = self.linear1(x).clamp(min=0)

y_pred = self.linear2(h_relu)

return y_pred
```

```python
N, D_in, H, D_out = 64, 1000, 100, 10

x = torch.randn(N, D_in)

y = torch.randn(N, D_out)

model = TwoLayerNet(D_in, H, D_out)

criterion = torch.nn.MSELoss()

optimizer = torch.optim.SGD(model.parameters(), lr=1e-4)

for t in range(500):

y_pred = model(x)

loss = criterion(y_pred, y)

print(t, loss.item())

optimizer.zero_grad()

loss.backward()
```

```
optimizer.step()
```

That brings us to the end of our quick tutorial on using PyTorch. For the final part in this guide, we take an in-depth look at LSTMs.

Part 5

A Look at LSTMs

———————◆———————

Sequence prediction problems have been in existence for as long as we can remember, considered to be one of the most complex and difficult of all data science problems to solve. These kinds of problems are wide-ranging, including sales predictions, stock market data patterns, speech recognition, language translation and much, much more.

In recent years, data science has seen a good many breakthroughs and, out of all the solutions to sequence prediction problems, one stands out head and shoulders above the rest – Long Short-Term Memory networks, better known as LSTMs.

LSTMs have more than a small edge over the standard feedforward network and over the RNN. Why? Because they have one very useful property – selectively memorizing a pattern for a long time period. In this last section of this guide, we are going to learn what LSTMs are and how to use them to solve real-world problems. It is important that you have a basic working knowledge of neural networks (you should have that by now) and a good understanding of the way that Keras works.

Flashback – The Recurrent Neural Network

To understand the LSTM, we need to go back over the RNN. First, let's take a good example of some sequential data – the data for a specific stock on the stock market. An artificial neural network (ANN) or a basic machine learning model could learn to predict the prices based on several features, such as opening value or stock volume, for example. While the stock price is dependent to a certain extent on features like those, it is also heavily dependent on the value in the preceding days. For market traders, those previous values make up something called a trend and that is one of the major features in their predictions.

In a standard feedforward network, every test case is treated independently which means that, when the model is fit for a given day, the previous few days prices are not taken into account. Recurrent neural networks (RNNs) are responsible for that time dependency.

An RNN is good at sequence handling but only to a certain extent. The RNN is a great model when it involves short contexts but, if you want to build up a story and remember the whole thing, the model has to understand and it has to remember what the context is behind each sequence, in much the same way that the human brain does. A simple RNN cannot do this.

Why not?

The Limitations of an RNN

The RNN works perfectly well when it works with the short-term dependencies, such as simple word prediction. For example, apply an RNN to this:

The color of the grass is _____.

And it will work perfectly well. That's because the problem doesn't have anything to do with the statement context. The RNN hasn't got to remember what came before, it hasn't got to remember what it all meant; all it has to remember is that, mostly, the grass is green and its prediction would be:

The color of the grass is green.

However, a vanilla RNN will not understand what an input's context is. For example, when making a prediction now, it will not remember anything that was said in the past. As an example:

I spent 20 years working with underprivileged children in Spain. Then I moved to Africa.

……..

I can speak _____ fluently.

We can understand from this that the author spent 20 years in Spain so it is a pretty good guess that he can speak Spanish fluently. But, for an RNN to make a good prediction, it would need to understand the context. The information that is pertinent is likely to have been separated from the point it is required by lots of data that isn't relevant and that is where an RNN will fail.

This is down to something called the Vanishing Gradient and, to understand that, you need to have a bit of knowledge about the feedforward neural network and how it works. We already know that, for a normal feedforward network, the updating of the weights on one specific layer is part of the learning rate, the error term from the layer before and the layer input. As such, the error term for one specific layer is the sum of all the errors for previous layers. When we come to deal with the sigmoid or other activation functions, its derivatives' small values are multiplied several times as we head to the starting layers and the result of this is the gradient pretty much vanishing and the layers become hard to train.

We can see something much like this is the recurrent neural network. An RNN will remember something for a short period of time but once we start to add more data in, that information will get lost. We can fix this by applying an LSTM, a tweaked version of an RNN.

LSTM – Improved RNN

When we set up our day's appointments or work, most us of prioritize, just in case we need to fit in something more important or just to know what really needs to be done that day. As it happens, an RNN doesn't do this. For new information to be added, an RNN will apply a function to transform all the existing information and that means any consideration for information that might be important is forgotten – the RNN can't tell what was and wasn't important.

Conversely, the LSTM uses addition and multiplication to change just part of the information in small ways. In an LSTM, data flows through something called 'cell states' and it is this that enables the LSTM to remember some things and forget others. At each cell state, there are three separate dependencies.

As an example of this, think about predicting the price of a certain stock. Today's prices will be dependent on certain things:

- The stock trend, i.e. the prices over the previous days – could be an up or downtrend

- How much the stock was the day before – a lot of traders compare that price before they purchase it

- Daily factors that have an effect on the stock price. The company could have issued new policies that are not being very well received, it could be a drop or a significant increase in profit, even a change in top management in the company.

All of these dependencies may be generalized, regardless of what the problem is, as:

- The last cell state – the information present in memory following the last time step

- The last hidden state – identical to the previous cell's output

- The current time step's input – new information fed to the network at that point in time

LSTMs have one more important feature – their comparison with the conveyor belt.

Yes, you did read that right!

Many industries use the conveyor belt to shift products around for all manner of processes; the LSTM uses much the same mechanism for moving information about. As the information goes through all the layers, there may be modifications, information removed or added, in much the same way as products can be modified while on the conveyor belt – painted, labeled, packed, for example.

This one LSTM property, their ability to modify bits of information rather than manipulating or transforming ALL the information, means that they can selectively remember and forget information. How they do this is what we are going to look at next.

LSTMs and Text Generation

That's enough of the theory behind the LSTM; now it's time to get practical and we'll do that by building a model. This model will predict n number of characters following the original Macbeth text. We can do this because most classical texts aren't copyright protected anymore. The text file can be found at https://s3-ap-south-

1.amazonaws.com/av-blog-media/wp-content/uploads/2017/12/10165151/macbeth.txt or at https://www.gutenberg.org/.

We're going to use Keras so make sure that it is installed on your system.

Now we can do some text generation:

Import Dependencies
The first thing we need to do is import the dependencies:

Importing dependencies numpy and keras

```
import numpy

from keras.models import Sequential

from keras.layers import Dense

from keras.layers import Dropout

from keras.layers import LSTM

from keras.utils import np_utils
```

Load Text File
Here, we load up the text file and then create the mappings for characters to integers:

load text

```python
filename = "/macbeth.txt"


text = (open(filename).read()).lower()


# mapping characters with integers

unique_chars = sorted(list(set(text)))


char_to_int = {}

int_to_char = {}


for i, c in enumerate (unique_chars):

    char_to_int.update({c: i})

    int_to_char.update({i: c})
```

Now we have our text file nicely opened and we have converted all our characters into lowercase. Then we mapped each of the characters to its respective number or integer; that step just makes it much easier for the LSTM to do the computation.

Prepare Dataset

Next, we prepare the dataset:

preparing input and output dataset

```
X = []

Y = []


for i in range(0, len(text) - 50, 1):

    sequence = text[i:i + 50]

    label =text[i + 50]

    X.append([char_to_int[char] for char in sequence])

    Y.append(char_to_int[label])
```

We've prepared the data in a format that makes it easy for the LSTM to predict the net letter. If, for example, we wanted our LSTM to predict the letter 'O' from the word 'HELLO', we would feed the LSTM with an input of ['H', 'E', 'L', 'L'] and an expected output of ['O']. In much the same way, in this example the sequence length that we want has been fixed to 50. We save the encodings for the characters 1 to 49 to X and the output we expect, the 50th character, to Y.

Reshape X

reshaping, normalizing and one hot encoding

X_modified = numpy.reshape(X, (len(X), 50, 1))

X_modified = X_modified / float(len(unique_chars))

Y_modified = np_utils.to_categorical(Y)

Any LSTM network will expect the input in a specific form – [sample, time steps, features]. Samples will be the number of the data points, the time steps is the number of the steps (time-dependent) in ne data point, and features is the number of variables for Y's corresponding True value. Next, the values are scaled to between 0 and 1 in _modified and the true values are one-hot encoded in Y_modified.

Define the Model

defining the LSTM model

model = Sequential()

model.add(LSTM(300, input_shape=(X_modified.shape[1], X_modified.shape[2]), return_sequences=True))

model.add(Dropout(0.2))

model.add(LSTM(300))

```
model.add(Dropout(0.2))

model.add(Dense(Y_modified.shape[1],
activation='softmax'))


model.compile(loss='categorical_crossentropy',
optimizer='adam')
```

We define a sequential model in which we use a linear stack of layers. Layer one is an LSTM layer that contains 300 memory units, returning sequences. We do this to make sure that the subsequent LSTM layer will get sequences and not data that has been randomly scattered. Each LSTM layer is followed by a dropout layer, thus reducing the chances of the model overfitting. The last layer is fully connected using a SoftMax activation and have a number of neurons equal to the unique characters – this is because the output needs to be one-hot encoded.

Fit the Model

```
# fitting the model

       model.fit(X_modified,    Y_modified,    epochs=1,
batch_size=30)


# picking a random seed
```

```
        start_index = numpy.random.randint(0, len(X)-1)

        new_string = X[start_index]


# generating characters

        for i in range(50):

        x = numpy.reshape(new_string, (1, len(new_string), 1))

        x = x / float(len(unique_chars))


#predicting

        pred_index = numpy.argmax(model.predict(x, verbose=0))

        char_out = int_to_char[pred_index]

        seq_in = [int_to_char[value] for value in new_string]

        print(char_out)


         new_string.append(pred_index)

        new_string = new_string[1:len(new_string)]
```

We fit our model over a series of 100 epochs using 30 as the batch size. Net, a random seed is fixed and we begin to generate our characters. The model prediction will be the character encoding of the character that was predicted, which is then decoded to the original value and appended to the data pattern.

Once sufficient epochs have been trained, the predicted results will improve.

That is how we solve sequence prediction tasks using an LSTM.

Using LSTM For Time Series Problems

To finish this guide, we are going to look at building two LSTM models for time series forecasting – a univariate LSTM model and a multivariate LSTM Model. We will be demonstrating these models on small, contrived, time series problems, just to give you an idea of how they work and the type of problem they can be used to address. The model configuration is discretionary and we have not optimized them for each of the problems – that is not the idea of this section; I just want to give you an idea of how they work.

Univariate LSTM Models

An LSTM can be used for modeling problems for univariate time series forecasting. These problems are made up of one sequence of observations and the model used has got to learn past observations from the sequence in order to correctly predict the next value.

I have split this into six sections, which are:

- Preparing the Data

- Vanilla LSTM

- Stacked LSTM

- Bidirectional LSTM

- CNN LSTM

- ConvLSTM

Each one of the models is shown to you for the purpose of univariate time series forecasting but you can adapt them quite easily and use them as input models for any other type of time series forecasting problems.

Preparing the Data

Before we can model a univariate series, we need to prepare it. Our LSTM model will need to learn a specific function, one that maps the sequences of previous observations that are input into one output observation. The observation sequence will need to be transformed into several examples that the LSTM can learn from.

Think about this univariate sequence:

[10, 20, 30, 40, 50, 60, 70, 80, 90]

The sequence can be divided down into several different patterns of inputs and outputs, each known as a sample. The prediction being learned is a one-step prediction and for this we use three time steps as the input and one time step for the output:

X,	y
10, 20, 30	40
20, 30, 40	50
30, 40, 50	60

...

The function we use below, called the split_sequence() function, will implement the behavior we specify and will divide the univariate sequence into a series of samples – each of these samples has got a specific number of time steps and, each time, the output will be just one time step:

```
# split the univariate sequence down into samples
    def split_sequence(sequence, n_steps):
    X, y = list(), list()
    for i in range(len(sequence)):
        # find the end of the pattern
```

```
        end_ix = i + n_steps
        # check if we have gone beyond the sequence
        if end_ix > len(sequence)-1:
            break
        # gather the input and output sections of the pattern
        seq_x, seq_y = sequence[i:end_ix], sequence[end_ix]
        X.append(seq_x)
        y.append(seq_y)
    return array(X), array(y)
```

This function can be easily demonstrated on the small but contrived dataset from above and you can see the entire example below:

```
# univariate data preparation
from numpy import array


# split the univariate sequence into samples
def split_sequence(sequence, n_steps):
    X, y = list(), list()
```

```
for i in range(len(sequence)):

    # find the end of the pattern

    end_ix = i + n_steps

    # check if we have gone beyond the sequence

    if end_ix > len(sequence)-1:

        break

    # gather the input and output bits of the pattern

    seq_x, seq_y = sequence[i:end_ix], sequence[end_ix]

    X.append(seq_x)

    y.append(seq_y)

return array(X), array(y)


# define the input sequence

raw_seq = [10, 20, 30, 40, 50, 60, 70, 80, 90]

# choose the number of time steps

n_steps = 3

# split into samples
```

```
X, y = split_sequence(raw_seq, n_steps)
```

summarize the data

```
for i in range(len(X)):

print(X[i], y[i])
```

When we run this example, it will divide our univariate series down into six separate samples. Each of the samples has the three time steps for input and the single time step for the output:

```
[10 20 30] 40

[20 30 40] 50

[30 40 50] 60

[40 50 60] 70

[50 60 70] 80

[60 70 80] 90
```

Now you are aware of how a univariate series can be prepared for modeling, we can go further and look at how to develop different LSTM models that can learn how to map inputs to outputs. We start with the Vanilla LSTM.

Vanilla LSTM

A Vanilla LSTM is a model that has just one hidden layer containing the LSTM units and one output layer that is used for making the prediction.

A Vanilla LSTM model can be defined for a univariate time series forecasting problem like this:

define the model

```
model = Sequential()

model.add(Dense(100,                          activation='relu',
input_dim=n_steps))

model.add(Dense(1))

model.compile(optimizer='adam', loss='mse')
```

The input shape is the key part of this definition because that shape is what our model is expecting as the input for each of the samples; this is in terms of the number of the features and the number of the time steps. As our model is working on a univariate time series, we have just one feature for one variable.

The number of the time steps that is input is the number chosen when we prepared the dataset and it is input as an argument to the function called split_sequence(). The input shape for each of the sample is specified in the argument called input_shape on the first hidden layer's definition.

Almost all of the time, we would have several samples so the model is going to expect that the input part of any training data will have the following shape or dimensions:

[samples, features]

The function, split_sequence(), from the previous part will output and it will have the shape of [samples, time steps]. This is very easy to reshape so it has the extra dimension for the single feature.

reshape from [samples, time steps] into [samples, time steps, features]

n_features = 1

X = X.reshape((X.shape[0], X.shape[1], n_features))

In our case, we have defined a model that has a hidden layer containing 50 LSTM units and an output layer that will predict one numerical value. We used the Adam optimizer, which is a highly efficient version of stochastic gradient descent to fit the model, and we used the MSE (mean squared error) loss function to optimize it.

As soon as the model has been defined, it can be fit on our training dataset:

fit the model

model.fit(X, y, epochs=200, verbose=0)

When the model has been fit, it can be used for making the prediction and, to get a prediction of the next sequence value, we simply provide it with the input:

[70, 80, 90]

And what we are expecting is a prediction on the lines of:

[100]

The model will expect a three-dimensional input shape of [samples, time steps, features] and that means the input sample must be reshaped before the prediction can be made:

```
# demonstrate the prediction
    x_input = array([70, 80, 90])
    x_input = x_input.reshape((1, n_steps, n_features))
    yhat = model.predict(x_input, verbose=0)
```

All of this can be ties together and demonstrate how a Vanilla LSSTM can be developed for making one single prediction on a univariate time series forecasting problem:

```
# univariate lstm example
    from numpy import array
```

```python
from keras.models import Sequential

from keras.layers import LSTM

from keras.layers import Dense


# split the univariate sequence into samples
def split_sequence(sequence, n_steps):
    X, y = list(), list()
    for i in range(len(sequence)):
        # find the end of the pattern
        end_ix = i + n_steps
        # check if we have beyond the sequence
        if end_ix > len(sequence)-1:
            break
        # gather the input and output bits of the pattern
        seq_x, seq_y = sequence[i:end_ix], sequence[end_ix]
        X.append(seq_x)
        y.append(seq_y)
```

```python
        return array(X), array(y)


# define the input sequence
        raw_seq = [10, 20, 30, 40, 50, 60, 70, 80, 90]
# choose the number of time steps
        n_steps = 3
# split into samples
        X, y = split_sequence(raw_seq, n_steps)
# reshape from [samples, time steps] into [samples, time steps, features]
        n_features = 1
        X = X.reshape((X.shape[0], X.shape[1], n_features))
# define the model
        model = Sequential()
        model.add(LSTM(50,                              activation='relu',
        input_shape=(n_steps, n_features)))
        model.add(Dense(1))
        model.compile(optimizer='adam', loss='mse')
```

```
# fit the model

        model.fit(X, y, epochs=200, verbose=0)

# demonstrate the prediction

        x_input = array([70, 80, 90])

        x_input = x_input.reshape((1, n_steps, n_features))

        yhat = model.predict(x_input, verbose=0)

        print(yhat)
```

When you run the example, it will prepare the date, fit the model and then make the prediction.

Given that the algorithm is of a stochastic nature, you may find that the results are different so try running it a few times.

You should be able to see that the net sequence value is predicted:

        [[102.09213]]

Stacked LSTM

To build a Stacked LSTM model, all we need to do is stack several hidden LSTM layers on top of each other.

Each LSTM layer will require the input to be three-dimensional and, by default, the LSTM will produce an output that is two-dimensional

– this is the interpretation the model gains from the end of the input sequence.

This can be solved by having our LSTM model output one value for every time step that is in the input data and, to do this, the return_sequences=True argument is set on the layer. This will ensure that the output from the hidden layer is a three-dimensional input to the next layer.

In that way, a Stacked LSTM can be defined like this:

define the model

```
model = Sequential()

model.add(LSTM(50,                          activation='relu',
return_sequences=True, input_shape=(n_steps, n_features)))

model.add(LSTM(50, activation='relu'))

model.add(Dense(1))

model.compile(optimizer='adam', loss='mse')
```

This can be tied together as in the entire code example here:

univariate stacked lstm example

```
from numpy import array

from keras.models import Sequential
```

```python
from keras.layers import LSTM

from keras.layers import Dense


# split the univariate sequence
    def split_sequence(sequence, n_steps):
    X, y = list(), list()
    for i in range(len(sequence)):
        # find the end of the pattern
        end_ix = i + n_steps
        # check if we have gone beyond the sequence
        if end_ix > len(sequence)-1:
            break
        # gather the input and output bits of the pattern
        seq_x, seq_y = sequence[i:end_ix], sequence[end_ix]
        X.append(seq_x)
        y.append(seq_y)
    return array(X), array(y)
```

define the input sequence

```
raw_seq = [10, 20, 30, 40, 50, 60, 70, 80, 90]
```

choose the number of time steps

```
n_steps = 3
```

split into samples

```
X, y = split_sequence(raw_seq, n_steps)
```

reshape from [samples, time steps] into [samples, time steps, features]

```
n_features = 1

X = X.reshape((X.shape[0], X.shape[1], n_features))
```

define the model

```
model = Sequential()

model.add(LSTM(50,                              activation='relu',
return_sequences=True, input_shape=(n_steps, n_features)))

model.add(LSTM(50, activation='relu'))

model.add(Dense(1))

model.compile(optimizer='adam', loss='mse')
```

fit the model

```
model.fit(X, y, epochs=200, verbose=0)
```

demonstrate the prediction

```
x_input = array([70, 80, 90])

x_input = x_input.reshape((1, n_steps, n_features))

yhat = model.predict(x_input, verbose=0)

print(yhat)
```

When you run this example, you will get a prediction of the next sequence value and we would expect it to be 100:

[[102.47341]]

Bidirectional LSTM

There are some sequence problems where you can gain significant benefit by allowing the LSTM model to learn what the input sequence is in both directions – forward and backward – and then concatenate both of the interpretations. This is known as a Bidirectional LSTM.

We can implement a Bidirectional LSTM model for a univariate time series problem very easily – the first hidden layer is wrapped up in a wrapper layer known as Bidirectional. Below is an example of the definition of a bidirectional LSTM that reads input in both directions:

define the model

```python
model = Sequential()

model.add(Bidirectional(LSTM(50, activation='relu'),
input_shape=(n_steps, n_features)))

model.add(Dense(1))

model.compile(optimizer='adam', loss='mse')
```

And you can see a whole Bidirectional LSTM example below:

```python
# univariate bidirectional lstm example

from numpy import array

from keras.models import Sequential

from keras.layers import LSTM

from keras.layers import Dense

from keras.layers import Bidirectional


# split the univariate sequence

def split_sequence(sequence, n_steps):

X, y = list(), list()

for i in range(len(sequence)):
```

```
        # find the end of the pattern

        end_ix = i + n_steps

        # check if we have gone beyond the sequence

        if end_ix > len(sequence)-1:

            break

        # gather the input and output bits of the pattern

        seq_x, seq_y = sequence[i:end_ix], sequence[end_ix]

        X.append(seq_x)

        y.append(seq_y)

    return array(X), array(y)


# define the input sequence

    raw_seq = [10, 20, 30, 40, 50, 60, 70, 80, 90]

# choose the number of time steps

    n_steps = 3

# split into samples

    X, y = split_sequence(raw_seq, n_steps)
```

```
# reshape from [samples, time steps] into [samples, time steps,
features]

    n_features = 1

    X = X.reshape((X.shape[0], X.shape[1], n_features))

# define the model

model = Sequential()

    model.add(Bidirectional(LSTM(50, activation='relu'),
    input_shape=(n_steps, n_features)))

    model.add(Dense(1))

    model.compile(optimizer='adam', loss='mse')

# fit the model

    model.fit(X, y, epochs=200, verbose=0)

# demonstrate the prediction

    x_input = array([70, 80, 90])

    x_input = x_input.reshape((1, n_steps, n_features))

    yhat = model.predict(x_input, verbose=0)

    print(yhat)
```

And if you run this example, the model will predict the next sequence value and we would expect to see 100 as the output:

[[101.48093]]

CNN LSTM

A CNN or Convolutional Neural Network is a neural network that has been specifically developed to work with image data that is two-dimensional. CNNs can be very effective when used for the automatic extraction of features from one-dimensional data sequences like the data for the univariate time sequence, and then learning that data.

We can use a CNN model in a kind of hybrid model where we have an LSTM backend. The CNN in this type of model is used for interpretation of the input subsequences; together, these are all provided to the LSTM model as a single sequence for the model to interpret. We call this hybrid a CNN-LSTM.

The first step in this model is to divide our sequences down into subsequences that the CNN model can interpret. As an example, the univariate time series data can be split into input samples with four time steps and output samples with one time step. Each of these samples is then split down into two sub-samples, each of which has got two time steps. The CNN interprets every subsequence with two time steps and outputs a time series of subsequence interpretations that the LSTM model can then process as the input.

This can be parameterized and the number of subsequences is defined as n_seq, with the number of time steps for each subsequence defined as n_steps. We can then reshape the input data so it has the correct structure:

[samples, subsequences, time steps, features]

As an example:

choose the number of time steps

    n_steps = 4

split into samples

    X, y = split_sequence(raw_seq, n_steps)

reshape from [samples, time steps] into [samples, subsequences, time steps, features]

    n_features = 1

    n_seq = 2

    n_steps = 2

    X = X.reshape((X.shape[0], n_seq, n_steps, n_features))

We want to be able to reuse this CNN model when each of the data subsequences is read in separately. To do this, the whole CNN model is wrapped in a wrapper called TimeDistributed and, for each input, this applies the whole model once. In our case, this would be once for every input subsequence.

First, the CNN model has got a convolutional layer which is used to read across the subsequence. This layer must be given a specified number of filters and a specified kernel size. The number of filters is how many times the input sequence is read or interpreted and the kernel size is how many time steps are in each of the input sequence 'read' operations.

After this layer comes a max pooling layer. This reduces the filter maps down so they are a quarter of their original size but still contain the important features. We then flatten the structures down to a one-dimensional vector that the LSTM layer will get as one input step.

```
model.add(TimeDistributed(Conv1D(filters=64,
kernel_size=1, activation='relu'), input_shape=(None,
n_steps, n_features)))

model.add(TimeDistributed(MaxPooling1D(pool_size=2)))

model.add(TimeDistributed(Flatten()))
```

Next, the LSTM section of our model can be defined. This will interpret the input sequence reading from the CNN model and the prediction will be made:

model.add(LSTM(50, activation='relu'))

model.add(Dense(1))

Again, all of this can be put together and you can see the entire example below:

univariate cnn lstm example

from numpy import array

from keras.models import Sequential

from keras.layers import LSTM

from keras.layers import Dense

from keras.layers import Flatten

from keras.layers import TimeDistributed

from keras.layers.convolutional import Conv1D

from keras.layers.convolutional import MaxPooling1D

split a univariate sequence into samples

```python
def split_sequence(sequence, n_steps):

    X, y = list(), list()

    for i in range(len(sequence)):

        # find the end of the pattern

        end_ix = i + n_steps

        # check if we have gone beyond the sequence

        if end_ix > len(sequence)-1:

            break

        # gather the input and output bits of the pattern

        seq_x, seq_y = sequence[i:end_ix], sequence[end_ix]

        X.append(seq_x)

        y.append(seq_y)

    return array(X), array(y)


# define the input sequence

    raw_seq = [10, 20, 30, 40, 50, 60, 70, 80, 90]

# choose the number of time steps
```

```
n_steps = 4
```

split into samples

```
X, y = split_sequence(raw_seq, n_steps)
```

reshape from [samples, time steps] into [samples, subsequences, time steps, features]

```
n_features = 1

n_seq = 2

n_steps = 2

X = X.reshape((X.shape[0], n_seq, n_steps, n_features))
```

define the model

```
model = Sequential()

model.add(TimeDistributed(Conv1D(filters=64,
kernel_size=1, activation='relu'), input_shape=(None,
n_steps, n_features)))

model.add(TimeDistributed(MaxPooling1D(pool_size=2)))

model.add(TimeDistributed(Flatten()))

model.add(LSTM(50, activation='relu'))

model.add(Dense(1))
```

```
model.compile(optimizer='adam', loss='mse')
```

fit the model

```
model.fit(X, y, epochs=500, verbose=0)
```

demonstrate the prediction

```
x_input = array([60, 70, 80, 90])

x_input = x_input.reshape((1, n_seq, n_steps, n_features))

yhat = model.predict(x_input, verbose=0)

print(yhat)
```

And, when you run this, the next sequence value is predicted; we expect this to be 100:

```
[[101.69263]]
```

ConvLSTM

A ConvLSTM is an LSTM model that is related to the CNN-LSTM. In a ConvLSTM, we build the convolutional input reading straight into each of the LSTM units. This type of LSTM was originally developed to read data classed as two-dimension spatial-temporal but we can easily adapt it to work with univariate time series problems.

The layer will expect the input to be a sequence containing two-dimensional images and that means the input data shape must be:

[samples, time steps, rows, columns, features]

For our example, we are going to split each of our samples down into subsequences. In each of these, the number of subsequences is the number of time steps, defined as n_seq, and the number of the time steps for each of the subsequences becomes the columns, defined as n_steps. Because this is one-dimensional data, we fix the number of rows as 1.

Now the samples can be reshaped into the structure needed:

choose the number of time steps

    n_steps = 4

split into samples

    X, y = split_sequence(raw_seq, n_steps)

reshape from [samples, time steps] into [samples, time steps, rows, columns, features]

    n_features = 1

    n_seq = 2

    n_steps = 2

    X = X.reshape((X.shape[0], n_seq, 1, n_steps, n_features))

The ConvLSTM can be defined as one layer. This is done in terms of how many filters there are and what size the two0dimensional kernel is in terms of (rows, columns). Because the data series is one-dimensional, we fix the number of rows in the kernel as 1.

We then flatten the model output; this must be done before interpretation and prediction:

```
model.add(ConvLSTM2D(filters=64, kernel_size=(1,2),
activation='relu', input_shape=(n_seq, 1, n_steps,
n_features)))

model.add(Flatten())
```

You can see the full ConvSLTM example below:

```
# univariate convlstm example

from numpy import array

from keras.models import Sequential

from keras.layers import LSTM

from keras.layers import Dense

from keras.layers import Flatten

from keras.layers import ConvLSTM2D
```

```python
# split the univariate sequence into samples
def split_sequence(sequence, n_steps):
    X, y = list(), list()
    for i in range(len(sequence)):
        # find the end of the pattern
        end_ix = i + n_steps
        # check if we have gone beyond the sequence
        if end_ix > len(sequence)-1:
            break
        # gather the input and output bits of the pattern
        seq_x, seq_y = sequence[i:end_ix], sequence[end_ix]
        X.append(seq_x)
        y.append(seq_y)
    return array(X), array(y)

# define the input sequence
raw_seq = [10, 20, 30, 40, 50, 60, 70, 80, 90]
```

```
# choose the number of time steps
    n_steps = 4
# split into samples
    X, y = split_sequence(raw_seq, n_steps)
# reshape from [samples, time steps] into [samples, time steps, rows,
columns, features]
    n_features = 1
    n_seq = 2
    n_steps = 2
    X = X.reshape((X.shape[0], n_seq, 1, n_steps, n_features))
# define the model
    model = Sequential()
    model.add(ConvLSTM2D(filters=64, kernel_size=(1,2),
    activation='relu', input_shape=(n_seq, 1, n_steps,
    n_features)))
    model.add(Flatten())
    model.add(Dense(1))
    model.compile(optimizer='adam', loss='mse')
```

```
# fit the model
```

```
model.fit(X, y, epochs=500, verbose=0)
```

```
# demonstrate the prediction
```

```
x_input = array([60, 70, 80, 90])
```

```
x_input = x_input.reshape((1, n_seq, 1, n_steps, n_features))
```

```
yhat = model.predict(x_input, verbose=0)
```

```
print(yhat)
```

And running this will result in a prediction of the next sequence value, expected to be 100:

```
[[103.68166]]
```

That completes our look at univariate data models, we can finish off by looking at the multivariate data models.

Multivariate LSTM Models

Multivariate time series data is nothing more than data where we have multiple observations for each of the time steps. There are two models that we will be discussing, both that may be required for use with multivariate time series data:

- **Multiple Input Series**

- **Multiple Parallel Series**

Let's discuss each of these models.

Multiple Input Series

A time series problem may have at least inputs and one output that is wholly dependent on the input. All the input time series are classed as parallel because each has one observation at each of the same time steps.

This can easily be demonstrated with an example showing two parallel inputs where the output is nothing more than the inputs added together:

define the input sequence

```
in_seq1 = array([10, 20, 30, 40, 50, 60, 70, 80, 90])

in_seq2 = array([15, 25, 35, 45, 55, 65, 75, 85, 95])

out_seq    =    array([in_seq1[i]+in_seq2[i]    for    i    in
range(len(in_seq1))])
```

These three data arrays can be reshaped into one dataset in which each of the rows is one time step and each of the columns is a separate time series. This is the usual way that parallel time series are stored in a CSV file:

convert to [rows, columns] structure

```
in_seq1 = in_seq1.reshape((len(in_seq1), 1))
```

```python
in_seq2 = in_seq2.reshape((len(in_seq2), 1))

out_seq = out_seq.reshape((len(out_seq), 1))
```

horizontally stack the columns

```python
dataset = hstack((in_seq1, in_seq2, out_seq))
```

And you can see the entire example here:.

multivariate data preparation

```python
from numpy import array

from numpy import hstack

# define the input sequence

in_seq1 = array([10, 20, 30, 40, 50, 60, 70, 80, 90])

in_seq2 = array([15, 25, 35, 45, 55, 65, 75, 85, 95])

out_seq    =    array([in_seq1[i]+in_seq2[i]    for    i    in
range(len(in_seq1))])
```

convert to [rows, columns] structure

```python
in_seq1 = in_seq1.reshape((len(in_seq1), 1))

in_seq2 = in_seq2.reshape((len(in_seq2), 1))

out_seq = out_seq.reshape((len(out_seq), 1))
```

horizontally stack the columns

```
dataset = hstack((in_seq1, in_seq2, out_seq))

print(dataset)
```

When you run this example, you should see the dataset printed; each time step has one row and the inputs and the output parallel time series all have one column each.

```
[[ 10  15  25]

 [ 20  25  45]

 [ 30  35  65]

 [ 40  45  85]

 [ 50  55 105]

 [ 60  65 125]

 [ 70  75 145]

 [ 80  85 165]

 [ 90  95 185]]
```

As we saw with the univariate time series, the data has to be structured into samples that have both input elements and output elements.

LSTM models require enough context that they can learn a mapping sequence of the input sequence to the output value. An LSTM is capable of supporting parallel time series as separate features or variables and that means the data needs to be split into samples that maintain the observation order across a pair of input sequences.

If we were to go with a number of three input steps, our first sample would look like this:

The input:

10, 15

20, 25

30, 35

The output:

65

What this means is that the input to the model is the first three time steps of each of the parallel series and the model will associate that with output value at the third of the time steps, 65 in this example.

What we can see is that, when we transform our time series into the input and output samples needed to train the model, some of the output values will need to be discarded. Those values come from the output time series where there are no values at prior time steps in the input series. In turn, that means the number of input steps chosen is going to have a significant impact on the amount of training data that gets used.

A function called split_sequences can be defined to take a dataset that we have defined with time steps as rows and the parallel series as columns; the input and output samples will be returned.

```
# split a multivariate sequence into samples

        def split_sequences(sequences, n_steps):

        X, y = list(), list()

        for i in range(len(sequences)):

                # find the end of the pattern

                end_ix = i + n_steps

                # check if we have gone beyond the dataset

                if end_ix > len(sequences):

                        break

                # gather the input and output bits of the pattern

                seq_x,    seq_y    =    sequences[i:end_ix,    :-1],
sequences[end_ix-1, -1]

                X.append(seq_x)
```

```
        y.append(seq_y)

    return array(X), array(y)
```

This function can be tested on the dataset and we will use three time steps as the input for each of the input time series. You can see the entire example here:

```
# multivariate data preparation

    from numpy import array

    from numpy import hstack


# split a multivariate sequence into samples

    def split_sequences(sequences, n_steps):

    X, y = list(), list()

    for i in range(len(sequences)):

        # find the end of the pattern

        end_ix = i + n_steps

        # check if we have gone beyond the dataset

        if end_ix > len(sequences):

            break
```

```python
        # gather the input and output bits of the pattern
        seq_x, seq_y = sequences[i:end_ix, :-1], sequences[end_ix-1, -1]
        X.append(seq_x)
        y.append(seq_y)
    return array(X), array(y)


# define the input sequence
in_seq1 = array([10, 20, 30, 40, 50, 60, 70, 80, 90])
in_seq2 = array([15, 25, 35, 45, 55, 65, 75, 85, 95])
out_seq = array([in_seq1[i]+in_seq2[i] for i in range(len(in_seq1))])
# convert to [rows, columns] structure
in_seq1 = in_seq1.reshape((len(in_seq1), 1))
in_seq2 = in_seq2.reshape((len(in_seq2), 1))
out_seq = out_seq.reshape((len(out_seq), 1))
# horizontally stack the columns
dataset = hstack((in_seq1, in_seq2, out_seq))
```

choose the number of time steps

```
n_steps = 3
```

convert into input/output

```
X, y = split_sequences(dataset, n_steps)

print(X.shape, y.shape)
```

summarize the data

```
for i in range(len(X)):

print(X[i], y[i])
```

When we run this example, we get the X and y component shape and we can see from this that X has got a three-dimensional shape. The first dimension is 7, which is the number of samples. The second dimension is 3, which is the function-specific value and the last dimension is 2, specifying the number of variables or parallel time series.

This three-dimensional structure is the exact shape that the LSTM expects as an input and is ready to be used without needing to be reshaped.

So, we can now see that both the input and the output for each of our samples are printed and they show each of the three time steps for the inputs and the associated output for each one.

(7, 3, 2) (7,)

[[10 15]

[20 25]

[30 35]] 65

[[20 25]

[30 35]

[40 45]] 85

[[30 35]

[40 45]

[50 55]] 105

[[40 45]

[50 55]

[60 65]] 125

[[50 55]

[60 65]

[70 75]] 145

[[60 65]

[70 75]

[80 85]] 165

[[70 75]

[80 85]

[90 95]] 185

The next step is to fit a model to all this data.

We can use any of the LSTM models we have already discussed – the Vanilla, Bidirectional, Stacked, Cnn or ConvLSTM. For our example, we will use the Vanilla LSTM. We specify the number of the time steps and parallel series or the features for the input layer by using the argument of input_shape:

define the model

```
model = Sequential()

model.add(LSTM(50,                          activation='relu',
input_shape=(n_steps, n_features)))

model.add(Dense(1))

model.compile(optimizer='adam', loss='mse')
```

When making a prediction, the model expects three time steps for two input time series.

We can predict the next value in the output series providing the input values of:

80,   85

90,   95

100, 105

The shape of the one sample with three time steps and two variables must be [1, 3, 2].

We would expect the next value in the sequence to be $100 + 105$, or 205.

```
# demonstrate prediction
x_input = array([[80, 85], [90, 95], [100, 105]])
x_input = x_input.reshape((1, n_steps, n_features))
yhat = model.predict(x_input, verbose=0)
```

The complete example is listed below.

```
# multivariate lstm example
from numpy import array
from numpy import hstack
from keras.models import Sequential
from keras.layers import LSTM
from keras.layers import Dense
```

```python
# split a multivariate sequence into samples

def split_sequences(sequences, n_steps):

    X, y = list(), list()

    for i in range(len(sequences)):

        # find the end of the pattern

        end_ix = i + n_steps

        # check if we have gone beyond the dataset

        if end_ix > len(sequences):

            break

        # gather the input and output bits of the pattern

        seq_x, seq_y = sequences[i:end_ix, :-1], sequences[end_ix-1, -1]

        X.append(seq_x)

        y.append(seq_y)

    return array(X), array(y)


# define the input sequence
```

```python
in_seq1 = array([10, 20, 30, 40, 50, 60, 70, 80, 90])

in_seq2 = array([15, 25, 35, 45, 55, 65, 75, 85, 95])

out_seq = array([in_seq1[i]+in_seq2[i] for i in
range(len(in_seq1))])
# convert to [rows, columns] structure

in_seq1 = in_seq1.reshape((len(in_seq1), 1))

in_seq2 = in_seq2.reshape((len(in_seq2), 1))

out_seq = out_seq.reshape((len(out_seq), 1))
# horizontally stack the columns

dataset = hstack((in_seq1, in_seq2, out_seq))
# choose the number of time steps

n_steps = 3
# convert into input/output

X, y = split_sequences(dataset, n_steps)
# the dataset knows the number of features, e.g. 2

n_features = X.shape[2]
# define the model
```

```
model = Sequential()

model.add(LSTM(50,                    activation='relu',
input_shape=(n_steps, n_features)))

model.add(Dense(1))

model.compile(optimizer='adam', loss='mse')
# fit the model
model.fit(X, y, epochs=200, verbose=0)
# demonstrate the prediction
x_input = array([[80, 85], [90, 95], [100, 105]])

x_input = x_input.reshape((1, n_steps, n_features))

yhat = model.predict(x_input, verbose=0)

print(yhat)
```

Run this example and the data is prepared, fitted to the model and the prediction is made:

[[208.13531]]

Multiple Parallel Series

An alternative type of time series problem is one that has multiple parallel time series with a value prediction required for each one. For example, let's take the data from the last section:

```
[[ 10  15  25]

 [ 20  25  45]

 [ 30  35  65]

 [ 40  45  85]

 [ 50  55 105]

 [ 60  65 125]

 [ 70  75 145]

 [ 80  85 165]

 [ 90  95 185]]
```

We might need to predict the value for all three time series on the next time step, something that is called 'multivariate forecasting'. Once again, we need to split the data into input/output samples so our model can be trained.

The first dataset sample would look like this:

The input:

    10, 15, 25

    20, 25, 45

    30, 35, 65

The output:

40, 45, 85

Using the function called split_sequences(), we can split our multiple parallel time series into rows for the time steps and columns each containing one series into the input/output shape required:

split the multivariate sequence into samples

```
def split_sequences(sequences, n_steps):

X, y = list(), list()

for i in range(len(sequences)):

    # find the end of the pattern

    end_ix = i + n_steps

    # check if we have gone beyond the dataset

    if end_ix > len(sequences)-1:

        break

    # gather the input and output bits of the pattern

    seq_x,    seq_y    =    sequences[i:end_ix,    :],
sequences[end_ix, :]

    X.append(seq_x)
```

```
        y.append(seq_y)

    return array(X), array(y)
```

This can be demonstrated on our contrived problem and you can see the entire example here:

```
# multivariate output data prep

from numpy import array

from numpy import hstack


# split the multivariate sequence into samples

def split_sequences(sequences, n_steps):

    X, y = list(), list()

    for i in range(len(sequences)):

        # find the end of the pattern

        end_ix = i + n_steps

        # check if we have gone beyond the dataset

        if end_ix > len(sequences)-1:

            break
```

```python
        # gather the input and output bits of the pattern
        seq_x, seq_y = sequences[i:end_ix, :], sequences[end_ix, :]
        X.append(seq_x)
        y.append(seq_y)
    return array(X), array(y)


# define the input sequence
    in_seq1 = array([10, 20, 30, 40, 50, 60, 70, 80, 90])
    in_seq2 = array([15, 25, 35, 45, 55, 65, 75, 85, 95])
    out_seq = array([in_seq1[i]+in_seq2[i] for i in range(len(in_seq1))])
# convert to [rows, columns] structure
    in_seq1 = in_seq1.reshape((len(in_seq1), 1))
    in_seq2 = in_seq2.reshape((len(in_seq2), 1))
    out_seq = out_seq.reshape((len(out_seq), 1))
# horizontally stack the columns
    dataset = hstack((in_seq1, in_seq2, out_seq))
```

choose the number of time steps

```
n_steps = 3
```

convert into input/output

```
X, y = split_sequences(dataset, n_steps)

print(X.shape, y.shape)
```

summarize the data

```
for i in range(len(X)):

print(X[i], y[i])
```

If you run this example, the shape for the prepared X and y components is printed. X is a three-dimensional shape with the first dimension being 6, the number of the samples. The second is 3, which is the number of time steps we chose for the samples and the final dimension is 3, which is the number of features or parallel time series.

y has a two-dimensional shape with 6 as the first dimension, which is the number of samples and 3 as the second dimension, the number of the time variables to be predicted per sample.

We can now use this data in an LSTM model that will expect to receive an input of three-dimensional shape and an output of two-dimensional shape for each sample's X and y component. Each sample will then be printed and will show the input and the output for each of the samples:

(6, 3, 3) (6, 3)

[[10 15 25]

[20 25 45]

[30 35 65]] [40 45 85]

[[20 25 45]

[30 35 65]

[40 45 85]] [50 55 105]

[[30 35 65]

[40 45 85]

[50 55 105]] [60 65 125]

[[40 45 85]

[50 55 105]

[60 65 125]] [70 75 145]

[[50 55 105]

[60 65 125]

[70 75 145]] [80 85 165]

[[60 65 125]

[70 75 145]

[80 85 165]] [90 95 185]

Now the data is ready to be fitted to an LSTM model and, once again, we can use any of the LST models we talked about at the start of the section. We'll use a Stacked LSTM where we specify the number of steps and the parallel series or features for the input layer using the argument of input_shape. We also use the number of parallel series in the number of values we specify the model to predict in the output layer – for this example, it is three:

define the model

```
model = Sequential()

model.add(LSTM(100, activation='relu',
return_sequences=True, input_shape=(n_steps, n_features)))

model.add(LSTM(100, activation='relu'))

model.add(Dense(n_features))

model.compile(optimizer='adam', loss='mse')
```

The next value can be predicted for each parallel series and we do this by providing a three time step input for each of the series:

70, 75, 145

80, 85, 165

90, 95, 185

The input shape for one prediction must be [1, 3, 3] which is [sample, time steps, features]:

demonstrate the prediction

```
x_input = array([[70,75,145], [80,85,165], [90,95,185]])

x_input = x_input.reshape((1, n_steps, n_features))

yhat = model.predict(x_input, verbose=0)
```

The vector output is expected to be:

[100, 105, 205]

Again, this can be tied together and the example below shows you a Stacked LSTM for the purpose of multivariate time series forecasting:

multivariate output stacked lstm example

```
from numpy import array
```

```python
from numpy import hstack

from keras.models import Sequential

from keras.layers import LSTM

from keras.layers import Dense


# split the multivariate sequence into samples

def split_sequences(sequences, n_steps):

X, y = list(), list()

for i in range(len(sequences)):

    # find the end of the pattern

    end_ix = i + n_steps

    # check if we have gone beyond the dataset

    if end_ix > len(sequences)-1:

        break

    # gather the input and output bits of the pattern

    seq_x,    seq_y    =    sequences[i:end_ix,    :],
sequences[end_ix, :]
```

```python
        X.append(seq_x)

        y.append(seq_y)

    return array(X), array(y)


# define the input sequence

    in_seq1 = array([10, 20, 30, 40, 50, 60, 70, 80, 90])

    in_seq2 = array([15, 25, 35, 45, 55, 65, 75, 85, 95])

    out_seq = array([in_seq1[i]+in_seq2[i] for i in range(len(in_seq1))])
# convert to [rows, columns] structure

    in_seq1 = in_seq1.reshape((len(in_seq1), 1))

    in_seq2 = in_seq2.reshape((len(in_seq2), 1))

    out_seq = out_seq.reshape((len(out_seq), 1))
# horizontally stack the columns

    dataset = hstack((in_seq1, in_seq2, out_seq))
# choose the number of time steps

    n_steps = 3
```

```python
# convert into input/output
        X, y = split_sequences(dataset, n_steps)
# the dataset knows the number of features, e.g. 2
        n_features = X.shape[2]
# define the model
        model = Sequential()
        model.add(LSTM(100, activation='relu',
        return_sequences=True, input_shape=(n_steps, n_features)))

        model.add(LSTM(100, activation='relu'))

        model.add(Dense(n_features))

        model.compile(optimizer='adam', loss='mse')
# fit the model
        model.fit(X, y, epochs=400, verbose=0)
# demonstrate the prediction
        x_input = array([[70,75,145], [80,85,165], [90,95,185]])

        x_input = x_input.reshape((1, n_steps, n_features))

        yhat = model.predict(x_input, verbose=0)
```

```
print(yhat)
```

Run this and the data is prepared, fitted to the model and the prediction is made:

```
[[101.76599 108.730484 206.63577 ]]
```

LSTMs are proving to be a great solution to both time series and sequence problems but they are not the easiest to train. It takes a great deal of both time and computing resource to train even the simplest of LSTM models but the results are genuinely worth it, making this a must-learn part of deep learning.

Conclusion

———— ◆ ————

I want to thank you for taking the time to read part 2 in my series on Deep Learning. Where the first guide gave you an overview of everything to do with Deep Learning, this time I have chosen a number of very important subjects and gone deeper into them. There are plenty of practical, hands-on examples for you here, examples that you should follow – you will learn far more by doing than just by reading alone.

Deep Learning with Python is a complex subject and there are many parts to it, a lot of learning, reading and doing to get the hang of things. Don't expect to read this and immediately think that you are an expert at the subject – you will have to trust me when I say that it will take an awful lot more than that. What I can do is give you a better understanding of the subject, of some of the concepts and the Python packages that you need to learn and understand before you can even think about getting to grips properly with Deep Learning.

Thank you once again for reading this guide; I hope that it has given you a deeper understanding of the main Deep Learning concepts.

References

https://medium.com

https://realpython.com

https://www.datacamp.com

https://dzone.com

https://www.kdnuggets.com

https://towardsdatascience.com

https://www.sitepoint.com

https://www.kaggle.com

https://skymind.ai

https://www.geeksforgeeks.org

http://ruder.io

https://mendeley.com

https://data.world/uci

http://www.patentsview.org/

https://nlp.stanford.edu/

https://machinelearningmastery.com

https://www.analyticsvidhya.com

https://s3-ap-south-1.amazonaws.com

https://www.gutenberg.org/

DEEP LEARNING

WITH PYTHON

A Comprehensive Guide for Experts

Travis Booth

Introduction

———————◆———————

Deep learning has become the most powerful field for solving real world problems regarding natural language processing, speech processing, and any other area which involves massive amounts of information. The purpose of *Deep Learning with Python: A Hands On Guide for Experts* is to cover the largest advancements made in deep learning in recent years. You will study several advanced theories and learn the background of the concepts behind them and then put everything into practice by implementing a number of algorithms.

This book is written to be a continuation of the previous books in the series, therefore before continuing you should at the very least master the basic theories of deep learning, as well as some of the more advanced ones. This expert guide will cover a number of advanced concepts behind deep learning, together with the use of the Keras library. You will expand your knowledge about optimization, regularization, and loss functions among other key notions.

At the core of this guide, you will explore some of the most powerful advanced deep neural network architectures, such as the Residual Neural Network and the Densely Connected Convolutional Neural

Network. Furthermore you will learn how to work with autoencoders, which are used to unveil the representation of input information. You will go through two practical applications, known as denoising and colorization. Each chapter will provide you with real world examples that are useful at solving real problems.

This guide also provides you with some of the most powerful techniques devised recently, such as the Generative Adversarial Networks. GANs are a relatively new way of generating manufactured data that mimics the real data. In the chapter about these networks you will explore two different examples, namely the deep convolutional GANs and the conditional GANs. Furthermore, you will learn about cross domain GANs and understand how they differ from the other models.

Finally, in the last chapter, you will explore the Variational Autoencoders, where you will learn about some highly important progress made to deep learning. This type of autoencoder is also a generative model that is used to create manufactured data. However, in this chapter we will focus on a couple of variational models which are used on decodable continuous latent space for variational inference.

How to Get the Most Out of It

In order to get the most out of this hands on guide for experts, you should already have enough knowledge of deep learning, Python, as well as know how to work with tools such as Keras and Tensorflow. However, while having experience will certainly help you understand these advanced concepts and techniques, the guide is prepared in such a way that you can understand the applications with a minimum of basic knowledge.

Furthermore, make sure to work together with the guide when it comes to the application of the concepts and models in code. Reading the theory is not enough, especially when exploring such advanced concepts. The code itself is well-researched by those who have developed the models and have written scientific papers on them. This guide makes sure to explain these models step by step so that it is easy for anyone to understand, even without the highest skill in mathematics and deep learning.

With that being said, let's get right to it by starting with everything you will need to work with the advance deep learning techniques and models.

Chapter 1

Advanced Deep Learning Prerequisites

————————◆————————

Throughout this book, we are going to work with the tree artificial neural networks you briefly studied in the other books. The foundation for advanced deep learning projects is nearly always built using recurrent neural networks, multilayer perceptrons, and convolutional neural networks. We will use them in combination with autoencoders and generative adversarial networks. For the purpose of constructing such models, we will also need a new tool, namely the Keras library. You will learn why Keras is frequently used for advanced deep learning projects and how to install it.

Here's what you will explore in this chapter:

1. Why Keras is the perfect tool for expert deep learning.

2. How to work with multilayer perceptrons, convolutional neural networks, and recurrent neural networks together with Keras and Tensorflow in order to build new, advanced models.

3. How the implement the three neural network structures with Keras with practical examples.

4. How to implement advanced concepts such as optimization, the loss function and regularization.

The purpose of this chapter is to set up the building blocks in order to study advanced deep learning techniques and topics, such as autoencoders and deep networks. Let's get started!

The Keras Library

Keras is a neural network API that is constructed using the Python programming language and is normally used together with Tensorflow. This library is well-documented and supported by a community of over 250,000 developers at the time of writing. In addition, it is designed to be used together with Tensorflow, which is another popular tool among deep learners, machine learners, and data scientists. Tensorflow, developed by Google, is a powerful, open source library that connects to Keras in order to use it as a high level API.

So, why use Keras at all if so far you were just fine with Tensorflow, Scikit-learn and other popular libraries? In short, it is a powerful tool used by the most important tech giants that drive multiple industries. It is used by Google, Nvidia, Netflix, and many more, therefore if you seek to enter the industry as a professional, knowing how to work with Keras will prove to be an advantage.

The main purpose of Keras is to boost the implementation of deep learning techniques and models. It works best when applied on advanced deep learning models, however, you can use it together with the basic deep learning models as well, because in essence it simply improves your training models. The main reason why all models are so easily improved is because the library is constructed from interconnected layers. This will result in a clean model that is straightforward to work with. All you will need is data and a measurement system. As a result, you will spend a lot less time writing code in order to implement your models.

Keras improves your deep learning models by also improving your productivity. Instead of writing and maintaining code, you will mostly focus on the algorithms themselves. Furthermore, Keras allows you to quickly introduce the neural networks into your training model with only a few lines of code. The process so far may seem simple, however, don't expect it to be too easy. Keras is used for complex processes, but by simplifying them it doesn't mean you receive the results with the press of a few buttons. In some cases you will have to customize Keras' unique functions and adapt them to your specific requirements. You will also have to build graphic representations of your models and much more.

Now that you know a little bit about Keras, let's start installing it together with Tensorflow.

Installation
Keep in mind that Keras shouldn't be used by itself. It is designed with other components in mind because it is built on other libraries.

This means that you will first need a deep learning library like Tensorflow, or Theano, or CNTK, whatever you prefer. However, in this book we will focus on working with Tensorflow and therefore Python as our favorite programming language. The reason why you should consider Tensorflow, if you haven't already when reading the previous books, is because of its reputation and popularity.

Take note that you can also use Tensorflow together with other similar libraries because Keras allows you to easily swap between them as needed. Why is this an important feature? You are probably aware that not all libraries are created equal when it comes to system performance. For instance, when you implement an algorithm into a network you will achieve slightly different results depending on the library you are using. Keras operates using your computer processor and GPU together with Google's Tensor Processing Unit. In this case, a powerful GPU will prove to be an advantage when training your models. So whenever you choose your backend, make sure it takes full advantage of your hardware and operating system.

With that being said, let's take care of the installation process. There are a couple of ways of installing Keras and Tensorflow. Start with the following command and with "pip":

    sudo pip3 install tensorflow

You may have already dabled with Tensorflow, however, you probably worked with the basic version. Keep in mind that if you have an NVIDIA GPU, with updated drivers, CUDA extensions, as well as the cuDNN deep neural network library, you can install the GPU powered version of Tensorflow. This means that Tensorflow will now use your GPU in order to power your model and therefore speed up the training process, as well as the prediction. In this case, use the following command:

```
sudo pip3 install tensorflow-gpu
```

Now that Tensorflow is taken care of, let's install Keras:

```
sudo pip3 install keras
```

While Keras provides you with a great deal of functionality and model training acceleration, by itself it will not be enough when working with advanced deep learning models. You will need to also install a number of packages. Some of them you may have worked with already, while some may be new. Some of the most important ones include pydot and matplotlib. Type the following lines if you have already installed Tensorflow and Keras:

```
import tensorflow as tf

message = tf.constant('Hello world!')

session = tf.Session()

session.run(message) b'Hello world!'

import keras.backend as K
```

Using TensorFlow backend.

print(K.epsilon())

1e-07

At this point, if you receive an error regarding SSE4.2 AVX AVX2 FMA, you can simply ignore it, as it will not have any impact on your work. However, if it does bother you, you will have to to install Tensorflow from https://github.com/ tensorflow/tensorflow. tensorflow/core/platform/cpu_feature_guard.cc:137] instead of its homepage.

Now that your tools have been assembled, let's start quickly implementing the three deep learning neural networks we discussed in the previous books. Before continuing, you might consider taking some time to read the Keras documentation from the developer's official page. The purpose of this book is not to dive deep into the functions offered by the library. We will strictly focus on working with advanced deep learning models and techniques.

Neural Network Implementation

We discussed earlier that we will be using three neural networks for the purpose of this guide, namely the multilayer perceptron, recurrent neural network, and convolutional neural networks. So far you mostly focused on them as separate networks, however, in most real world situations you will use them together. As you know, each neural net comes with its own advantages and by combining the three models you will be able to improve your model significantly by taking advantage of each network's strengths.

In this section you will focus on each neural network in order to gain a deeper understanding of them. You will learn a number of advanced techniques and concepts that go hand in hand with specific models. For instance you will explore multilayer perceptrons together with optimizers and regularizers.

As you should already know from the previous books, multilayer perceptrons are interconnected networks that are mostly used as feedforward neural networks. In order to understand how advanced training models are created, you need to understand how these neural networks are used in real applications. For instance, multilayer perceptrons are often used when dealing with linear regression problems, as well as logistic regression. Take note that these networks are not recommended to be used when it comes to processing large sequences of data. Why? Multilayer perceptrons are known for having a bad memory. Remembering complex patterns of multidimensional data is not this network's strongest feature. This doesn't mean it's not possible to use them this way. Multilayer perceptrons are simply not the most optimal choice because you would have to prepare a large number of parameters in advance. Always remember to keep it simple. The more processes you need to prepare, the more time you waste and the more you risk introducing human error into the model.

Multidimensional data is best processed by recurrent neural networks. Their structure allows you to learn anything from the data's history that can be used to improve the prediction mode. However, if your data comes in the form of images and videos, you should consider focusing on a convolutional neural network instead because it offers you powerful features such as classification and segmentation that are particularly useful when dealing with such data.

As you can see, each type of neural network serves a specific purpose. However, in the real world your datasets will not be so clear and clean. That is why you will need to learn how to combine all three in order to obtain the best results. Furthermore, multilayer perceptrons, recurrent neural nets, and convolutional neural nets will not be able to fulfill all of your requirements even when used together. You will have to understand various components such as optimizers, regularizers, and loss functions. What does all of this mean? The loss function needs to be minimized and in order to do so, you will have to know how to implement an optimizer. The optimizer is an algorithm that can calculate how the training model adjusts the weights during each pass. Keep in mind, that with real world datasets it is not enough to just work with your training and test data. You will even have to take into account unpredictable data. In this case, you need to learn how to apply a regularizer.

With that being said, let's start discussing the multilayer perceptrons in more detail and learn about the concepts like regularizers and loss functions.

Multilayer Perceptrons with Keras

You have already worked with multilayer perceptrons, but in this section you will take a few extra steps. In this section, you will again encounter the popular MNIST dataset because this type of network is best used for identifying information based on handwritten symbols. The MNIST dataset is the best choice for learning purposes when it comes to handwritten digit classification. If you don't recall from the previous book, you should know that this dataset contains roughly 70,000 detailed writing samples that are classified into a training set which contains 60,000 data items and a test set which contains 10,000 items.

In order to use this dataset with Keras, all you need to do is download everything from the library because it provides you will all the tools you need and everything is done automatically. By typing the following code, you will download the dataset, plot 25 random images, and then count how many training and testing labels we have:

```
import numpy as np
```

```python
from keras.datasets import mnist

import matplotlib.pyplot as plt

(x_train, y_train), (x_test, y_test) = mnist.load_data()
# the number of training labels

unique, counts = np.unique(y_train, return_counts=True)

print("Train labels: ", dict(zip(unique, counts)))
# the number of testing labels

unique, counts = np.unique(y_test, return_counts=True)

print("Test labels: ", dict(zip(unique, counts)))
# accessing 25 random handwritten digits

indexes = np.random.randint(0, x_train.shape[0], size=25)

images = x_train[indexes]

labels = y_train[indexes]
# using matplotlib to plot the 25 random digits

plt.figure(figsize=(5,5))

for i in range(len(indexes)):

plt.subplot(5, 5, i + 1)
```

```
image = images[i]

plt.imshow(image, cmap='gray')

plt.axis('off')

plt.show()

plt.savefig("mnist-samples.png")

plt.close('all')
```

While some of this code should already be familiar to you, you will take note of our use of the load data function. In this case we are loading the entire dataset containing 70,000 items, however, they are labeled one by one and then stored inside an array. Afterwards we use matplot lib to plot only 25 randomly selected digits.

Next, we need to implement a multilayer perceptron with Keras, but first we also need to process the labels, reshape the data, and apply an optimizer. Here's the code:

```
import numpy as np

from keras.models import Sequential

from keras.layers import Dense, Activation, Dropout

from keras.utils import to_categorical, plot_model

from keras.datasets import mnist

(x_train, y_train), (x_test, y_test) = mnist.load_data()
```

```python
# process the labels
        num_labels = len(np.unique(y_train))
# performing a one-hot vector conversion
        y_train = to_categorical(y_train)

        y_test = to_categorical(y_test)
# process the dimension of the digits by presuming a square shape
        image_size = x_train.shape

        input_size = image_size * image_size
# resizing process
        x_train = np.reshape(x_train, [-1, input_size])

        x_train = x_train.astype('float32') / 255

        x_test = np.reshape(x_test, [-1, input_size])

        x_test = x_test.astype('float32') / 255
# multilayer perceptron parameters
        batch_size = 128

        hidden_units = 256

        dropout = 0.45
# we will have a multilayer perceptron with 3 layers
# between each layer we will implement a dropout and a rectified
linear unit
```

```python
model = Sequential()

model.add(Dense(hidden_units, input_dim=input_size))

model.add(Activation('relu'))

model.add(Dropout(dropout))

model.add(Dense(hidden_units))

model.add(Activation('relu'))

model.add(Dropout(dropout))

model.add(Dense(num_labels))
# one-hot vector output

model.add(Activation('softmax'))

model.summary()

plot_model(model, to_file='mlp-mnist.png',
show_shapes=True)
# loss function and optimizer
# we will use the accuracy metric to measure the classification

model.compile(loss='categorical_crossentropy',

optimizer='adam',
```

```
        metrics=['accuracy'])
```

training the model

```
        model.fit(x_train, y_train, epochs=20,
        batch_size=batch_size)
```

using the test set to validate the network model

```
        acc = model.evaluate(x_test, y_test, batch_size=batch_size)

        print("\nTest accuracy: %.1f%%" % (100.0 * acc))
```

Once we import the data we first need to calculate the number of labels. By default, they are presented from a scale of 0 to 9 and therefore this isn't good for the neural net's prediction layer. Therefore, we need to convert the labels to a different format, in this case a one-hot vector. The concept of One-hot refers to a collection of bits which hold a combination of values of either 1 or 0, but where there is only one "1" bit and the rest are 0. For instance, if we have 000 written in binary code, the one-hot version becomes 00000001. In one-hot vector follows the same principle, however, it is a 10 dimensional vector where the value of 1 represents the index of the item. Therefore, label 2 becomes a one-hot vector like so : 0, 0, 1, 0, 0, 0, 0, 0, 0, 0. The value of 1 occupies the third position because the first value is index 0.

After converting all the labels to one-hot vectors we continue by calculating the dimensions of each image. We take the input size of each dense layer in order to scale the value of each pixel. Take note that by default the values go from 0 to 255. By performing this process we change their dimensions to go from a value of 0 to 1. Keep in mind that if you want you can still use the basic pixel values, however, by changing their range you normalize the input data. The benefit of taking this step is that you can greatly limit the number of gradient values that would restrict the training process. After this step we also perform the same normalization process on the network for the same reasons.

Once the data has been prepared, we can create the multilayer perceptron model. You will notice that the multilayer perceptron layer is called "Dense" in Keras. The name refers to the fact that we're dealing with a densely connected layer. In our model we have determined that the first two multilayer perceptron layers are the same and they both hold 256 units, followed by a dropout unit and a rectified linear unit. If you're asking yourself why 256 is the chosen number, that is simply because of performance. If we have fewer units, like 128 for instance, then the test accuracy is much lower. However, if we increase the number of units to 512 or more, then the boost to test accuracy is barely noticeable. 256 is a comfortable sweet spot that combines performance with accuracy. Keep in mind that these units control the multilayer percepron's capacity. What do we mean by capacity? It is simply a way to determine how complex a function which a network calculates is.

You will notice in the model implementation we are using Keras' sequential model API. For the purpose of this chapter we are going to stick to this basic model because we only need to use an input and output that are required when processing with a sequence of Dense layers. Take note that a Dense layer is a linear operation, therefore a sequence of such layers can only be used to determine a linear function. As you probably know, the MNIST classification process is a non-linear one, however. To solve this problem, we are applying a rectified linear unit. Now our multilayer perceptron will be capable of modeling any nonlinear functions as well because the rectified linear unit is a nonlinear function that acts as a filter. The filter accepts positive inputs but everything else is set to zero. There are other nonlinear functions you can use in this case, however, the rectified linear unit is considered by most deep learners to be the industry standard. It is powerful, efficient, and easy to implement.

Regularization

With enough capacity any neural network can memorize the training data, however, when this happens the network will fail when processing the test data. This is known as a failure to generalize. To counteract this danger we need to add a regularization layer to the model. This layer is known as the dropout, which we already implemented into our example. So how does a dropout work?

If you establish a dropout value like in our implementation, for instance 0.45, then the regularization layer will remove that percentage of values from entering the neighboring layer. In our example, the first two layers hold 256 units. If we introduce the regularization process with a dropout value of 0.45, then we will have only 140 units ((1 - 0.45) * 256) passing from the first layer to the second. This means that the regularization layer will reinforce the neural network to make it more resistant to unpredictable information because it is capable of making correct predictions even if it has only a part of the data to work with.

Take note that the regularization layer is not applied to the output layer. Furthermore, it is only being used during the training phase, and not during the prediction. There are other regularization layers you can create instead of using the dropout. For instance, you can opt for l1 or l2 through Keras. These two work by determining and implementing a penalty system. L1 uses a part of the sum of values, while l2 uses the part of the square of values. This means that the regularization layer will push the optimizer to focus on small values because they are less sensitive to noise that comes from the input data. Here's how you can implement an l2 for instance:

```
from keras.regularizers import l2

model.add(Dense(hidden_units,

kernel_regularizer=l2(0.001),

input_dim=input_size))
```

You can use this method instead of the dropout if you'd like, without having to add an extra layer. However, keep in mind that with our model the dropout is more efficient and simply performs better than the l2.

Optimization

The purpose of optimization in this case is to reduce the loss function. The loss function itself is a method that evaluates how an algorithm performs when modeling the data. If the prediction is not close to the real result, then we have a high loss function. However, if we implement an optimization function, then the loss function will use it to learn how to lower the prediction error. In addition, we need to use various performance measures in order to see how well a model distributes the data. In this case, by using Keras we have the "loss" metric. Keep in mind that this doesn't mean you should be using only this metric. You can also use accuracy during various phases such as validation and testing, as well as other metrics. As you already know, there are a number of performance metrics in deep learning and you should choose them based on the purpose of the model's application.

As for optimizers, you can choose from a number of them when working with Keras. Some of the most popular ones are the stochastic gradient descent, adaptive moments (also known as Adam), and the root mean squared propagation. Each one will hold a number of parameters that include the learning rate, decay, and momentum. It's also worth taking note that the adaptive moments and root mean squared propagation optimizers are in fact variations of the stochastic gradient descent, with the exception that they have adaptive learning rates. In our example we have implemented the Adam optimizers due to its high testing accuracy. However, you can also use the stochastic gradient descent, which is the most basic optimizer you can implement. If you remember your calculus lessons, you will notice that it is an even more basic form of the gradient descent. The concept is that when you trace a function's curve on a downwards path, you will find the minimum value. The gradient descent isn't used in deep learning because of the millions of parameters you often have to work with. In such a case, the gradient descent is not efficient and that is why the stochastic gradient descent is used instead.

Optimization is based on the requirement of a differentiable loss function, because it is based on differentiation. You always need to keep this limitation in mind whenever you work with a new loss function. Once you are all set with the dataset, loss function, optimizer and regularizer, you can start training your model:

loss function and optimizer

we will use the accuracy metric to measure the classification

```
    model.compile(loss='categorical_crossentropy',

    optimizer='adam',
```

```
metrics=['accuracy'])
```

training the model

```
model.fit(x_train, y_train, epochs=20,
batch_size=batch_size)
```

Here we use the fit function, which is available to us through Keras. All we need to do is provide the data, establish how many epochs need to be trained, and the batch size. Everything else is done automatically. This is a perfect example of Keras significantly reducing your workload and making each step simpler to implement. Normally you would have to perform other tasks like formatting your input and output data, loading and many more. All of these processes take place here as well, however, they occur behind the curtain by using the fit function. In our example an epoch is represented by the sampling of the training data, while the batch size is the sample size of the inputs we need to process during every single phase. One epoch is processed when the function divides the training set by the batch size. In addition, we add a value of 1 in order to compensate for additional fractional values.

Now that the model is complete, we have to evaluate the performance in order to see if we have the best solution or not.

Performance

In this scenario we have performed the training process over 20 epochs in order to gain enough metrics that we can compare. We used the default values for the optimizers, however, we will notice what changes occured when we varied them, as well as the regularizer and the total number of units that we have observed in each layer. The first thing we will conclude is that having a large neural network doesn't automatically mean that the performance is better. You will notice that by increasing the size of the network you will in fact gain nothing of value. The accuracy of the training and testing sets changes only marginally. We also mentioned earlier that if we would have 128 units, the accuracy would be impacted greatly. However, we have used 256 units per layer and when we remove the regularizer you will see a training accuracy of around 99.9% and a testing accuracy of around 98%. The reason why the testing accuracy is considerably lower is because of overfitting.

However, once we implemented the optimizer with a Dropout value of 0.45, the testing accuracy improves by approximately half a percent. This is already a significant change, even though the overfitting problem hasn't been fully eliminated. Now if you would experiment by also removing the regularizer with the rectified linear unit, you will notice that the accuracy for both sets will go down by a large margin. Furthermore, you can perform another test by using the l2 instead of the Dropout layer, however, again you will notice significantly less performance.

In conclusion, we can establish that using a multilayer perceptron with a number of techniques that improve the model is simply not enough. The problem is with the neural network structure itself. What we need to do is use a convolutional neural network in order to improve the testing accuracy.

Convolutional Neural Networks

In this section we are going to focus on the same problem using the MNIST dataset, however, this time we will work with a convolutional neural network. Take note that before we can implement this network we have to modify the model we built earlier. For instance, we will no longer have an input vector, but an input tensor instead, with a height, width, and number of channels. Furthermore, we will have to change the dimension of the images in order to fulfill the requirements for the input.

We're now going to move on to the second artificial neural network, Convolutional Neural Networks (CNNs). In this section, we're going to solve the same MNIST digit classification problem, this time using CNNs. Let's go through the code using Keras, the MNIST dataset and the convolutional neural network and then discuss:

```
import numpy as np

from keras.models

import Sequential

from keras.layers import Activation, Dense, Dropout
```

```python
from keras.layers import Conv2D, MaxPooling2D, Flatten

from keras.utils import to_categorical, plot_model

from keras.datasets import mnist

# loading our dataset

(x_train, y_train), (x_test, y_test) = mnist.load_data()

# process the labels

num_labels = len(np.unique(y_train))

# one-hot vector

y_train = to_categorical(y_train)

y_test = to_categorical(y_test)

# image dimensions

image_size = x_train.shape[1]

# resize and normalize

x_train = np.reshape(x_train,[-1, image_size, image_size, 1])

x_test = np.reshape(x_test,[-1, image_size, image_size, 1])

x_train = x_train.astype('float32') / 255

x_test = x_test.astype('float32') / 255
```

486

```
# image is processed the way it is

    input_shape = (image_size, image_size, 1)

    batch_size = 128

    kernel_size = 3

    pool_size = 2

    filters = 64

    dropout = 0.2

# model is built using a convolutional neural network

# with a rectified linear unit and max pooling

    model = Sequential()

    model.add(Conv2D(filters=filters,

    kernel_size=kernel_size,

    activation='relu',

    input_shape=input_shape))

    model.add(MaxPooling2D(pool_size))

    model.add(Conv2D(filters=filters,

    kernel_size=kernel_size,
```

```
        activation='relu'))

        model.add(MaxPooling2D(pool_size))

        model.add(Conv2D(filters=filters,

        kernel_size=kernel_size,

        activation='relu'))

        model.add(Flatten())
# using a dropout
        model.add(Dropout(dropout))
# using a 10 dimensional one-hot vector for the output layer
        model.add(Dense(num_labels))

        model.add(Activation('softmax'))

        model.summary()

        plot_model(model, to_file='cnn-mnist.png',
        show_shapes=True)
# the loss function
# using an adam optimizer
# using the accuracy metric for classification
```

```
model.compile(loss='categorical_crossentropy',

optimizer='adam',

metrics=['accuracy'])

# training the neural network

model.fit(x_train, y_train, epochs=10,
batch_size=batch_size)

loss, acc = model.evaluate(x_test, y_test,
batch_size=batch_size)

print("\nTest accuracy: %.1f%%" % (100.0 * acc))
```

The biggest difference you will notice is the fact that we used 2D convolutional layers. The rectified linear unit is a part of the Conv2D layers and it is used as an activation layer if the model has a batch normalization layer present. In our example we use batch normalization in order to prevent potential instability during the model training stage when we use a large rate of learning.

When building the multilayer perceptron model you saw that the Dense layer is represented by the number of units. In the case of a convolutional neural network, it's the kernel that represents all the processes. The process known as convolution can be imagined as a box that scans through the entire MNIST digit image from left to right and from top to bottom. The image is converted to a number of feature maps which are in fact constructed from the information that the kernel extracts from the image. Then these features maps are converted into a different set of feature maps when shifted to the next layer. The process continues this way from layer to layer and in order to manipulate how many feature maps we generate we use a "filters" argument.

Imagine the process we discussed above by looking at a 5 x 5 image to which we apply a 3 x 3 kernel. Once we obtain a feature map after the convolution process, we will see that it is in fact smaller in dimension that the image we started with. This happens because the convolution is only applied to valid data and therefore the kernel cannot process anything outside of the original image. If the size of the image would be identical to that of the feature map, then the Conv2D class can have "padding = same", and therefore pad the space around the input with zeroes in order to maintain the size after the convolution process is over.

Furthermore, we can make another change by adding a MaxPolling layer with a pool size equal to 2. The purpose of this layer is to compress the feature map because it would allow the kernel to cover a wider area. For instance, if we have a pooling value of two and a 2 x 2 kernel, then the kernel will convolve a 4 x 4 area. The convolutional neural network will now be capable of covering different sets of feature maps. However, you can use other methods to apply compression or a max pooling layer. For instance you can create an average pooling layer instead, which will take the average size of an area, instead of going with the maximum value. This way you automatically reduce the size by 50%.

In addition, you can work with a strided convolution with a stride value of 2, which means you will skip over two pixels during the process, however, maintain the identical 50% compression. These reduction methods achieve the same thing, however, there are some differences between them, mainly in how effective they are in various situations.

Recurrent Neural Networks

Now that we covered the first two neural networks, let's discuss the implementation of the recurrent neural network. If you recall from the previous books, this type of network is best used when working with sequential data. In other words, it is useful when handling text for natural language processing or processing data extracted from various instruments that take measurements. While you may look at the MNIST dataset and think that this is not the case of sequential data, you might be right, however, you can think of an image as a sequence of pixels arranged in rows and columns. Therefore you can benefit from working with a recurrent neural network.

For our example we are going to use the recurrent neural network to process all of our images as a sequence of 28 input vector elements. Let's take a look at the code and analyze it:

```python
import numpy as np

from keras.models import Sequential

from keras.layers import Dense, Activation, SimpleRNN

from keras.utils import to_categorical, plot_model

from keras.datasets import mnist
```

loading our dataset

```python
(x_train, y_train), (x_test, y_test) = mnist.load_data()
```

processing the number of labels

```python
num_labels = len(np.unique(y_train))
```

performing a one-hot vector conversion

```python
y_train = to_categorical(y_train)

y_test = to_categorical(y_test)
```

normalization and resizing dimensions

```python
image_size = x_train.shape[1]

x_train = np.reshape(x_train,[-1, image_size, image_size])

x_test = np.reshape(x_test,[-1, image_size, image_size])
```

```python
x_train = x_train.astype('float32') / 255 x_test =
x_test.astype('float32') / 255

input_shape = (image_size, image_size)

batch_size = 128

units = 256

dropout = 0.2
```

using a recurrent neural network with 256 units

the input will be a 28 dimensional vector with 28 timestamps

```python
model = Sequential()

model.add(SimpleRNN(units=units,

dropout=dropout,

input_shape=input_shape))

model.add(Dense(num_labels))

model.add(Activation('softmax'))

model.summary()

plot_model(model, to_file='rnn-mnist.png',
show_shapes=True)
```

loss function

\# applying a stochastic gradient descent optimizer

\# measuring with the accuracy metric

```
model.compile(loss='categorical_crossentropy',

optimizer='sgd',

metrics=['accuracy'])
```

\# training the neural network

```
model.fit(x_train, y_train, epochs=20,
batch_size=batch_size)

loss, acc = model.evaluate(x_test, y_test,
batch_size=batch_size)

print("\nTest accuracy: %.1f%%" % (100.0 * acc))
```

If you analyze the code you will see that there are two differences between the three neural network implementations. The most obvious one is the fact that our input shape is in fact a sequence of dimension vectors with a timestamp length. The second one is the fact that we used a simple recurrent neural network that represents a network cell with a value of 256 output units.

Our previous model was represented by the convolution of the kernel over a feature map, however, in the case of our recurrent neural network, the output is a function of the input, as well as the output from the hidden state. The former output is the previous input's function, therefore the current output is also the previous output's function. In addition, you should know that the simple recurrent neural network layer we implemented is a more simplistic version of a real recurrent neural network and it is a feature offered by Keras. Here's how you can determine the output of this layer:

$$h_t = \tanh(b + Wh_{t-1} + Ux_t)$$

In this mathematical equation we have a bias (b), and the weights of the previous output and those of the current input (W and U). The position inside the sequences is determined by "t", and if we have 256 units like in our model, then we can calculate the number of parameters like so : $256 + 256 \times 256 + 256 \times 28 = 72,960$.

If you still find it somewhat difficult to understand recurrent neural networks, that's perfectly alright because they are more difficult to grasp than multilayer perceptrons and convolutional neural networks. When it comes to the multilayer perceptron all you have to do is understand the perceptron itself because after that you are just dealing with a collection of perceptrons. In the case of convolutional neural networks you can simply look at the kernel as a box that moves through the feature map in order to analyze it and create a new map. On the other hand, with recurrent neural networks you have to understand something referred to as a self loop. You need to understand that all we have is actually one cell. The collection of cells is in fact an illusion created by the fact that the cell appears based on the timestep. In reality there is only one cell that is used again and again. All the neural networks under the recurrent neural networks will be distributed across the cells. With that in mind, the reason why we implemented Keras' simple recurrent neural network is in order to have fewer parameters to deal with, however, you will notice that by using this model on its own we would have the lowest accuracy when compared to the other two implementations.

Summary

In this chapter you were provided with a brief re-introduction to working with the three main neural networks, but this time through the Keras library. In addition, you hopefully gained some insight into how to use the library's sequential API, however, for advanced deep learning you will be using the Functional API instead, which we will discuss in the next chapter.

The purpose of this chapter was to help you explore the three neural networks together with a number of advanced techniques such as optimization, regularization, and the loss function. In order to gain a better understanding of these concepts, you worked once again with the popular MNIST dataset. You have used each different model in order to perform the digit classification and see the exact difference between the three when it comes to performance.

Now that you have everything you need to understand deep learning networks, we can continue with the advanced deep learning models and concepts

Chapter 2

Deep Neural Networks

----------◆----------

In this chapter, we are going to focus on deep neural networks due to their high-performing capabilities and classification accuracy. This type of network is best used on datasets that are considered advanced, such as ImageNet and CIFAR100. You will learn about two of the most powerful deep neural networks, namely the residual network and the densely connected convolutional network, also known as ResNet and DenseNet. Before we dive straight into the core of the problem, let's briefly examine these neural networks.

The residual network came to be by looking to solve the problem of the vanishing gradient that appears in deep convolutional networks. This type of network is what introduced the idea of residual learning in order to create deep networks. The dense network, on the other hand, simply sought to polish the residual network concept by enabling the convolutions to access the inputs certain feature maps found in the lower layer. Furthermore, it created the possibility of having a low number of parameters with the help of two new layers referred to as the bottleneck and the transition layers.

These two deep neural networks were only the beginning. Since then, newer, improved versions came to be, such as the fractal network. The reason why you are going to focus on ResNet and DenseNet is because once you understand them you will also be able to understand all the networks that were modeled after them. After all, they are the ones that inspired everything else that came after them. In addition, you will also be able to create your own custom models by using them as the starting point. Furthermore, you will learn about the concept of transfer learning and therefore understand how to apply a pre trained residual or dense network to your project. All of these advantages, plus the fact that the two deep neural networks are compatible with Keras, will allow you to leave the basics behind and enter the world of advanced deep learning.

Keep in mind that while the purpose of this section is to teach you about deep neural networks, you will first focus on the Functional API from Keras. The reason why you need to know about this API is because it is in fact an alternative method for creating neural networks that are a great deal more complex than what you have built so far. The Functional API will become a powerful tool that you will use to implement a deep residual network, as well as the densely connected convolutional network.

The Functional API

In the first chapter you worked using a sequential model where a layer is placed on top of another layer where you access it with the input and output layers. In this section you also concluded that it can be quite a challenge to add an additional input inside the center of the network. Furthermore, you weren't able to work with graph-based models and you couldn't share the layers between a number of different models.

There are quite a few disadvantages of working with the model you learned to use in the previous section, and that is why you need to learn how to adapt the Functional API into your workflow if you want to create deep learning models.

Before we get started, you need to understand that there are two general ideas behind the Functional API:

1. First, the layer takes a tensor as the argument and the output is a different tensor. When you create a model, the instances of each layer become objects that are interconnected via the tensors. This process is nearly the equivalent of stacking several layers when working with the sequential model. However, in this case you will not have a problem implementing additional layers or inputs and outputs because the inputs and outputs of every single layer are always ready to be accessed.

2. Keep in mind that the model is in fact a function between a number of tensors and between the input and the output there are layer instances that are connected through the input and

output tensor. Therefore, you can say that the model is a function of at least one input layer and output layer and the model instance will define the graph of the flow of data between the input and output.

Once you create the model, everything else is similar to the sequential model. The evaluation and the training processes remain the same. For instance, if you have a conv2d convolutional layer with 32 filters and one layer input tensor, as well as one layer output tensor, you can write the formula like so:

$y = Conv2D(32)(x)$

Keep in mind that you can also have a multitude of layers on top of eachother when constructing the model. This allows you to write the convolutional neural network you used earlier for the MNIST dataset and convert it with the Functional API like so:

```
import numpy as np

from keras.layers import Dense, Dropout, Input

from keras.layers import Conv2D, MaxPooling2D, Flatten

from keras.models import Model

from keras.datasets import mnist

from keras.utils import to_categorical
```

```python
# process the labels

    num_labels = len(np.unique(y_train))

# perform the one-hot vector conversion

    y_train    =    to_categorical(y_train)    y_test    =
to_categorical(y_test)

# modify the input images

    image_size = x_train.shape[1]

    x_train = np.reshape(x_train,[-1, image_size, image_size, 1])

    x_test = np.reshape(x_test,[-1, image_size, image_size, 1])

    x_train = x_train.astype('float32') / 255

    x_test = x_test.astype('float32') / 255

# process the image in square greyscale

    input_shape = (image_size, image_size, 1)

    batch_size = 128

    kernel_size = 3

    filters = 64

    dropout = 0.3
```

```
# create the convolutional neural network layers by using the
Function API

        inputs = Input(shape=input_shape)

        y = Conv2D(filters=filters,

        kernel_size=kernel_size,

        activation='relu')(inputs)

        y = MaxPooling2D()(y)

        y = Conv2D(filters=filters,

        kernel_size=kernel_size,

        activation='relu')(y)

        y = MaxPooling2D()(y)

        y = Conv2D(filters=filters,

        kernel_size=kernel_size,

        activation='relu')(y)

# before you connect the dense layer you need to transform the image
to a vector

        y = Flatten()(y)

# work in the dropout and the regularization
```

```
        y = Dropout(dropout)(y)

        outputs = Dense(num_labels, activation='softmax')(y)

# creating the model

        model = Model(inputs=inputs, outputs=outputs)

        model.summary()

# use the Adam optimizer and the accuracy metric for the classifier

        model.compile(loss='categorical_crossentropy',

         optimizer='adam',

        metrics=['accuracy'])

# model training

        model.fit(x_train,

        y_train,

        validation_data=(x_test, y_test),

        epochs=20,

        batch_size=batch_size)

# use the test set to obtain the model accuracy
```

```
score = model.evaluate(x_test, y_test,
batch_size=batch_size) print("\nTest accuracy: %.1f%%" %
(100.0 * score[1]))
```

If you analyse the code you will notice that every single layer will generate a tensor for the output. This output tensor becomes the input for the layer that follows. In order to build this model all you need to do is use the Model function and then specify the tensors. All the other processes are similar or identical. Take note that you can also use the evaluate and fit functions as well, just like you did when working on the sequential model in the previous chapter.

The 2-Input / 1-Output Model

In this section you are going to build your first advanced deep learning model, which will have two inputs and an output. However, before we begin exploring this mode, you should know that there is one aspect of it that isn't as clear cut as what you worked with when setting up the sequential model. Let's say that you create a model for the MNIST dataset, called N-Network. This network will be able to use one input twice, on each side of the convolutional neural network. The results that we obtain with it will be concatenated in a special concatenate layer. This process is similar to stacking two tensors in order to create a single tensor. Keep in mind that in this case the tensors need to have the same shape in order to be combined. Now let's say that we have two (3, 3, 16) tensors. They will combine in the shape of a (3, 3, 32) tensor. After this concatenation phase, everything will be the same as with the convolutional network model.

This new model we have, however, needs to be improved with a few modifications. First of all, we have double the number of filters due to the N-Network's branches because we need to compensate for the fact that our feature maps are half the size. This is caused by the pooling function. If we have an output of (28, 28, 32), with max pooling it becomes half the size. However, the next convolution will change the size of the filter to 64, thus turning the output's new shape to (14, 14, 64). Secondly, we have the dilation rate with a value of 2 for the right branch. Keep in mind that this happens even though the branches have a kernel with the size value of 3. However, if the value of the kernel coverage goes up, then the convolutional neural network will force the right branch to learn a different feature map. In our example we also use the "padding = same" declaration in order to guarantee that there will be no tensors with a negative size. As you already know from the previous chapter, this works by padding the input with zeroes and therefore force the output to have an identical dimension.

The two branches in the model are built by using two for loops and both of them require an input with the same shape. The loops are used to form two stacks of Conv2D, each one containing three layers. One thing we could do here is use certain merge functions on top of the concatenation process that is used to merge the outputs of both branches together. These merge functions are part of Keras and they include multiply, add and dot functions, among others. In our N-Network the concatenate layer will not eliminate any of the features maps. However, the Dense layer is the one that decides how to handle the feature maps that were already concatenated. Let's finally take a look at the N-Network model's code and the Functional API:

```
import numpy as np

from keras.layers import Dense, Dropout, Input

from keras.layers import Conv2D, MaxPooling2D, Flatten

from keras.models import Model

from keras.layers.merge import concatenate

from keras.datasets import mnist

from keras.utils import to_categorical

from keras.utils import plot_model
```

using the MNIST dataset once again

```
(x_train, y_train), (x_test, y_test) = mnist.load_data()
```

processing labels

```
num_labels = len(np.unique(y_train))
```

performing one-hot vector conversion

```python
    y_train = to_categorical(y_train)

    y_test = to_categorical(y_test)
# change the shape of the images
    image_size = x_train.shape[1]

    x_train = np.reshape(x_train,[-1, image_size, image_size, 1])

    x_test = np.reshape(x_test,[-1, image_size, image_size, 1])

    x_train = x_train.astype('float32') / 255

    x_test = x_test.astype('float32') / 255

    input_shape = (image_size, image_size, 1)

    batch_size = 32

    kernel_size = 3

    dropout = 0.4

    n_filters = 32
# here's the left branch of the model
    left_inputs = Input(shape=input_shape)

    x = left_inputs filters = n_filters

    for i in range(3):
```

```python
        x = Conv2D(filters=filters,

        kernel_size=kernel_size,

        padding='same',

        activation='relu')(x)    x = Dropout(dropout)(x)

        x = MaxPooling2D()(x)

        filters *= 2

# this is the right branch of our model

        right_inputs = Input(shape=input_shape)

        y = right_inputs filters = n_filters

        for i in range(3):

        y = Conv2D(filters=filters,

        kernel_size=kernel_size,

         padding='same', activation='relu', dilation_rate=2)(y)

        y = Dropout(dropout)(y)

        y = MaxPooling2D()(y)

        filters *= 2

# here we need to combine the outputs of the two branches
```

```python
        y = concatenate([x, y])

        y = Flatten()(y)

        y = Dropout(dropout)(y)

        outputs = Dense(num_labels, activation='softmax')(y)
# using the Functional API we create the model

        model = Model([left_inputs, right_inputs], outputs)
# validate the model with the help of graph

        plot_model(model, to_file='cnn-y-network.png',
        show_shapes=True)

        model.summary()

        model.compile(loss='categorical_crossentropy',

        optimizer='adam',

        metrics=['accuracy'])
# training the model with the labels and the input images

        model.fit([x_train, x_train],

        y_train,

        validation_data=([x_test, x_test], y_test),
```

```
epochs=20,

batch_size=batch_size)
```

the accuracy score

```
score = model.evaluate([x_test, x_test], y_test,
batch_size=batch_ size)

print("\nTest accuracy: %.1f%%" % (100.0 * score[1]))
```

Now that we have the model in front of us we can see the the N-Network requires two inputs in order to perform the training and validation process. Keep in mind that these inputs are the same. The accuracy, however, did improve by working with a 3 layer stack convolutional network because we achieved up to 99.4% accuracy. The downside is that in order to gain these results we had to have twice the amount of parameters and a higher architectural complexity.

Now that you understand how to work with various features offered by the Functional API, we can continue with the advanced deep neural networks. You can now start working with the ResNet and DenseNet, however, you might want to study Keras' Functional API in more detail at some point in the near future. For the purpose of this chapter we will not dig deeper into the API, but only focus on the components we truly need to build our models.

The Deep Residual Network

The main advantage of working with deep networks is that they can learn and adapt from inputs as well as feature maps. This means that whether you are working on classification and detection problems, among others, you will obtain a better performance and better results by being able to adapt to various learning levels.

Unfortunately, there is one major problem you will encounter during the training process of these networks. The gradient vanishes during the backpropagation. During backpropagation the gradients diminish gradually from layer to layer until they reach the shallow layers. That's where they run the risk of vanishing, also referred to as exploding. This issue occurs because of the small values that are multiplied, namely the error values. Take note that there are as many multiplication processes taking place as the network is deep. Furthermore, when the gradient degrades, the parameters will start having trouble updating themselves. In order to reduce the gradient degradation issue, we are provided with the deep residual learning framework. This is done by allowing the information to pass through a shortcut connection.

In the previous chapter we mentioned the stride and the fact that when its value is greater than one it means that it will skip a number of pixels during the convolution process. For instance if the value is equal to two, we will jump over every second pixel. When developing a ResNet you need to have a full understanding of all of its components in order to perform image classification. You need to know how to train the deep layers in such a way to return as few errors as possible, in order to prevent the shallow layers from returning an even higher count of errors. In order to discuss the foundation of a ResNet and the more complex elements that are part of its foundation, we are going to work with a more complex dataset, namely the CIFAR10. This dataset is a compilation of pictures that contain 60,000 color images, 32 x 32 pixels in size. They are distributed in ten classes, such as cars, birds, horses, and so on, with 6,000 images per class. Keras provides us with an easy way to access the CIFAR10 dataset with the following line:

from keras.datasets import cifar10

(x_train, y_train), (x_test, y_test) = cifar10.load_data()

The fact that this dataset holds ten classes, or categories, makes it similar to the MNIST dataset you are so familiar with. The 60,000 images it contains are distributed in a collection of 50,000 used for the training set and 10,000 for the test set. You can build a ResNet with this data by using a number of slightly different neural network structures. For instance, you can have a network where the values of "n" and those of the ResNet implementation are validated by using a shortcut connection as we discussed earlier. Take note that there will also be three groups of residual blocks where each one of them has "2n" layers that match with the residual blocks. The kernel will have a size value of three, minus the part where the transition occurs during two feature maps that differ in dimension. For instance, we will have a Conv2D with a size of one and the strides value equal to two. In order to maintain consistency we are going to implement a transition layer in order to combine the different residual blocks. When backpropagation occurs, the ResNet will rely on setting the kernel initializer to "he_normal" to help with the convergence process. Finally, the last layer will be an AveragePooling2D-Flatten-Dense setup.

Keep in mind that the ResNet architecture will not require a dropout. Furthermore, the convolution and the merging process have the ability to regulate themselves. Let's take a look at a simple example on how to implement this type of network with Keras. This will only be a partial implementation. Take note that by modifying the value of "n" we can control the network's depth. For instance, if we set the variable to be equal to 18, we will obtain a network 110 layers deep. In our example we are going to use a value of 3 in order to construct a 20 layer ResNet. Here's how the code looks:

```
n = 3

version = 1

if version == 1:

depth = n * 6 + 2

elif version == 2:
```

```python
depth = n * 9 + 2

if version == 2:

model = resnet_v2(input_shape=input_shape, depth=depth)

else:

model = resnet_v1(input_shape=input_shape, depth=depth)
```

The ResNet is built by declaring the n value and you will notice that there's a resnet_v1 method used, which is in fact a builder for the network. This is version one of the ResNet. In the next example we are going to improve it by adding a residual block in order to obtain a better performance. Let's continue with the code and then discuss:

```python
def resnet_v1(input_shape, depth, num_classes=10):

 if (depth - 2) % 6 != 0:

raise ValueError('depth should be 6n+2 (eg 20, 32,   44 in [a])')

# This is the definition of the model

num_filters = 16

num_res_blocks = int((depth - 2) / 6)

inputs = Input(shape=input_shape)

x = resnet_layer(inputs=inputs)
```

```python
# Next we need to instantiate the stack of residual units

    for stack in range(3):

    for res_block in range(num_res_blocks):

    strides = 1

    if stack > 0 and res_block == 0:

    strides = 2

# Downsampling process

    y   =   resnet_layer(inputs=x,   num_filters=num_filters,
    strides=strides)

    y   =   resnet_layer(inputs=y,   num_filters=num_filters,
    activation=None)

    if stack > 0 and res_block == 0

# linear projection residual shortcut connection

    x = resnet_layer(inputs=x,

    num_filters=num_filters,

    kernel_size=1,

    strides=strides,

    activation=None,
```

```
batch_normalization=False)

x = add([x, y])

x = Activation('relu')(x)

num_filters *= 2
```

Adding a classifier

Once we have a shortcut connection implemented,

version 1 will not use a BN at the end

```
x = AveragePooling2D(pool_size=8)(x)      y = Flatten()(x)

outputs = Dense(num_classes,

activation='softmax', kernel_initializer='he_normal')(y)
```

Model instantiation

```
model = Model(inputs=inputs, outputs=outputs)

return model
```

This version of ResNet is slightly different from the one that was originally created. The first thing you'll notice is that we are using Adam for the convergence, while with the old model we'd be using a stochastic gradient descent. The reason behind this change is simply the fact that it's easier to go with Adam. Furthermore, we have a learning rate scheduler in order to set the epochs at different values, down from the 1e-3 which is the default setting. This function will be initiated during the training process after each epoch. The learning rate scheduler is a component of the "callbacks" variable.

A second callback is used in order to save a checkpoint when we advance with the validation accuracy. This process is considered standard practice and you should always save your model whenever you make some kind of progress. Training deep neural networks, especially advanced ones, takes a lot more time than working with the basic techniques you learned in the previous books. So, make sure to always save your progress to avoid losing a massive amount of time and effort. Once the checkpoint is saved you can always reload it and restore your progress. You can do this with Keras' handy load model function.

Another important function is the learning rate reducer. During the schedule reduction, the measure can reach a certain limit, which isn't a good thing. That's what this function is for. It allows you to lower the learning rate if the validation loss is still too great after the five epochs. The callback is provided with the model.fit method. Furthermore, Keras relies on the image data generator function, which means using data augmentation, in order to obtain training data for the regularization processes. When we have more training data, the generalization will receive a boost. This data augmentation refers to something as simple as flipping a picture with a simple "horizontal_flip = True" declaration. The image of a car, for instance, will still represent a car, no matter how you flip it. In addition, you can also rotate or scale the image and nothing will change regarding the label of the data item.

Now, let's see the version 2 of ResNet with its differences. The model we just discussed is known as version 1 because new methods of improving it were discovered since it was first written. These improvements mainly consist in how the layers are arranged inside the residual block. The structure is changed and can be written with the following formula: 1 x 1 - 3 x 3 - 1 x 1 BN-ReLU-Conv2D. Furthermore the 2D convolution in this variant is after the batch normalization and the activation of ReLU. Analyze the code to understand this model:

```
def resnet_v2(input_shape, depth, num_classes=10):

if (depth - 2) % 9 != 0:

raise ValueError('depth should be 9n+2 (eg 56 or 110 in [b])')

# The definition of the model

num_filters_in = 16   num_res_blocks = int((depth - 2) / 9)

inputs = Input(shape=input_shape)

# The Conv2D is performed with the BN-ReLU during the input

# before it is divided into two branches
```

```python
        x = resnet_layer (inputs=inputs, num_filters=num_filters_in,
        conv_first=True)
# The block of residual units is instantiated
        for res_block in range(num_res_blocks):
        activation = 'relu'
        batch_normalization = True
        strides = 1
        if stage == 0:
        num_filters_out = num_filters_in * 4
        if res_block == 0:
# This is the first layer and the first phase
        activation = None
        batch_normalization = False
        else:
        num_filters_out = num_filters_in * 2
        if res_block == 0:
# this is the first layer but without the first stage
```

```
        strides = 2

# use downsampling and bottleneck the residual unit

        y = resnet_layer(inputs=x,

        num_filters=num_filters_in,

        kernel_size=1,

        strides=strides,

        activation=activation,

        batch_normalization=batch_normalization,

        conv_first=False)

        y = resnet_layer(inputs=y,

        num_filters=num_filters_in,

        conv_first=False)

        y = resnet_layer(inputs=y,

        num_filters=num_filters_out,

        kernel_size=1,

        conv_first=False)

        if res_block == 0:
```

\# This is the linear projection for the shortcut link

\# in order to pair with the changed dims

```
        x = resnet_layer(inputs=x,

        num_filters=num_filters_out,

        kernel_size=1,

        strides=strides,

        activation=None,

        batch_normalization=False)

        x = add([x, y])

        num_filters_in = num_filters_out
```

\# The classifier needs to be at the top

\# In version 2 of the implementation the BN-ReLu comes before the pooling

```
        x = BatchNormalization()(x)

        x = Activation('relu')(x)

        x = AveragePooling2D(pool_size=8)(x)

        y = Flatten()(x)
```

```
outputs = Dense(num_classes,

activation='softmax',

kernel_initializer='he_normal')(y)
```

Model instantiation

```
model = Model(inputs=inputs, outputs=outputs)

return model
```

On top of the performance, you will also notice a slight accuracy increase of around 1%, depending on how many layers your architecture will contain.

Now that you know about ResNet and how to implement it, let's discuss the DenseNet.

The Densely Connected Convolutional Network

Also known as DenseNet, this model focuses on the issue of the vanishing gradient from another point of view. Unlike with ResNet, there will be no shortcut connections in order to solve this problem. Instead, all the old feature maps will be transformed into the input in the following layer.

The kernel size of Conv2D will be with a value of 3 and we will have "k" as the number of feature maps which can be generated for each layer. This is known as the growth rate, and normally it is set to a value of 12, sometimes 24. Therefore if the feature maps x_o are k_o, then after passing through a four layer dense structure, we will have $4 \times k + k_0$. In addition, it is recommended for the dense section to come before the BN-ReLU-Conv2D block, together with the total number of features maps multiplied by the growth rate. This will lead to a total number of 72 feature maps. We will also have to implement an average pooling, as well as apply a dropout layer if we aren't using any kind of data augmentation.

Keep in mind that the deeper the network, the more problems we will encounter. For instance, we know that all the layers contribute with a k number of feature maps, which means that the layer will have the following number of inputs: $(1 - 1) \times k + k_0$. This means that the number of feature maps can expand greatly in the deep layers. The problem with this process is that it would greatly slow down our computing power. The second issue is almost the same as the one we encounter with a ResNet. The size of the feature maps decreases in order to expand the area which the kernel will cover. Therefore if our DenseNet will use concatenation during the merging process, then it will have to handle these dimension differences.

One of the solutions you will implement due to the inefficiency of the computation process is a Bottleneck layer. It works by applying a 4k sized filter with every 1 x 1 convolution at the end of each concatenation. This is in fact a dimensionality reduction method which will prevent the size of the feature maps from increasing during the Conv2D's processing. The Bottleneck's purpose is to also change the network's BN-ReLU-Conv2D(3) structure into a BN-ReLU-Conv2D(1)-BNReLU-Conv2D(3).

The other issue of the feature maps size difference can be solved by segmenting the network into a number of dense blocks that are connected together through transition layers. Inside every block, the height and the width of the feature map will stay constant. The transition layer's purpose is to move from the size of a feature map to a smaller one in between two blocks. This size reduction is normally a split in half which is performed through the average pooling layer. For instance, if we give the average pooling layer a default pool size value of 2, we will cut the size of a 64 by 64 by 256 feature map to 32 by 32 by 256. Take note that the transition layer's input will be the output of the concatenation layer from the previous block. In addition, the number of the feature maps will be reduced by a compression factor of $0 < \theta < 1$. In DenseNet θ is used with a value of 0.5. Therefore if we have the last concatenation's output with a value of 64 by 64 by 512, then the new size will become 64 x 64 x 256. This way by applying dimensionality reduction together with a compression factory we obtain a transition layer that is constructed with a set of BN-Conv2D(1)-AveragePooling2D layers.

Now let's create a DenseNet with Bottleneck and Compression. It will have a 100 layer structure and we will be using the CIFAR10 dataset once again. Keep in mind that in this example we are going to follow the exact same techniques we used when discussing the ResNet.

Defining the mod

The densenet convolutional neural networks are created with BN-ReLU-Conv2D

```
inputs = Input(shape=input_shape)

x = BatchNormalization()(inputs)

x = Activation('relu')(x)

x = Conv2D(num_filters_bef_dense_block,

kernel_size=3,

padding='same',

kernel_initializer='he_normal')(x)

x = concatenate([inputs, x])
```

Using transition layers to connect a collection of dense blocks

```
    for i in range(num_dense_blocks):
```

the dense block is defined as a set of bottleneck layers

```
        for j in range(num_bottleneck_layers):

y = BatchNormalization()(x)
```

```python
        y = Activation('relu')(y)

        y = Conv2D(4 * growth_rate,

                   kernel_size=1,

                   padding='same',

                   kernel_initializer='he_normal')(y)

        if not data_augmentation:

            y = Dropout(0.2)(y)

        y = BatchNormalization()(y)

        y = Activation('relu')(y)

        y = Conv2D(growth_rate,

                   kernel_size=3,

                   padding='same',

                   kernel_initializer='he_normal')(y)

        if not data_augmentation:

            y = Dropout(0.2)(y)

        x = concatenate([x, y])

    # no transition layer after the last dense block
```

```
        if i == num_dense_blocks - 1:

        continue

# Compress the feature maps with the transition layer

        num_filters_bef_dense_block += num_bottleneck_layers *
        growth_rate

        num_filters_bef_dense_block                              =
        int(num_filters_bef_dense_block*

        compression_factor)

        y = BatchNormalization()(x)

        y = Conv2D(num_filters_bef_dense_block,

        kernel_size=1,

        padding='same',

        kernel_initializer='he_normal')(y)

        if not data_augmentation:

        y = Dropout(0.2)(y)   x = AveragePooling2D()(y)

# The classifier needs to be at the top

# The size of a feature map will be 1 x 1 once average pooling is
performed
```

```
x = AveragePooling2D(pool_size=8)(x)

y = Flatten()(x) outputs = Dense(num_classes,

kernel_initializer='he_normal', activation='softmax')(y)
```

Model instantiation

Using an RMSprop optimizer because it works better with the DenseNet

However, you can also use a stochastic gradient descent instead

```
model = Model(inputs=inputs, outputs=outputs)

model.compile(loss='categorical_crossentropy',

optimizer=RMSprop(1e-3),

metrics=['accuracy'])

model.summary()
```

By training this model we can achieve approximately 93.7% accuracy. We used data augmentation and the same callbacks as we did with version 1 of the DenseNet. Keep in mind that the training of this model does take a great deal of time, however. One epoch can take over an hour if you have at least a GTX 1060 GPU and you have to train over 200 epochs.

Summary

In this chapter you learned about the Functional API and how it is used to create advanced deep neural networks together with Keras. In addition, you used this tool in practice by building your very own double input / single output network and also used it to create even more complex models. Keep in mind that the Functional API is a powerful component which you will use later in order to create and implement various decoders or autoencoders.

Furthermore, you explored two advanced neural networks, namely the ResNet and DenseNet, which are invaluable for solving classification problems. Take note that while we mostly used them for the purpose of classification, they can also be used for detection, generation, tracking, and much more. The purpose of this chapter was to help you understand how these two networks are designed and implemented.

Chapter 3

Autoencoders

---◆---

In this chapter we are going to focus on autoencoders, which represent neural network structures that seek to discover a compressed version of the input data they receive. This data can be anything from text to speech and video. The purpose of the autoencoders is to change the data in such a way that it becomes more useful and easy to work with. An example of an autoencoder that achieves this is the denoising autoencoder. This tool allows the neural network to clean up the noisy data and convert it to something it can use and process. In this case, noisy data refers to the static noise from an audio file, which can be cleaned with an autoencoder and turned into sound we can understand. Take note that the autoencoders can learn the code which it will use to convert the noisy data completely by itself without you labeling anything. This means that you can place this type of network in the category of unsupervised learning algorithms.

An autoencoder, when it's used in the most basic way, learns the code by attempting to copy the input to the output, however, the process is not as straightforward as simply copying. The neural network cannot discover the hidden structure inside the input distribution, therefore it will encode the distribution to a vector, which is in fact a low dimensional tensor. The hidden structure is then determine with approximation. The operation that represents the encoding is actually an approximation of the vector, also known as the latent representation. This latent vector is then decoded in order to access the former state of the input. Because the latent representation is a low dimensional compressed version of the input distribution, it means that the output which the decoder can recover will only approximate the input. There's a difference between the input and the output and we can detect it and measure it through the loss function.

Now the question is, why bother to use autoencoders at all? They are simply useful, whether you use them on their own in their basic form or as a component of an advanced deep neural network. They are used to understand certain concepts behind deep learning because of the latent vector component. In addition, you can use it to perform other operations on the input data, such as denoising, detection, segmentation, colorization, and so on.

In this chapter you will learn the concepts behind the autoencoders in order to understand how they work. Then you will use the Keras library in order to implement them in a practical model. Finally, you will explore the most important characteristics of denoising, as well as colorization autoencoders.

Creating Autoencoders

In this section you will learn about the concept behind autoencoders and how to implement them with the MNIST dataset. However, before we get started, you need to understand the two components, or operators, that make an autoencoder:

1. Encoder: This is what turns the input into a low dimensional vector. If the input is "x", the formula for this process can be written like so: $z = f(x)$. Take note that the low dimension part is important. This is what forms the condition that forces the encoder to focus only on the most important features of the input. For instance, when working with the MNIST dataset, these features would be the writing style, thickness of the strokes, etc. Basically, the most important information is learned while the rest is ignored.

2. Decoder: This component's purpose is to extract the original input from the vector. Keep in mind that even if it's low in dimension, the latent representation still provides the decoder with just enough information to obtain the data. The decoder seeks to essentially reconstruct x as close as possible to the original x.

Take note that the encoder and decoder are nonlinear functions and the "z" dimension can be seen as a metric for the number of features that it represents. Furthermore, the dimension is smaller than the input dimension. In order to limit the latent vector to force it to learn the most important features of the input distribution, we need high efficiency and that is why we have a reduced dimension.

Now, let's start with the practical side of things. We are going to create an autoencoder using Keras. As mentioned earlier, we are going to use the MNIST dataset once again. We will use the autoencoder to use the input data in order to produce the latent vector. Then the decoder is used to recover the input data. In our scenario, the latent vector will have a 16-dim size.

First, we will create the encoder, which will be a block of two Conv2D, then we will generate the latent vector using a Dense layer. The output's structure of the final Conv2D will be reserved in order to process the size of the decoder input layer. This way we can recreate a MNIST image a lot easier. Now, let's take a look at the code for the autoencoder implementation:

```
from keras.layers import Dense, Input

from keras.layers import Conv2D, Flatten

from keras.layers import Reshape, Conv2DTranspose

from keras.models import Model

from keras.datasets import mnist

from keras.utils import plot_model

from keras import backend as K
```

```python
import numpy as np

import matplotlib.pyplot as plt
```

Loading the dataset

```python
(x_train, _), (x_test, _) = mnist.load_data()

# Resize the input images to 28, 28, 1

image_size = x_train.shape[1]

x_train = np.reshape(x_train, [-1, image_size, image_size, 1])

x_test = np.reshape(x_test, [-1, image_size, image_size, 1])

x_train = x_train.astype('float32') / 255

x_test = x_test.astype('float32') / 255

input_shape = (image_size, image_size, 1)

batch_size = 32 kernel_size = 3

latent_dim = 16
```

Establish the number of filters for each convolutional neural network layer

```python
layer_filters = [32, 64]
```

Building the autoencoder model by first starting with the encoder model

```
inputs = Input(shape=input_shape, name='encoder_input')

x = inputs
```

stack of Conv2D(32)-Conv2D(64)

```
    for filters in layer_filters:

    x = Conv2D(filters=filters,
```

kernel_size=kernel_size, activation='relu', strides=2, padding='same')(x)

We don't want manual processing,

so we shape the information needed to construct the decoder model

the input to the decoder's first Conv2DTranspose will have the following shape

shape is (7, 7, 64) which is processed by the decoder back to (28, 28, 1)

```
    shape = K.int_shape(x)
```

latent vector generation

```
    x = Flatten()(x) latent = Dense(latent_dim,
    name='latent_vector')(x)
```

```python
# encoder model instantiation
    encoder = Model(inputs, latent, name='encoder')

    encoder.summary()

    plot_model(encoder,                    to_file='encoder.png',
    show_shapes=True)
# build the decoder model
    latent_inputs = Input(shape=(latent_dim,),
    name='decoder_input')
# use  (7, 7, 64) which we saved
    x = Dense(shape[1] * shape[2] * shape[3])(latent_inputs)
# convert from a vector to a shape that is acceptable for transposed
    conv x = Reshape((shape[1], shape[2], shape[3]))(x)
# stack of Conv2DTranspose(64)-Conv2DTranspose(32)
    for filters in layer_filters[::-1]:

    x = Conv2DTranspose(filters=filters,

    kernel_size=kernel_size, activation='relu',  strides=2,
    padding='same')(x)
# input reconstruction
```

```python
        outputs = Conv2DTranspose(filters=1,

        kernel_size=kernel_size,activation='sigmoid',

        padding='same',name='decoder_output')(x)
# decode model instantiation

        decoder = Model(latent_inputs, outputs, name='decoder')

        decoder.summary()

        plot_model(decoder,                    to_file='decoder.png',
        show_shapes=True)

# autoencoder = encoder + decoder

# autoencoder model instantiation

        autoencoder = Model(inputs,

        decoder(encoder(inputs)),

        name='autoencoder')

        autoencoder.summary()

        plot_model(autoencoder, to_file='autoencoder.png',
        show_shapes=True)

# Mean Square Error (MSE) loss function, Adam optimizer

        autoencoder.compile(loss='mse', optimizer='adam')
```

autoencoder training process

```
autoencoder.fit(x_train,

x_train, validation_data=(x_test, x_test), epochs=1,
batch_size=batch_size)
```

using test data to predict the autoencoder output

```
x_decoded = autoencoder.predict(x_test)
```

displaying the first 8 test input and decoded images

```
imgs = np.concatenate([x_test[:8], x_decoded[:8]])

imgs = imgs.reshape((4, 4, image_size, image_size))

imgs = np.vstack([np.hstack(i)

for i in imgs]) plt.figure() plt.axis('off')

plt.title('Input: 1st 2 rows, Decoded: last 2 rows')
plt.imshow(imgs, interpolation='none',

cmap='gray') plt.savefig('input_and_decoded.png')
plt.show()
```

As you can see, the latent vector is decompressed in order to find the MNIST digit. Take note that the decoder input phase is in fact a dense layer that only accepts a latent vector. Furthermore, the total number of units has to be equal to the result of the Conv2D output dimensions that are obtained from the encoder and saved. The output of the layer can then be resized in order to recover the initial MNIST digit dimensions.

The structure of the decoder holds three Conv2DTranspose layers that are stacked on top of each other. In this example we are using a transposed convolutional neural network, also known as deconvolution, which is in fact the opposite of a convolutional network. This means that if the convolutional network turns an image to a number of feature maps, the transposed network will create an image using feature maps.

The autoencoder is then constructed by attaching the encoder model to the decoder. The encoder's output becomes the decoder's input and therefore generates the autoencoder's output. In our example we are also applying a loss function and an Adam optimizer. In addition, during the training phase the input is equal to the output. Another aspect to take into account is that the validation loss is driven down to 0.01 with a single epoch and only a small number of layers are capable of doing that. Fortunately this dataset is a simple one. Otherwise, we would need a deeper encoder, as well as decoder, in addition to a larger number of training epochs.

Once the training is complete, we can check whether we can encode and decode the dataset's unknown information. You will notice that our model is capable of decoding the images, with only some slight blurring effect to them. The images can easily be recognized, therefore we can verify that the input can be recovered without too much quality loss. Keep in mind that our results can be significantly improved by training for more epochs.

Denoising Autoencoders

In this section we are going to create an autoencoder with a real world purpose and application. We are going to take into account the possibility of dealing with data that is corrupted by noise. For instance, our MNIST images could easily be affected by this issue. When it comes to images especially, noise makes it difficult to read the data, both for humans as well as machines. Therefore we are going to create a denoising autoencoder in order to eliminate this noise.

A denoising autoencoder has the same architecture as the basic autoencoder we constructed in the previous example. Keep in mind that the purpose of the encoder is to create a latent representation which will allow the decoder to recover "x" by reducing the loss function. In order to create a denoising autoencoder, however, it is required that we make some modifications to the autoencoder we used earlier. One of the largest differences will be in the training process because the input data contains corrupted information. The output data, however, will be represented by the original images which are free of any noise. We are going to use this information to teach the autoencoder how the images should look like after correction is applied and to instruct it to learn on its own how to eliminate the noise corruption from a specific image. Finally, the autoencoder has to be validated based on the test data set.

We are going to use the MNIST digits dataset once again in order to create a simulation of corrupted data. We will do this with some random noise, which will be of a Gaussian distribution with a mean of 0.5 ($\mu = 0.5$) and a standard deviation with a value of 0.5 as well ($\sigma = 0.5$). Keep in mind that with the random noise addition we might encounter invalid values when it comes to pixel information. These are values that go lower than zero or higher than one. That is why we are also going to limit these values to a range between 0.1 and 1. Most of the operations and processes will be similar to those used with the regular autoencoder. Take note that for the noise autoencoder it is advisable to use an Adam optimizer, as well as a Mean Square Error as the regression loss function. Furthermore, we are going to perform the training process over ten epochs in order to make sure the autoencoder will be well-optimized and accurate.

With that being said, you should be able to create your own denoising autoencoder with the knowledge of how to build a regular encoder. You should try on your own, however, if you don't manage, take a look at the following code:

```
from keras.layers import Dense, Input

from keras.layers import Conv2D, Flatten

from keras.layers import Reshape, Conv2DTranspose
```

```python
from keras.models import Model

from keras import backend as K

from keras.datasets import mnist

import numpy as np

import matplotlib.pyplot as plt

from PIL import Image

np.random.seed(1337)

# Loading the dataset

(x_train, _), (x_test, _) = mnist.load_data()

# Changing the dimension of the images to 28, 28, 1

image_size = x_train.shape[1]

x_train = np.reshape(x_train, [-1, image_size, image_size, 1])

x_test = np.reshape(x_test, [-1, image_size, image_size, 1])

x_train = x_train.astype('float32') / 255

x_test = x_test.astype('float32') / 255

# adding noise to the images
```

```
noise = np.random.normal(loc=0.5, scale=0.5,
size=x_train.shape)

x_train_noisy = x_train + noise

noise = np.random.normal(loc=0.5, scale=0.5,
size=x_test.shape)

x_test_noisy = x_test + noise
```

make sure to limit the pixel values within a range

because the noise can go over the valid values

```
x_train_noisy = np.clip(x_train_noisy, 0., 1.)

x_test_noisy = np.clip(x_test_noisy, 0., 1.)
```

neural net parameters

```
input_shape = (image_size, image_size, 1)

batch_size = 32 kernel_size = 3 latent_dim = 16
```

establish the number of encoder/decoder layers

plus the number of filters for each layer

```
layer_filters = [32, 64]
```

creating the autoencoder model by first building the encoder

```
inputs = Input(shape=input_shape, name='encoder_input')
```

```python
    x = inputs
# stack of Conv2D(32)-Conv2D(64)
    for filters in layer_filters:       x = Conv2D(filters=filters,
    kernel_size=kernel_size, strides=2, activation='relu',
    padding='same')(x)
# We need to obtain the shape data in order to create the decoder
# In order to avoid performing manual processing
# The shape of the decoder's first Conv2DTranspose will be 7, 7,
64
# and it will be computed with the decoder to a dimension of 28,
28, 1
    shape = K.int_shape(x)
# The latent vector needs to be created
    x = Flatten()(x) latent = Dense(latent_dim,
name='latent_vector')(x)
# Encoder instantiation
    encoder = Model(inputs, latent, name='encoder')
    encoder.summary()
```

creating the decoder

```python
latent_inputs = Input(shape=(latent_dim,),
name='decoder_input')

x = Dense(shape[1] * shape[2] * shape[3])(latent_inputs)

x = Reshape((shape[1], shape[2], shape[3]))(x)

for filters in layer_filters[::-1]:

x = Conv2DTranspose(filters=filters,
kernel_size=kernel_size,

strides=2,activation='relu', padding='same')(x)
```

rebuilding the input without the noise

```python
outputs = Conv2DTranspose(filters=1,
kernel_size=kernel_size,

padding='same', activation='sigmoid',
name='decoder_output')(x)
```

decoder instantiation

```python
decoder = Model(latent_inputs, outputs, name='decoder')

decoder.summary()
```

autoencoder instantiation

```python
autoencoder = Model(inputs, decoder(encoder(inputs)),
name='autoencoder')

autoencoder.summary()
# Mean Square Error loss function, Adam optimizer
autoencoder.compile(loss='mse', optimizer='adam')
# training process
autoencoder.fit(x_train_noisy, x_train,
validation_data=(x_test_noisy, x_test), epochs=10,
batch_size=batch_size)
```

using the noisy test images in order to predict the output of the autoencoder

```python
x_decoded = autoencoder.predict(x_test_noisy)
```

three rows of images containing nine digits

first row contains the original images

second row contains the noisy images

third row contains the cleaned up images

```python
rows, cols = 3, 9

num = rows * cols
```

```
imgs = np.concatenate([x_test[:num], x_test_noisy[:num],
x_ decoded[:num]])

imgs = imgs.reshape((rows * 3, cols, image_size,
image_size))

imgs = np.vstack(np.split(imgs, rows, axis=1))

imgs = imgs.reshape((rows * 3, -1, image_size,
image_size))

imgs = np.vstack([np.hstack(i) for i in imgs])

imgs = (imgs * 255).astype(np.uint8)

plt.figure() plt.axis('off') plt.title('Original images: top rows,
' 'Corrupted Input: middle rows, ' '

Denoised Input: third rows') plt.imshow(imgs,
interpolation='none', cmap='gray')

Image.fromarray(imgs).save('corrupted_and_denoised.png')

plt.show()
```

That's it! As you can see, there are more similarities between a basic autoencoder and a denoising autoencoder than there are differences. Go through the model and apply it on your own on some noisy data to see different results.

In the next section we are going to discuss the second type of autoencoders, namely the colorization autoencoders.

Colorization Autoencoders

Another useful scenario in which we can use autoencoders is when we want to turn a black and white image, or a grayscale image, into a colored one. As the name suggests, colorization autoencoders allow us create a technique of applying color automatically. Certain objects always have the same color or color range. Humans can tell that the grass should be green, the sky should be blue, and the clouds should be white or gray. With the help of an autoencoder, a machine can gain the same ability and automatically detect which object should be a certain color.

Autoencoders are a powerful way of implementing colorization algorithms. The way this works is by feeding the autoencoder with a large enough number of grayscale images as the input. The output will then consist of the colored version of the same images. This way the algorithm can eventually learn to which patterns certain colors should be applied. This entire process of colorization is actually backwards denoising, therefore you will see some familiarity in the implementation of the autoencoder.

From the perspective of a denoising autoencoder, you can look at the colorization encoder as a method of applying good noise, also known as color. In order to incorporate this technique we first need to access a dataset which contains a sufficiently large number of both grayscale as well as colored images. For our practical example we are going to use the CIFAR10 dataset once again because it suits our purposes precisely. It contains 50,000 training images, as well as 10,000 testing images and they can easily be turned to grayscale. In order to convert an image from color to grayscale we can use the "rgb2gray" function. This function will simply adjust the RGB elements until we remove all the color.

With that being said, let's go through the entire implementation of a colorization autoencoder and discuss the steps as we look at the code:

```
from keras.layers import Dense, Input

from keras.layers import Conv2D, Flatten

from keras.layers import Reshape, Conv2DTranspose

from keras.models import Model

from keras.callbacks import ReduceLROnPlateau,
ModelCheckpoint

from keras.datasets import cifar10

from keras.utils import plot_model

from keras import backend as K

import numpy as np

import matplotlib.pyplot as plt
```

```
import os
```

As mentioned earlier, the first step is to transform our colored photos from RGB to # # grayscale. This can be achieved by simply setting the grayscale levels to a combination # like this: 0.299*red + 0.587*green + 0.114*blue.

```
def rgb2gray(rgb):

return np.dot(rgb[...,:3], [0.299, 0.587, 0.114])
```

Loading the dataset

```
(x_train, _), (x_test, _) = cifar10.load_data()
```

Establish the input image shapes by assuming the data format as "channels_last"

```
img_rows = x_train.shape[1]

img_cols = x_train.shape[2]

channels = x_train.shape[3]
```

create saved_images folder

```
imgs_dir = 'saved_images'

save_dir = os.path.join(os.getcwd(), imgs_dir)

if not os.path.isdir(save_dir):
```

```
os.makedirs(save_dir)
```

Let's see the first 100 images, both in color and grayscale

```
imgs = x_test[:100]

imgs = imgs.reshape((10, 10, img_rows, img_cols,
channels))

imgs = np.vstack([np.hstack(i)

for i in imgs])

plt.figure()

plt.axis('off')

plt.title('Test color images (Ground Truth)')

plt.imshow(imgs, interpolation='none')

plt.savefig('%s/test_color.png' % imgs_dir)

plt.show()
```

Transform the training and testing image sets from color to grayscale

```
x_train_gray = rgb2gray(x_train) x_test_gray =
rgb2gray(x_test)
```

Display the testing images that are set to grayscale

```python
        imgs = x_test_gray[:100]

        imgs = imgs.reshape((10, 10, img_rows, img_cols))

        imgs = np.vstack([np.hstack(i) for i in imgs])

        plt.figure()

        plt.axis('off')

        plt.title('Test gray images (Input)')

        plt.imshow(imgs, interpolation='none', cmap='gray')

        plt.savefig('%s/test_gray.png' % imgs_dir)

        plt.show()

# This is the normalization of the testing and

# training output images that are in color only

        x_train = x_train.astype('float32') / 255

        x_test = x_test.astype('float32') / 255

# This is the normalization of both the training

# and testing input images that are in grayscale only

        x_train_gray = x_train_gray.astype('float32') / 255

        x_test_gray = x_test_gray.astype('float32') / 255
```

Change the shape of the images to the following structure : row x col x channel

This is necessary for the validation of the convolutional neural network

```
x_train = x_train.reshape(x_train.shape[0], img_rows,
img_cols, channels)

x_test = x_test.reshape(x_test.shape[0], img_rows,
img_cols, channels)
```

Change the shape of the images to the following structure : row x col x channel

This time it's for the input of the network

```
x_train_gray = x_train_gray.reshape(x_train_gray.shape[0],
img_rows, img_cols, 1) x_test_gray =
x_test_gray.reshape(x_test_gray.shape[0], img_rows, img_
cols, 1)
```

neural net parameters

```
input_shape = (img_rows, img_cols, 1) batch_size = 32
kernel_size = 3

latent_dim = 256
```

establish the number of encoder/decoder layers

```python
# plus the number of filters for each layer

    layer_filters = [64, 128, 256]

# setup the autoencoder model by first creating the encoder

    inputs = Input(shape=input_shape, name='encoder_input')

    x = inputs

# block of Conv2D(64)-Conv2D(128)-Conv2D(256)

for filters in layer_filters:    x = Conv2D(filters=filters, kernel_size=kernel_size,

strides=2, activation='relu', padding='same')(x)

# We need to obtain the shape data in order to create the decoder

# In order to avoid performing manual processing

# The shape of the decoder's first Conv2DTranspose will be 4, 4, 256

# and it will be computed with the decoder to a dimension of 32, 32, 3

    shape = K.int_shape(x)

# generate a latent vector

x = Flatten()(x) latent = Dense(latent_dim, name='latent_vector')(x)
```

```python
# instantiating the decoder

        encoder = Model(inputs, latent, name='encoder')
encoder.summary()

# building the decoder

        latent_inputs = Input(shape=(latent_dim,),
        name='decoder_input')

        x = Dense(shape[1]*shape[2]*shape[3])(latent_inputs)

        x = Reshape((shape[1], shape[2], shape[3]))(x)

# block of Conv2DTranspose(256)-Conv2DTranspose(128)

# Conv2DTranspose(64)

        for filters in layer_filters[::-1]:

        x = Conv2DTranspose(filters=filters,
        kernel_size=kernel_size, strides=2,

        activation='relu', padding='same')(x)

        outputs = Conv2DTranspose(filters=channels,
        kernel_size=kernel_size,

        activation='sigmoid', padding='same',
        name='decoder_output')(x)

# instantiating the decoder
```

```python
decoder = Model(latent_inputs, outputs, name='decoder')
decoder.summary()
```

instantiating the autoencoder, which is the sum of the decoder and encoder

```python
autoencoder = Model(inputs, decoder(encoder(inputs)),
name='autoencoder')

autoencoder.summary()
```

prepare method for saving checkpoints

```python
save_dir = os.path.join(os.getcwd(), 'saved_models')

model_name = 'colorized_ae_model.{epoch:03d}.h5'

if not os.path.isdir(save_dir):

os.makedirs(save_dir)

filepath = os.path.join(save_dir, model_name)
```

lower the learning rate by a value of sqrt(0.1)

this reduction is performed only if we can't see an improvement

to the loss over 5 epochs

```python
lr_reducer = ReduceLROnPlateau(factor=np.sqrt(0.1),
cooldown=0, patience=5,
```

```
            verbose=1, min_lr=0.5e-6)
```

keep the weights for use down the road

we can reload the neural network parameters without the training
process

```
        checkpoint = ModelCheckpoint(filepath=filepath,
        monitor='val_loss', verbose=1,        save_best_only=True)
```

Mean Square Error (MSE) loss function, Adam optimizer

```
        autoencoder.compile(loss='mse', optimizer='adam')

        callbacks = clr_reducer, checkpoint]
```

autoencoder training operation

```
        autoencoder.fit(x_train_gray, x_train,
        validation_data=(x_test_gray, x_test),

        epochs=30, batch_size=batch_size, callbacks=callbacks)
```

use the test data set to predict the output of the autoencoder

```
        x_decoded = autoencoder.predict(x_test_gray)
```

show the first 100 images in color

```
        imgs = x_decoded[:100]
```

```
imgs = imgs.reshape((10, 10, img_rows, img_cols,
channels))

imgs = np.vstack([np.hstack(i)

for i in imgs])

plt.figure()

plt.axis('off')

plt.title('Colorized test images (Predicted)')

plt.imshow(imgs, interpolation='none')

plt.savefig('%s/colorized.png' % imgs_dir)

plt.show()
```

You will notice that for this model we have added an increase to the capacity with the addition of another convolution block, as well as a transposed convolution block. In addition, we have double the amount of filters for each convolutional neural network section. We also have a 256 dim latent vector which is used to boost the number of important features that can be represented. Last but not least, we have also created an output filter with a size value of 3, or in other words, with a size equal to the number of channels, namely RGB. Take note that colorization encoder is trained using the grayscale for the input and the colored images for the output. This means that the training process will take longer to compute. However, we do use a learning rate reducer in order to lower the rate when we can't improve the validation loss over a series of epochs.

If you followed through with this example, you will notice that the results are quite satisfying. The autoencoder does its job remarkably well and image sections like the sea are colorized automatically to blue, while clouds are white and animals are of a variety of shades of brown. Unfortunately, the model isn't perfect and you will also notice some faults with the implementation. The most obvious mistakes are various vehicles that were originally blue, but they were colorized red.

Summary

In this chapter you learned how to work with autoencoders which are a type of advanced neural network with the capability of compressing the input into a low dimensional representation, making them extremely powerful in operations such as colorization and denoising. You learned how to use an encoder and a decoder to build an autoencoder, as well as how to uncover the latent vector in order to perform various operations on the initial input distribution. Keep in mind that in order to understand the input distribution, you need to visualize the latent vector with the help of low level embedding, or dimensionality reduction.

While in this chapter you focused only on denoising and colorization, you can also use an autoencoder to convert the input distribution to a latent vector which you can then use in various processes that involve segmentation or reconstruction.

In the next chapter you are going to learn about some of the most powerful innovations in the field of artificial intelligence. You will be introduced to the Generative Adversarial Networks and learn about their function and application.

Chapter 4

Generative Adversarial Networks

---•◆•---

In this chapter you are going to explore the generative adversarial networks, namely three powerful deep learning and artificial intelligence algorithms. This type of network is part of the neural network category of generative models.

In this chapter you are going to explore the theory and the concepts behind generative adversarial networks, and you will also go through a number of implementations using Keras. Furthermore, you will observe the practical implementation and the techniques needed for a balanced training process.

The purpose of this chapter is to explore two main generative implementations, namely the deep convolutional generative adversarial network, and the conditional generative adversarial network. But before we dive into the technical implementations, let's gain an understanding of the theory.

The Theory Behind GANs
In order to understand the complexity of GANs, you need to start with the basics. These networks are undoubtedly powerful and

efficient. This statement can be backed up with the fact that these networks can be used to create faces that don't exist, all because of the latent space interpolations they can process. These networks can be used to produce real looking humans that don't actually exist, however, we aren't going to go that deep into such an example because it would take a whole book on its own.

Generative adversarial networks are some of the most powerful networks you will work with because they can achieve various purposes that autoencoders simply could not accomplish. These networks work by modeling the input distribution by training two networks that either compete or collaborate. The two components are known as a discriminator and a generator.

The purpose of the generator is to continue processing new methods of creating fake audio or visual information that can trick the discriminator into believing it. On the other hand, the discriminator learns how to spot differences between fake and real data. However, at some point a barrier is reached where the discriminator can no longer determine which data is real and which is fake. At this stage the discriminator is removed. The generator is ready to build the more realistic data possible.

As you can see, the concept itself is quite easy to understand. However, the biggest challenge you will encounter is establishing a well-balanced training of the generator / discriminator structure. We know that these two systems need to be able to compete against each other in order for them to learn properly at the same time. Take note that with this type of network the loss function is processed from the discriminator's output. The faster the discriminator can converge, the fewer gradient updates the generator receives until it eventually can no longer converge.

Another challenge with GANs, aside from the training difficulty, is the risk of partial failure where the generator creates nearly identical outputs for each encoding. Imagine the two components as a policeman for the discriminator, and a counterfeiter as the generator. During training courses at the police academy, the policeman learns the difference between a real banknote and a fake one. He gets to analyse both real money as well as counterfeited in order to train how to tell the difference. Every now and then, the counterfeiter will act like he creates real banknotes, but the policeman won't be convinced and he will manage to come up with an explanation as to why the money is fake. Now that the counterfeiter has the explanation, he will know how to improve his skills and have a better attempt at creating counterfeit banknotes. The process then repeats, and the policeman will still realize that the money is fake and then explain why it is fake. This cycle keeps repeating, however, a point will be reached when the counterfeiter's skills will outmatch the policeman and his fake bills will look identical to the real ones. Now the counterfeiter can print as much money as he wants because he can't be caught by the policeman because the policeman is unable to spot the difference between his bills and the real ones.

As already mentioned, the GAN is created from two network components, the generator and the discriminator. The input of the generator is the noise and the output is a manufactured signal. However, the discriminator's input can also be a manufactured signal, or a real one. Real signals are the result from true data and the manufactured signals are obtained from the generator. We can label the real signals with a value of 1.0 which represents the fact that they are 100% legitimate. At the same time, the manufactured signals are labeled with a value of 0 to show that they have a 0% chance of being legitimate. Keep in mind that this process is automatic, therefore GANs are an unsupervised deep learning approach. The purpose of the discriminator is to learn from the dataset it has access to and train itself on how to tell the difference between a legitimate signal and a manufactured one.

During this stage of the training only the parameters that belong to the discriminator are updated. The discriminator is trained in a similar way to a binary classifier with the ability to make predictions between a range of zero to one values, which represent the likelihood of having a real signal. However, this isn't the entire process. The generator will occasionally act as if the output is a real signal and it will tell the algorithm to mark it with a value of one. That means that when the manufactured signal is sent to the discriminator it is marked as fake with a value of zero. Next, we have the optimizer which determines that the generator parameter will be updated based on the value obtained from the label, which is one. During this training phase it also takes its prediction into consideration and therefore the discriminator does experience a form of doubt which is then marked by the algorithm.

At this point, the GANs will allow gradients to backpropagate from the discriminator's final layer to the generator's first layer. Take note that at this stage the parameters belonging to the discriminator are locked for a time. The generator relies on the gradients for the parameter updated in other to learn better how to create a manufactured signal. As you can see, the entire system is basically a competition between two networks who always try to outmaneuver each other, but they still work together to some degree. When the network's training is fully assembled, the final result is the generator with its ability to manufacture signals and the discriminator will consider that they are in fact real. Even if they will not be marked with a value of one, they will be near one, which translates to the fact that the discriminator can be eliminated. The generator component will use the noise inputs in order to generate relevant outputs.

The generator and the discriminator can be enforced by designing a solid neural network structure. As long as the data is an image, for example, the generator and the discriminator components will rely on a convolutional neural network. However, if we have a one dimension sequence, then these two elements can be a recurrent neural network, with the possibility of having different architectures as well.

Deep Convolutional GANs

What you have learned so far are the basic concepts behind this type of network. In addition, you should remember that GANs need to be implemented through convolutional or recurrent neural networks. One of this network's main characteristics is somewhat negative because of the difficulty to train it. This means that even small modifications to the layers can lead to a longer, even unstable, training process.

In this section we are going to explore one of the simpler adaptations of GAN by using a deep convolutional neural network, which can be used to generate fake images. But before we switch to the practical implementation, you need to follow certain recommendations. Keep in mind that these aren't strict, however, your workflow and results would be more successful by doing what DCGANs prefer:

1. Instead of using max pooling or up sampling, you should use a convolution with strides greater than the value of one. With this setting the convolutional neural net can train itself to change the dimension of the feature maps.

2. Don't use Dense layers. Instead, you should only apply convolutional networks in every single layer. If you have to use a Dense layer, then you can use it in the generator's first layer. The output of this layer becomes the input of any convolutional networks that follow.

3. Stabilize the learning process with batch normalization in order to normalize every layer's input. This way the input will have zero mean and variance. However, there should be no batch normalization in the output layer that belongs to the generator and in the input layer of the discriminator. Again, this is not a rule. For instance, in the example you will be working with soon we will use batch normalization in the discriminator.

4. Use a rectified linear unit in the generator's layers with one exception being the output layer. In the output we will use a tanh activation instead, however, you can also use a sigmoid like we are going to do in the practical example. If we use the MNIST dataset, the sigmoid will lead to better results and a stable training process.

5. Apply a leaky rectified linear unit for each layer of the discriminator. The difference between this type of unit and the regular linear unit is that we don't zero out the output if the input is less than zero. The leaky version is used to create a gradient that is equal to the value of the alpha input. You will see that in our example we will have an alpha with the value of 0.2.

The generator will generate fake images using the 100 dim input vectors that have a random noise with a uniform distribution with a range from negative one to positive one. The discriminator will determine the real images from the fake ones, but it will also unintentionally train generator how to create real images during the training of the network.

The implementation of the deep convolutional GAN in our example will require a kernel size of five in order to boost the convolution's power and covering area. The generator will take a 100-dim z vector that is generated by a distribution ranging from a value of negative one to positive one. The generator's first layer will be a Dense layer with 6,272 units (7 * 7 * 128). These units are processed based on the dimension of the output image and the number of filters inside the Conv2DTranspose (128). The transposed network is basically a backwards version of the regular convolutional network. The convolutional network transforms an image to feature maps, while the transposed network will create an image from feature maps. Therefore the transposed convolutional network is ideal when working with decoders, like in the previous chapter, as well as with generators.

Once we process two transposed networks with strides equal to a value of two, we will have a number of feature maps with the dimension calculated with this formula: 28 * 28 * total number of filters. However, before the transposed network we will apply a rectified linear unit and batch normalization. In the last layer we will include an activation of the sigmoid type in order to create the fake images. Every single pixel will be normalized to a range between zero and one in order to match the grayscale levels ranging from zero to 255.

Now, let's take a look at how to implement the generator network. As usual, we are going to continue working using the Keras library. First we will define a function in order to create the model. Take note that because the code is quite long, for now we will only explore the lines of code that are directly related to the topic. With that being said, let's look at the function:

def build_generator(inputs, image_size):

""" Build a Generator Model

Use a block of BN-ReLU-Conv2DTranpose in order to generate fake images.

The output activation will be a sigmoid instead of tanh because a sigmoid converges easily.

Arguments

> **inputs (Layer):** this is the Input layer of the generator (the z-vector)

> **image_size:** with a target size of one side (we will assume a square image)

Returns

Model: Generator Model

"""

image_resize = image_size // 4

neural net parameters

kernel_size = 5

layer_filters = [128, 64, 32, 1]

x = Dense(image_resize * image_resize * layer_filters[0])(inputs)

x = Reshape((image_resize, image_resize, layer_filters[0]))(x)

for filters in layer_filters:

We will apply strides with a value of 2 for the first two convolution layers

The final two layers will have strides with a value of 1

if filters > layer_filters[-2]:

strides = 2

else:

strides = 1

```
x = BatchNormalization()(x)

x = Activation('relu')(x)

x = Conv2DTranspose(filters=filters,
kernel_size=kernel_size, strides=strides,

padding='same')(x)

x = Activation('sigmoid')(x)

generator = Model(inputs, x, name='generator')

return generator
```

You will notice in our example that the discriminator is nearly identical to other classifiers that are based on convolutional neural networks. The input of an image is classified as fake if the value is zero or real if the value is one. Keep in mind that we have four convolutional network layers, and with the exception of the last layer, the others use strides equal to two in order to downsample the feature maps. Before these layers, however, we have a leaky rectified linear unit layer. Furthermore, the starting filter size has a value of 32, but it doubles on each convolution layer, leading to a final filter size of 256. Take note that a filter with a size of 128 would do just fine as well. However, if we apply a filter with the size of 256 then the result, the final images, will simply look better.

Once the last output layer is flattened and the dense layer generates the prediction once the sigmoid activation is implemented, the output is processed as a Bernoulli distribution. This is the reason why we use a binary cross entropy loss function in this example. Once the generator and the discriminator are created, we develop the adversarial model through a concatenation between the two components.

As mentioned earlier, we use an RMSprop optimizer for the discriminator, as well as the adversarial networks. This provides a training rate of 2e-4 for the discriminator and 1e-4 for the network. Furthermore, the optimizer also applied a 6e-8 decay rate for the discriminator and 3e-8 for the adversarial network. This way we can gain a far more efficient training. Keep in mind that the training process for a GAN involves two phases. First we train the discriminator and then the generator. The generator's training is the one that is referred to as adversarial training. During this process, the weights of the discriminator are suspended.

Now, let's discuss the discriminator implementation with the Keras library. You will notice that we have to define a seperate function in order to create the model of our discriminator. Once the models for the discriminator and the generator are created, we can set up the adversarial model which is in fact the two components molded together. You will see that the implementation of the model is quite straightforward, however, it will be difficult to make changes in the design because this can break the training convergence.

We will start by building the discriminator with the builder function:

```
def build_discriminator(inputs):

""" Creating the Discriminator Model
```

In order to discriminate the real from the fake we apply a block of LeakyReLU-Conv2D. However, the network will not converge with batch normalization , therefore we will not use it like with the base model.

```
# Arguments
```

inputs (Layer): Input layer of the discriminator (the image)

```
# Returns
```

Model: Discriminator Model

```
    """

    kernel_size = 5

    layer_filters = [32, 64, 128, 256]

    x = inputs

    for filters in layer_filters:
```

For the first three convolution layers we will use strides with a value of 2

The last convolution layer will have strides with a value of 1

```
        if filters == layer_filters[-1]:

        strides = 1

        else:

        strides = 2

        x = LeakyReLU(alpha=0.2)(x)

        x = Conv2D(filters=filters, kernel_size=kernel_size,
        strides=strides, padding='same')(x)

        x = Flatten()(x)

        x = Dense(1)(x)

        x = Activation('sigmoid')(x)

        discriminator = Model(inputs, x, name='discriminator')

        return discriminator
```

Now that we have both component models, we can build the deep convolutional GAN and call for the training process with the following code:

```python
def build_and_train_models():
    # loading the dataset
    (x_train, _), (_, _) = mnist.load_data()
    # normalize and change the shape of the data for the convolutional network
    # with a dimension of 28, 28, 1
    image_size = x_train.shape[1]
    x_train = np.reshape(x_train, [-1, image_size, image_size, 1])
    x_train = x_train.astype('float32') / 255
    model_name = "dcgan_mnist"
    # neural net parameters
    # the latent vector will be 100-dim
    latent_size = 100 batch_size = 64 train_steps = 40000 lr = 2e-4 decay = 6e-8 input_shape = (image_size, image_size, 1)
    # creating the model for the discriminator
    inputs = Input(shape=input_shape, name='discriminator_input')
```

```python
    discriminator = build_discriminator(inputs)
```

You can use an Adam optimizer, however it is easier for the discriminator to converge # with an RMSprop instead

```python
    optimizer = RMSprop(lr=lr, decay=decay)

    discriminator.compile(loss='binary_crossentropy',
    optimizer=optimizer,

    metrics=['accuracy'])

    discriminator.summary()
```

creating the model for the generator

```python
    input_shape = (latent_size, )

    inputs = Input(shape=input_shape, name='z_input')

    generator = build_generator(inputs, image_size)

    generator.summary()
```

creating the adversarial model

```python
    optimizer = RMSprop(lr=lr * 0.5, decay=decay * 0.5)
```

suspending the discriminator's weights during the process of

training the adversarial network

```python
    discriminator.trainable = False
```

adversarial model is the generator plus the discriminator

```
adversarial = Model(inputs,
discriminator(generator(inputs)), name=model_name)

adversarial.compile(loss='binary_crossentropy',
optimizer=optimizer,

metrics=['accuracy'])

adversarial.summary()
```

the training phase for the discriminator and the adversarial networks

```
models = (generator, discriminator, adversarial)

params = (batch_size, latent_size, train_steps, model_name)

train (models, x_train, params)
```

Take note that because of the custom training process we will not be using the basic fit function as usual. We need to apply a "train on batch" function instead in order to run the gradient update for a specified batch of data. Then we use the adversarial network to train the generator. This works with the training process selecting a batch of real images at first and then labeling it with a value of 1, meaning real. Next, the generator will generate the fake images, which are labeled with a value of 0, meaning fake. Both image stacks are then concatenated in order to be used for the training process of the discriminator. Once this phase is finished, another round of fake images are generated, but this time they are labeled with a value of 1 even though they are fake. This group of images is needed for the training process of the adversarial network. Keep in mind that both networks will be training in an alternate fashion for around 40,000 rounds. At certain intervals we will establish checkpoints in order to save the generated images. Finally, the last phase of the training process involves the convergence of the network. Take note that the model for the generator will be saved separately in order to use it for future generations.

Keep in mind though that we will save only the generator because this is the component needed to generate new images. With that being said, here's how we would use it for this purpose:

```
def train(models, x_train, params):
```

""" Training the Discriminator and Adversarial Networks

You can also train the two components by batch. We can train the discriminator as usual with both real and fake images. Then the adversarial networks are trained using the fake images that pose as real images. Finally, we generate the images for every save interval we define.

Arguments

models (list): Generator, Discriminator, Adversarial models

```python
        x_train (tensor): Train images

        params (list) : Networks parameters

        """

# GAN models

        generator, discriminator, adversarial = models

# neural net parameters

        batch_size, latent_size, train_steps, model_name = params

# We save the generator in intervals of 500 steps

        save_interval = 500

# during training we check the noise vector

# to verify the output evolution of the generator

        noise_input  =  np.random.uniform(-1.0,  1.0,  size=[16,
        latent_size])

# total number of elements in the training set

        train_size = x_train.shape[0]

        for i in range(train_steps):

# For a single batch we need to train the discriminator.
```

```
# This batch will have real images labeled with a value of 1,

# as well as fake images with a value of 0

# Real images are randomly chosen from the dataset

        rand_indexes = np.random.randint(0, train_size, size=batch_
        size)

        real_images = x_train[rand_indexes]

# Use the generator to create fake images from the noise

# The noise is generated with a uniform distribution

        noise  =  np.random.uniform(-1.0,  1.0,  size=[batch_size,
        latent_ size])

# Fake image generation

        fake_images = generator.predict(noise)

# One batch of training data is equal to the sum of real and fake
images

        x = np.concatenate((real_images, fake_images))

# Both the fake and the real images need to be labeled

# The label for the real images is 1.0 and the label for the fake ones
is o.0
```

```python
    y = np.ones([2 * batch_size, 1])

    y[batch_size:, :] = 0.0
```

During the discriminator training process we note the loss and the accuracy

```python
    loss, acc = discriminator.train_on_batch(x, y)

    log = "%d: [discriminator loss: %f, acc: %f]" % (i, loss, acc)
```

The adversarial network needs to be trained for only 1 batch as well

This batch will consist of fake images with the 1.0 label

Keep in mind that only the generator will be trained here because the discriminator is suspended in the adversarial network

Noise is generated with a uniform distribution

```python
    noise = np.random.uniform(-1.0, 1.0, size=[batch_size, latent_size])
```

The fake images will now be labeled the same as the real ones

```python
    y = np.ones([batch_size, 1])
```

Adversarial network training phase

Notice that during this stage we will not store the fake images inside a variable

```python
# like we did during the discriminator training process

# In this case the fake images belong to the input of the discriminator

# which belongs to the adversarial

# For the classification purpose we need to log the loss and the
accuracy

        loss, acc = adversarial.train_on_batch(noise, y)

        log = "%s [adversarial loss: %f, acc: %f]" % (log, loss, acc)

        print(log)

        if (i + 1) % save_interval == 0:

        if (i + 1) == train_steps:

        show = True

        else:

        show = False

# On regular intervals we need to plot the generator images

        plot_images(generator,                  noise_input=noise_input,
        show=show, step=(i + 1),

        model_name=model_name)

# Once the generator is trained we save the model
```

This way we can reload the generator whenever we have to generate more images

    generator.save(model_name + ".h5")

We can now see how the fake images evolve from the generator as we progress through all the training steps. Once we reach 5,000 steps, we will already obtain images that can be identified. However, you will notice that some of the MNIST digits images will change when reaching certain steps. For instance, we can have an eight in one column which later becomes a zero.

Now, let's go to the next section and discuss the conditional GANs and see how they differ from the deep convolutional GANs.

Conditional GANs

You noticed in the previous section that when working with deep convolutional GANs, the fake images are generated randomly. You don't have the option of requesting certain images. This is an issue which can be easily solved by applying a conditional GAN. You can use the same GAN, but this time prepare a condition which acts on the inputs of the generator, as well as discriminator. This condition comes in the shape of a one-hot vector, instead of the image itself.

The major difference between the deep convolutional GAN and the conditional one is this one-hot vector type of input. In the case of the generator the one-hot label has to concatenate with the latent vector ahead of the implementation of the Dense layer. In the case of the discriminator, however, we have a new Dense layer which will process the vector and transform it in such a way that it can be concatenated to the input of the convolutional neural network layer that comes after.

The generator will be trained to create fake images based on a 100-dim input vector and a certain digit. The discriminator will then classify the real and the fake images based on the ones that correspond to their labels. You will notice that the foundation of the conditional GAN is the same as the GAN you already work with. However, the inputs of the discriminator and the generator are trained on the one-hot labels. Furthermore, we have a new discriminator loss function, which has the purpose of reducing the error of the real image prediction with images sourced from the dataset, and the fake images that are sourced from the generator based on their one-hot labels. The loss function of the generator, however, has the purpose of reducing the accurate prediction of the discriminator on the fake images that are trained on certain one-hot labels. In this case the generator is trained to create specific images in order to trick the discriminator.

Now, let's start going through the practical implementation of a conditional GAN to observe the differences when compared to the deep convolutional GAN. Take note that we will process a one-hot vector with the help of a Dense layer and then concatenate it with the image. With that being said, here's the code with comments regarding each step:

```
def build_discriminator(inputs, y_labels, image_size):
```

""" Creating a Discriminator Model

Take note that we concatenate the inputs right after the Dense layer. Furthermore, we will have a block of LeakyReLU-Conv2D to discriminate the real images from the fake ones. The network will not converge with batch normalization, therefore we will not apply it in this implementation like with did with the deep convolutional GAN

Arguments

inputs (Layer): This will be the Input layer of the discriminator, the image

y_labels (Layer): This will be the Input layer for the one-hot vector to condition the inputs

image_size: The target size of one side. We will assume a square image.

Returns

Model: Discriminator Model

"""

```
kernel_size = 5

layer_filters = [32, 64, 128, 256]

x = inputs

y = Dense(image_size * image_size)(y_labels)

y = Reshape((image_size, image_size, 1))(y)

x = concatenate([x, y])

for filters in layer_filters:
```

We will have strides with a value of 2 for the first 3 convolution layers

The final layer will use strides with a value of 1

```
    if filters == layer_filters[-1]:

    strides = 1

    else:

    strides = 2     x = LeakyReLU(alpha=0.2)(x)

    x = Conv2D(filters=filters, kernel_size=kernel_size,
    strides=strides, padding='same')(x)

    x = Flatten()(x)

    x = Dense(1)(x)
```

```
    x = Activation('sigmoid')(x)
```

We need to condition the input by y_labels

```
    discriminator = Model([inputs, y_labels], x,
    name='discriminator')

    return discriminator
```

Next, let's see how we implement the one-hot labels for conditioning inside the generator function. Keep in mind that the model will be modified for the latent vector input, as well as the one-hot vector input.

```
    def build_generator(inputs, y_labels, image_size):
```

""" Creating the Generator Model

Before the Dense layer we need to concatenate the inputs. We then use a block of BN-ReLU-Conv2DTranpose to generate the fake images. Furthermore, we use a sigmoid output activation because it converges so easily.

Arguments

inputs (Layer): This is the input layer of the generator, which is the latent vector.

y_labels (Layer): This is the input layer for the one-hot vector that is needed to condition the inputs.

image_size: The target size of one side where we assume we are dealing with square images.

Returns

Model: Generator Model

```
    """

    image_resize = image_size // 4
# neural net parameters
    kernel_size = 5 layer_filters = [128, 64, 32, 1]

    x = concatenate([inputs, y_labels], axis=1)

    x = Dense(image_resize * image_resize *
    layer_filters[0])(x)

    x = Reshape((image_resize, image_resize,
    layer_filters[0]))(x)

    for filters in layer_filters:
# The first two convolution layers will use strides with a value of two
# and the final layers will have strides with a value of one
        if filters > layer_filters[-2]:

        strides = 2
```

```
        else:

        strides = 1

        x = BatchNormalization()(x)

        x = Activation('relu')(x)

        x = Conv2DTranspose(filters=filters,
        kernel_size=kernel_size, strides=strides,

        padding='same')(x)

        x = Activation('sigmoid')(x)

# the input will be conditioned by y_labels

        generator = Model([inputs, y_labels], x, name='generator')

        return generator
```

Take note of the modifications that are needed for the train function in order to adapt the one-hot vector for both the discriminator and the generator. First we train the conditional GAN with one stack of real and fake images that are conditioned with their matching one-hot labels. The generator parameters will be updated when training the adversarial network. In this case the conditioned fake data will act as if it's real. You will also notice that the discriminator weights are suspended during the adversarial network's training process, just like in the case of the deep convolutional GAN. With that being said, let's take a look at the code for the training process of the conditional GAN:

```
def train(models, data, params):
```

""" Train the Discriminator and Adversarial Networks

You can also train the two components by batch. We can train the discriminator as usual with both real and fake images. Then the adversarial networks are trained using the fake images that pose as real images. Finally, we generate the images for every save interval we define. Keep in mind that train labels of the real images will condition the discriminator inputs. The same thing happens with the random labels for the fake images. The adversarial inputs are also conditioned by the random labels.

Arguments

models (list): Generator, Discriminator, Adversarial models

data (list): x_train, y_train data

params (list): Network parameters

```
    """
```

```
    # These are the GAN models
        generator, discriminator, adversarial = models
        # Images and labels
```

590

```
        x_train, y_train = data

# neural net parameters

        batch_size,    latent_size,    train_steps,    num_labels,
        model_name = params

# In intervals of 500 steps we save the generator image

        save_interval = 500

# Apply a noise vector to see the evolution of the generator output

# during the training process

        noise_input  =  np.random.uniform(-1.0,  1.0,  size=[16,
        latent_size])

# The noise needs to be conditioned to a one-hot label

        noise_class  =  np.eye(num_labels)[np.arange(0,  16)  %
        num_labels]

# The total number of elements within the training set

        train_size = x_train.shape[0]

        print(model_name,  "Labels  for  generated  images:  ",
        np.argmax(noise_class, axis=1))

        for i in range(train_steps):
```

```python
# Discriminator training for one batch of real and fake images

# The real images are chosen randomly from the dataset
        rand_indexes    =    np.random.randint(0,    train_size,
        size=batch_size)

        real_images = x_train[rand_indexes]
# We will have matching one-hot labels for the real images
        real_labels = y_train[rand_indexes]
# Use the generator to create fake images from the noise
# which will use a uniform distribution
        noise   =   np.random.uniform(-1.0,   1.0,   size=[batch_size,
        latent_size])
# One-hot labels need to be assigned
        fake_labels =
        np.eye(num_labels)[np.random.choice(num_labels,

        batch_size)]
# The generated fake images are conditioned on fake labels
        fake_images = generator.predict([noise, fake_labels])
# One batch of training data contains real and fake images
```

```python
        x = np.concatenate((real_images, fake_images))
```

One batch of training one-hot labels contain real and fake one-hot labels

```python
        y_labels = np.concatenate((real_labels, fake_labels))
```

Both the real and fake images need to be labeled

```python
        y = np.ones([2 * batch_size, 1])

        y[batch_size:, :] = 0.0
```

Logging the loss and the accuracy while training the discriminator network

```python
        loss, acc = discriminator.train_on_batch([x, y_labels], y)

        log = "%d: [discriminator loss: %f, acc: %f]" % (i, loss, acc)
```

Use one batch to train the adversarial network

The batch of fake images will be conditioned on fake one-hot labels

One single generator is trained because

the discriminator weights are suspended within the adversarial network

With a uniform distribution we generate the noise

```python
    noise = np.random.uniform(-1.0, 1.0, size=[batch_size,
    latent_size])
```

One-hot labels are distributed

```python
    fake_labels = np.eye(num_labels)[np.random.choice
    (num_labels,batch_size)]
```

The fake images are now labeled as real

```python
    y = np.ones([batch_size, 1])
```

Training the adversarial network

Keep in mind that we will not save the fake images inside a variable like we did during # the discriminator training process.

#These images will go to the input of the adversarial network

for the classification process

The accuracy and the loss need to be logged

```python
    loss, acc = adversarial.train_on_batch([noise, fake_labels], y)

    log = "%s [adversarial loss: %f, acc: %f]" % (log, loss, acc)

    print(log

    if (i + 1) % save_interval == 0:

    if (i + 1) == train_steps:
```

```
        show = True

    else:

        show = False

# During regular intervals we need to plot generator images

        plot_images(generator, noise_input=noise_input,
        noise_class=noise_class,

        show=show, step=(i + 1), model_name=model_name)

# The model is saved once the generator is trained

# This way we can reuse the generator at any point to generate more
images

        generator.save(model_name + ".h5")
```

Take note the the conditional GAN can be compared to a robot that can draw the handwritten digits similarly to humans. The main advantage in using it instead of a deep convolutional GAN is that we can tell the robot specifically the digit we want it to draw. If you recall, this isn't possible with the deep convolutional model.

The Least-Squared GAN

As mentioned earlier, the basic GAN model isn't easy to train. The problem here lies with the GAN's ability to optimize the loss function. That's because in reality it's attempting to optimize the information radius instead. Optimizing the information radius, also known as the Jensen-Shannon divergence, is extremely problematic because of the lack of sufficient overlap between two distribution functions. Other GAN models attempt to fix this issue with the help of a Wasserstein loss function because of the smooth differentiable function it has even if the overlap is lacking. However, this solution again isn't optimal because this model doesn't focus on the quality of the image. The other option is using a Least-Squared GAN.

The theory behind the LSGAN is that the two problems regarding the quality of the image and the optimization can be solved at the same time. This model relies on the least squares loss to avoid poorly generated data. Furthermore, the fake samples distribution needs to be near the distribution of the real samples. Regular GANs have the issue of vanishing gradients when the fake samples are on the right side of the decision limit. This means that the generator has issues finding the "motive" to boost the quality of the fake data. The fake samples that come from the edge of the decision limit will not seek to shift to a closer position near the distribution of the real samples. By using a square loss function, however, these gradients will not vanish when the fake samples distribution is further away from the other distribution. The goal of the generator here is to boost the estimation of the density distribution even if the fake samples are in position.

If we compare the standard GAN to the LASGAN we will see that the discriminator loss function forces the MSE between the real data and the true label to be near a value of zero. Furthermore, the LSGAN discriminator has to learn how to distinguish real data from fake data. By having a minimizing equation the discriminator, however, could be fooled to see the fake samples as real. By implementing the LSGAN model, together with the DCGAN code we worked with earlier, we can obtain an improved model. The DCGAN model in this case serves as the foundation. Some of the key differences involve the elimination of the sigmoid activation and the replacement of the adversarial loss function and discriminator with an MSE. With that being said, let's take a look at the code:

```
def build_and_train_models():
```

we are using the MNIST dataset once again

```
(x_train, _), (_, _) = mnist.load_data()
```

the first step is to reshape data for CNN as (28, 28, 1) and normalize it

```
image_size = x_train.shape[1]

x_train = np.reshape(x_train, [-1, image_size, image_size, 1])
```

```python
x_train = x_train.astype('float32') / 255

model_name = "lsgan_mnist"
```

these are the neural network parameters

the latent or z vector is 100-dim   latent_size = 100

```python
input_shape = (image_size, image_size, 1)

batch_size = 64

lr = 2e-4

decay = 6e-8    train_steps = 40000
```

creating the discriminator model

```python
inputs = Input(shape=input_shape,
name='discriminator_input')

discriminator = gan.discriminator(inputs, activation=None)
```

we could be using the Adam optimizer, but the discriminator converges

easily with RMSprop as well

```python
optimizer = RMSprop(lr=lr, decay=decay)
```

LSGAN uses MSE loss

```python
    discriminator.compile(loss='mse',optimizer=optimizer,
    metrics=['accuracy'])

    discriminator.summary()
# creating the generator model
    input_shape = (latent_size, )

    inputs    =    Input(shape=input_shape,    name='z_input')
            generator    =    gan.generator(inputs,    image_size)
    generator.summary()
# creating the adversarial model = generator + discriminator
    optimizer = RMSprop(lr=lr*0.5, decay=decay*0.5)
# we need to suspend the weights of discriminator
# during the adversarial training process
    discriminator.trainable = False

    adversarial = Model(inputs,
    discriminator(generator(inputs)), name=model_name)
#LSGAN uses MSE loss
    adversarial.compile(loss='mse',optimizer=optimizer,
    metrics=['accuracy'])

    adversarial.summary()
```

```
# training the discriminator and adversarial networks

    models = (generator, discriminator, adversarial)

    params = (batch_size, latent_size, train_steps, model_name)

    gan.train(models, x_train, params)
```

As you can see we have trained the LSGAN successfully by using the MNIST dataset to perform 40,000 training steps. The output images are now of a higher quality than those we obtained with the DCGAN model.

Summary

In this chapter you learned about two different types of Generative Adversarial Networks and the concepts behind them. You now have the necessary foundation to continue studying even more complex models, such as improved GANs, Cross Domain GANs, and much more.

The purpose of this chapter is to teach you the structure of a GAN, which is made from a generator and a discriminator. Keep in mind that the discriminator's role is to discriminate between the fake and real signals, such as our image data from the MNIST dataset. The generator, on the other hand, is supposed to act as its opponent, always trying to fool it. This is why, to form a typical GAN, you need to combine the generator with the discriminator. By training this adversarial network, the generator becomes capable of manufacturing its own signals until the discriminator can no longer tell the difference from reality.

Furthermore, you learned that GANs are not that easy to train, even though they are quite simple in architecture and therefore you should be able to build them on your own. The implementations we worked with show that deep convolutional GANs are useful for image generation when working with deep convolutional neural networks. In our case these fake images were MNIST handwritten digits. However, the problem with this model is that you cannot control which image is drawn. In order to solve this problem we have implemented and conditional GAN. Remember that the condition comes as a one-hot label and this type of GAN is powerful when we need to generate a certain data item.

In the next chapter we are going to focus on Cross-Domain GANs and put some of the general concepts you learned into application.

Chapter 5

Cross Domain GANs

---◆---

In many tech fields you will encounter tasks that require you to transform an image from a certain type of information to another. Whether you're dealing with image processing, computer graphics, or computer vision, you need to know how you can translate an image to a different shape. We already had such type of application where we colorized a number of grayscale images. This is one application example of many. You may also be required to convert various terrain scans into maps, modify the digital art of someone to obtain a different style, turn night time photos into daytime ones, transform winter images to summer ones, and so on. All of these assignments are known as cross domain transfers, which involve a source image to be transferred to a target and therefore gain a translated image.

Cross domain transfers are applied often in real world scenarios, not just theoretical ones. For instance, this method is used to gather vehicle driving information in order to make advances in autonomous driving systems. Collecting this kind of data can be extremely time consuming because of the many variations in the scene. For instance, the weather is a variable on its own because it changes the scene due to the various conditions caused by the seasons. By using cross domain transfers, however, you can generate these scenes. Even though they are manufactured and "fake", they are accurate enough so that we can translate the real data that is recorded. For instance, you might have to record summer scenes from a certain road and winter scenes from another road. Once you have access to this data, you can turn the summer images from one scene to winter and vice versa. This simple example already shows how you can benefit from this system because you can cut your workflow in half, and as you already know, GANs are excellent at generating manufactured images.

GANs are optimal for cross domain translation and in this chapter we are going to focus on this aspect. You will learn how to work with the cross domain GAN algorithm known as CycleGAN, which is somewhat simpler than other translation algorithms because it doesn't need the training images to be aligned before the processing. For instance, other algorithms would require two images, one which is the source and the other which is that target. If we consider a terrain image, you would also need the map which corresponds to the image. On the other hand, with CycleGAN, you only need the initial terrain image plus any maps that come from other sources.

With that in mind, in this chapter you will learn about the concept behind cross domain GANs and CycleGan and how to implement it using Keras. Let's get to it!

Cross Domain GANs Concepts

As mentioned earlier, one of the most frequent tasks encountered in image processing and computer vision is translating images from a domain to another. An even more common tasks is edge detection. For instance, we can look at the source image on one side and the edge detected image on the other side. The second image can be considered to be a sample within the target domain. Keep in mind that there are many other cross domain translation operations you can perform in the real world, such as: image to caricature, turning a medical scan into a photo, turning a photo into a drawing and so on.

Every technical field has such examples. However, in image processing, the translation can be done with a particular algorithm that seeks to obtain certain features from the source image and use them to create the target image. For instance, an operator known as "canny edge" is a perfect example for this. The problem is that the translation is highly complex and finding the right algorithm to automate the process is close to impossible because the source and target distributions are high dimensional and simply too complex.

A solution to this problem, however, is using deep learning methods instead. As long as we have access to a quality dataset that offers an adequate source and target domains, then we can construct a neural network for the translation process. Take note that the target images need to be generated automatically by using the source images. However, they also need to look like real images. This is why GANs are the perfect type of network for this job. An example of such an algorithm is "pix2pix" which in many ways is similar to a conditional GAN. Remember that when it comes to conditional GANs, the generator's output is limited by a condition that comes as a one-hot vector. For instance, if we want to output the handwritten MNIST digit eight, we need to set the one-hot vector [0, 0, 0, 0, 0, 0, 0, 0, 1, 0] as the restricting condition. This condition, however, will be translated when using the pix2pix algorithm, and the translation becomes the output for the generator. Then the algorithm is trained through the optimization of the GANs loss. Take note that a L1 type of loss is needed in order to reduce any potential blurring in the images.

There is, however, a disadvantage when working with this type of neural networks. We need to align the training input and output. In this case, we need a pair of aligned images that will contain the target image which is created using the source image. Keep in mind that in most cases these pairs are hard, if not impossible, to generate by relying on the source photos. There's also the possibility of our inability to figure out how to generate an image from a certain source image. Fortunately, we can use an algorithm like CycleGAN instead, in order to learn image translation from a large enough dataset that contains plenty of source and target images. For example you can have a real photo of a flower and a target domain, which is a certain artstyle, like Van Gogh's flower painting styles. They don't need to align. The CycleGAN algorithm can learn the source and target images in order to be able to make any translation based on the given data. Furthermore, you don't need to supervise the process. All you truly need is large datasets contain thousands of images of the same type of subject, like a sunflower, and then thousands of variations of an artist's representations of a sunflower. Once the training process is complete, we can translate a sunflower image to a particular artist's painting style of a sunflower.

The CycleGAN Model

Now that you know the theory behind Cross Domain GANs, let's discuss one of the most popular models we mentioned, namely the CycleGAN. In this section we are going to handle a problem which CycleGAN is perfect for addressing. Remember that in the third chapter, when we discussed autoencoders, we worked with a model which was designed to turn grayscale images into colorized images. In that example we used the CIFAR10 dataset which contains 50,000 trained RGB images and 10,000 test images that are categorized in ten different classes. All of these images can be converted to grayscale with the same function we used earlier, rgb2gray, and then we can use them to train source images, while the color images become the target.

Keep in mind that even if the dataset is aligned, the algorithm's input is a combination of random color and grayscale images. Therefore, CycleGAN will not detect this data to be aligned. Once the training is complete however, the grayscale photos will be used to check how the model performs overall.

In order to implement the CycleGAN algorithm you will have to create two generators, as well as two discriminators. The GAN's generator has the purpose of learning the latent vector that belongs to the source input and then translate it to the target output. You will notice here that there is a similarity between this method and the application of autoencoders. There is a difference, however. The autoencoder will downsample the input with an encoder until the decoder flips the bottleneck layer. This kind of model isn't the best choice for translating images because there are a number of features shared between the two autoencoder components. For instance, when it comes to colorization tasks, the architecture, the shape, and the edges of the grayscale photos are identical to those of the colored photos. In order to solve this issue, the CycleGAN model relies on its generators to use a U-Net architecture. This type of architecture involves the concatenation of the encoder layer's output with the decoder layer's output. Keep in mind that with U-Net we will require a deeper structure if we have high-dimensional inputs and outputs.

A U-Net allows the continuous data flow between the two network components. The encoder layer is constructed using a

Normalization(IN)-LeakyReLU-Conv2D structure, and the decoder layer is formed with a IN-ReLU-Conv2D. Furthermore, we have instance normalization, which is in fact a batch normalization for each data sample. In other words, you can classify the instance normalization as the batch normalization of individual images. Take note that the sample contrast is therefore normalized for each sample instead of a batch.

Now let's start with the coding by looking at the implementation of the layers containing the encoder and decoder.

Encoder and Decoder Implementation

First, we are going to create the basic encoder layer with a Conv2D-IN-LeakyReLU structure. Keep in mind that the Leaky ReLU is actually optional and you can also use a regular ReLU instead. Next, we will create the basic decoder layer that is constructed using the Conv2D-IN-LeakyReLU structure. Again, the leaky ReLU is optional and it can be replaced with the basic version.

```
def encoder_layer(inputs, filters=16, kernel_size=3,
strides=2, activation='relu',

instance_norm=True):

conv = Conv2D(filters=filters, kernel_size=kernel_size,
strides=strides,

padding='same')
```

```python
x = inputs

if instance_norm:

x = InstanceNormalization()(x)

if activation == 'relu':

x = Activation('relu')(x)

else:

x = LeakyReLU(alpha=0.2)(x)

x = conv(x)

return x

def decoder_layer(inputs, paired_inputs, filters=16,
kernel_size=3, strides=2,  activation='relu',
instance_norm=True):

conv = Conv2DTranspose(filters=filters,

kernel_size=kernel_size,  strides=strides, padding='same')

x = inputs

if instance_norm:

x = InstanceNormalization()(x)

if activation == 'relu':

x = Activation('relu')(x)

else:
```

```
x = LeakyReLU(alpha=0.2)(x)

x = conv(x)

x = concatenate([x, paired_inputs])

return x
```

The next step of the process, like with regular GANs, is the implementation of the generator.

Generator Implementation

The generator will be a U-Net, constructed with an encoder with four layers, as well as a decoder with four layers. The "n-i" layer will communicate with the "i" layer.

```
def build_generator(input_shape, output_shape=None, kernel_size=3,

name=None):

inputs = Input(shape=input_shape)

channels = int(output_shape[-1])

e1 = encoder_layer(inputs, 32, kernel_size=kernel_size,
activation='leaky_relu', strides=1)

e2 = encoder_layer(e1, 64, activation='leaky_relu',
kernel_size=kernel_size)
```

```
e3 = encoder_layer(e2, 128, activation='leaky_relu',
kernel_size=kernel_size)

e4 = encoder_layer(e3, 256, activation='leaky_relu',
kernel_size=kernel_size)

d1 = decoder_layer(e4, e3, 128, kernel_size=kernel_size)

d2 = decoder_layer(d1, e2, 64, kernel_size=kernel_size)

d3 = decoder_layer(d2, e1, 32, kernel_size=kernel_size)

outputs = Conv2DTranspose(channels,
kernel_size=kernel_size, strides=1,

activation='sigmoid', padding='same')(d3)

generator = Model(inputs, outputs, name=name)

return generator
```

When implementing this model, you will notice that the discriminator of the CycleGAN is close in design to the GAN discriminator. We downsample the input image multiple times and we have a Dense layer as a final layer in order to make a probability prediction that shows whether the input is real or not. All the layers are nearly identical when compared to the encoder layer which is part of the generator. However, there is one difference. There is no instance normalization. Take note that if we have large photos and we use only one number to compute them as fake or real, we are dealing with ineffective parameters and therefore the generator will offer images of substandard quality. In order to solve this problem we can use a PatchGAN algorithm. This will help by splitting the image into a number of patches that will be arranged in the form of a grid. The grid will be able to perform a probability prediction on the patches and determine whether they are real or not. Keep in mind that these patches can sometimes overlap, but other times they simply connect at their limits instead.

At this point, you might be thinking that the PatchGAN is another type of GAN that we are building inside the CycleGAN. That isn't the case. We are simply using it to avoid having one output for the discrimination process and instead have four of them with the help of the PatchGAN. This will lead to a better quality of generated photos. Furthermore, we should not see any modifications to the loss functions, and therefore see the entire image as if it's real, as long as all the patches seem real as well.

Discriminator Implementation

In this section we are going to implement the discriminator. You will observe how it defines the possibility of a patch being a colorized photo. Take note that we are using the CIFAR10 image dataset which contains very small images with a size of 32 by 32. Therefore we will only use one scalar to represents the probability of the image being real. Furthermore, we will check the results after applying the PatchGAN.

```python
def build_discriminator(input_shape, kernel_size=3,
patchgan=True, name=None):
```

""" The discriminator will be an encoder with four layers which will output a 1-dim or n-dim probability patch that measures how real the input is. """

```python
    inputs = Input(shape=input_shape)

    x = encoder_layer(inputs, 32, kernel_size=kernel_size,
    activation='leaky_relu',        instance_norm=False)

    x = encoder_layer(x, 64, kernel_size=kernel_size,

    activation='leaky_relu', instance_norm=False)

    x = encoder_layer(x, 128, kernel_size=kernel_size,
    activation='leaky_relu',

    instance_norm=False)

    x = encoder_layer(x, 256, kernel_size=kernel_size,
    strides=1, activation='leaky_relu',  instance_norm=False)
```

If the PatchGAN is true then then we will have an n-dim output

If not, then the 1-dim output is used instead

```python
    if patchgan:

    x = LeakyReLU(alpha=0.2)(x)
```

```python
outputs = Conv2D(1, kernel_size=kernel_size, strides=1, padding='same')(x)

else:

x = Flatten()(x)

x = Dense(1)(x)

outputs = Activation('linear')(x)

discriminator = Model(inputs, outputs, name=name)

return discriminator
```

Now that we have the generator and discriminator elements, we can create the CycleGAN builder model. The two generators are g_source and g_target, and the two discriminators are d_source and d_target. Take note that both discriminators are instantiated. Then we have two cycles, namely the forward cycle which can be represented as reco_source = g_source(g_target(source_input)), and the backward cycle as reco_target = g_target(g_source (target_input)). Both of the inputs belong to the source, as well as the target information. In this model, we don't have an identity network because there's a difference between the channels of the color images and grayscale images.

The CycleGAN Builder

Take note that just like with the basic GANs we will apply an RMSprop optimizer for the discriminator, which will have a learning rage equal to 23-4 and a decay rate equal to 6e-8. Both of these values will be half of those of the discriminator.

In this section we will have three steps. We will create the source and the target discriminators. Then we create the two generators, as well as the adversarial network.

> def build_cyclegan(shapes, source_name='source', target_name='target',
>
> kernel_size=3, patchgan=False, identity=False):

Arguments:

shapes (tuple): we will have both the source and the target shapes

(string): this will be the string that needs to be appended to the generator and discriminator models

target_name (string): the target name string also needs to be appended to the discriminator and generator models

kernel_size (int): this is the kernel size for the generator and discriminator

> models

patchgan (bool): we establish whether to use a patchgan on discriminator

identity (bool): we establish whether to use identity loss

Returns: (list): 2 generator, 2 discriminator, and 1 adversarial models

"""

source_shape, target_shape = shapes

lr = 2e-4

decay = 6e-8   gt_name = "gen_" + target_name
        gs_name = "gen_" + source_name   dt_name =
"dis_" + target_name ds_name = "dis_" + source_name

build target and source generators

g_target = build_generator(source_shape, target_shape,
kernel_size=kernel_size,   name=gt_name) g_source =
build_generator(target_shape, source_shape,
        kernel_size=kernel_size, name=gs_name)

print('---- TARGET GENERATOR ----')
        g_target.summary()   print('---- SOURCE
GENERATOR ----') g_source.summary()

create the source and target discriminators

```python
    d_target = build_discriminator(target_shape,
            patchgan=patchgan, kernel_size=kernel_size,
    name=dt_name)

    d_source = build_discriminator(source_shape,
    patchgan=patchgan,

    kernel_size=kernel_size, name=ds_name)

    print('---- TARGET DISCRIMINATOR ----')

    d_target.summary()

    print('---- SOURCE DISCRIMINATOR ----')
    d_source.summary()

    optimizer = RMSprop(lr=lr, decay=decay)

    d_target.compile(loss='mse', optimizer=optimizer,
    metrics=['accuracy'])

    d_source.compile(loss='mse', optimizer=optimizer,
    metrics=['accuracy'])

# the discriminator weights need to be suspended in the adversarial
network

    d_target.trainable = False     d_source.trainable = False

# create a graph that will represent the adversarial network
```

```python
# this will be the forward cycle network and target discriminator
    source_input = Input(shape=source_shape)
    fake_target = g_target(source_input)
    preal_target = d_target(fake_target)
    reco_source = g_source(fake_target)
# this will be the backward cycle network and source discriminator
    target_input = Input(shape=target_shape)
    fake_source = g_source(target_input)
    preal_source = d_source(fake_source)
    reco_target = g_target(fake_source)
# if we use identity loss, add 2 extra loss terms
# and outputs
    if identity:
    iden_source = g_source(source_input)
    iden_target = g_target(target_input)
    loss = ['mse', 'mse', 'mae', 'mae', 'mae', 'mae']
    loss_weights = [1., 1., 10., 10., 0.5, 0.5]
```

```python
inputs = [source_input, target_input]

outputs = [preal_source, preal_target, reco_source,
reco_target, iden_source, iden_target]

else:    loss = ['mse', 'mse', 'mae', 'mae']

loss_weights = [1., 1., 10., 10.]

inputs = [source_input, target_input]

outputs = [preal_source, preal_target, reco_source,
reco_target]
```

creating the adversarial model

```python
adv = Model(inputs, outputs, name='adversarial')

optimizer = RMSprop(lr=lr*0.5, decay=decay*0.5)

adv.compile(loss=loss, loss_weights=loss_weights,
optimizer=optimizer,          metrics=['accuracy']) print('---
- ADVERSARIAL NETWORK ----')

adv.summary()

return g_source, g_target, d_source, d_target, adv
```

The Training Process

You will notice that we are going to use the same training process as
we did in the previous section. However, there will be one important

difference when compared to the basic GAN. The discriminators need to be optimized. With every 2000 steps the source and the target image predictions are saved. Furthermore, we will use a batch size of 32 and not a size of one. This is because the training process will take a longer time with a batch size of one.

We will do three things in this section. We will train the source and target discriminators and then train backward and forward cycles that belong to the adversarial networks.

Now let's go through the code:

```
def train_cyclegan(models, data, params, test_params,
test_generator):
```

"""Arguments:

models (Models): Source/Target Discriminator/Generator, Adversarial Model

data (tuple): source and target training data

params (tuple): network parameters

test_params (tuple): test parameters

test_generator (function): used for generating predicted target and source images """

the models

```python
        g_source, g_target, d_source, d_target, adv = models
# network parameters
        batch_size, train_steps, patch, model_name = params
# training
        source_data, target_data, test_source_data, test_target_data =
        data
        titles, dirs = test_params
# we save the generator image every 2000 steps
        save_interval = 2000
        target_size = target_data.shape[0]
        source_size = source_data.shape[0]
# We need to determine whether we should use patchgan
        if patch > 1:
        d_patch = (patch, patch, 1)
        valid = np.ones((batch_size,) + d_patch)
        fake = np.zeros((batch_size,) + d_patch)
        else:    valid = np.ones([batch_size, 1])        fake =
        np.zeros([batch_size, 1])
```

```python
        valid_fake = np.concatenate((valid, fake))

        start_time = datetime.datetime.now()

        for step in range(train_steps):
# sample a batch of real target data
            rand_indexes = np.random.randint(0, target_size,
            size=batch_size)

            real_target = target_data[rand_indexes]
# sample a batch of real source data
            rand_indexes = np.random.randint(0, source_size,
            size=batch_size)

            real_source = source_data[rand_indexes]
# generating a batch of fake target data
            fake_target = g_target.predict(real_source)
# compiling the real and fake into the same batch
            x = np.concatenate((real_target, fake_target))
# training process for the discriminator with fake and real data
            metrics = d_target.train_on_batch(x, valid_fake)

            log = "%d: [d_target loss: %f]" % (step, metrics[0])
```

```python
# generating a batch of fake source data

    fake_source = g_source.predict(real_target)

    x = np.concatenate((real_source, fake_source))

# training process for the discriminator with fake and real data

    metrics = d_source.train_on_batch(x, valid_fake)

    log = "%s [d_source loss: %f]" % (log, metrics[0])

# training the adversarial network using forward and backward
cycles

# the generated fake source and target data attempts to fool the
discriminators

    x = [real_source, real_target]

    y = [valid, valid, real_source, real_target]

    metrics = adv.train_on_batch(x, y)

    elapsed_time = datetime.datetime.now() - start_time

    fmt = "%s [adv loss: %f] [time: %s]"

    log = fmt % (log, metrics[0], elapsed_time)

    print(log)

    if (step + 1) % save_interval == 0:
```

```
if (step + 1) == train_steps:

    show = True

else:  show = False

test_generator((g_source, g_target), (test_source_data,
test_target_data),

    step=step+1, titles=titles,   dirs=dirs,  show=show)
```

once the training process is complete we save the models

```
g_source.save(model_name + "-g_source.h5")
        g_target.save(model_name
+ "-g_target.h5")
```

Before we train all the functions we need to prepare the data. We have two cifar modules that need to be loaded for the CIFAR10 training and test data. Once the data is loaded, we can convert both the training and the test photos to grayscale in order to create the source data and test data that are necessary for the process.

Solving the Colorization Problem

In this section we are going to use the CycleGAN model to create a generator network in order to solve the colorization of the grayscale images problem. Take note that CycleGAN is symmetric, which means that we need to create and train a second generator network in order to convert the data from color to grayscale. The two CycleGAN networks are trained and the first one will use discriminators that have nearly the same scalar output as the basic GAN. The second network, however, will use a PatchGAN with a size of 2 x 2 instead.

```
def graycifar10_cross_colorcifar10(g_models=None):

model_name = 'cyclegan_cifar10'     batch_size = 32

train_steps = 100000

patchgan = True

kernel_size = 3

postfix = ('%dp' % kernel_size) if patchgan else  ('%d' % kernel_size)

data, shapes = cifar10_utils.load_data()      source_data,
_,test_source_data,

test_target_data = data

titles = ('CIFAR10 predicted source images.', 'CIFAR10 predicted target images.', 'CIFAR10 reconstructed source images.', 'CIFAR10 reconstructed target images.')

dirs = ('cifar10_source-%s' % postfix, 'cifar10_target-%s' % postfix)
```

we need to generate the predicted target, which is the color,

```
# and source source target which is the grayscale

    if g_models is not None:

    g_source, g_target = g_models

    other_utils.test_generator((g_source, g_target),
    (test_source_data, test_target_

    data),  step=0, titles=titles, dirs=dirs, show=True)

    return

# creating the cyclegan used for the colorization process

    models = build_cyclegan(shapes,      "gray-%s" % postfix,

    "color-%s" % postfix,

    kernel_size=kernel_size, patchgan=patchgan)

# take note the input is not scaled down in the discriminator, therefore
the patch size is divided by 2^n

    patch = int(source_data.shape[1] / 2**4) if patchgan else 1

    params = (batch_size, train_steps, patch, model_name)

    test_params = (titles, dirs)     # train the cyclegan
            train_cyclegan(models, data,

    params, test_params, other_utils.test_generator)
```

As you already know, the source images come from the testing set. In order to make the comparison, we need to show the reality and therefore the colorization results, by using the simple autoencoder we discussed in the chapter about autoencoders. All of the colorized images turned out to be acceptable even though the technique we used has its disadvantages. The main problem is that not all the techniques are accurate in assigning the correct color, usually for objects like the sky and vehicle. For instance, if you have worked alongside with this example, you will notice that the background sky of a plane image turns out white. While the autoencoder has performed admirably and knows that it's correct, the CycleGAN algorithm considers it light brown or blue. Another example can be found in the image with a boat on dark waters. Even though there's an overcast sky, it was colored blue together with the sea by the autoencoder. However, CycleGAN colored the sky white instead. Both of these colorization predictions are understandable in the real world though.

You will notice, however, the CycleGAN together with Patchgan offer the most accurate reality that is close to the actual truth. However, there are some problematic exceptions. For instance, neither of our methods could predict that the car on the second last row and second column should be red. However, when it comes to animals both GAN applications are fairly close in determining the real color.

Keep in mind that CycleGAN is symmetric, therefore it can also use colored images in order to predict the grayscale images. If you run the model for this process you will notice that the predictions will be accurate. By using the target images from the test set, the model will show the reality of the images, with only some small inaccuracies regarding the shades of gray.

CycleGAN and MNIST

In this section we are going to attempt to solve a different problem. Let's say that the MNIST handwritten digits images are in grayscale for the source data and we want to obtain the style from the SVHN dataset, which will be the target data. In case you haven't worked with the SVHN dataset yet, you should know it is called the Street View House Numbers dataset and it complements the MNIST dataset as well as other computer vision datasets.

For this problem we can use the same build and train functions that we worked with in the previous section. Transfering the style can be done with the same CycleGAN algorithm. However, we will need to create various routines that will load the information from the two datasets. The CycleGAN will maintain its architecture, but we will also have to change the kernel size because the domains differ greatly. With that being said, let's go through the code and discuss it:

```
def mnist_cross_svhn(g_models=None):
```

```python
    model_name = 'cyclegan_mnist_svhn' batch_size = 32b
    train_steps = 100000

    patchgan = True kernel_size = 5 postfix = ('%dp' %
    kernel_size)

    if patchgan else ('%d' % kernel_ size)

    data, shapes = mnist_svhn_utils.load_data()

    source_data, _, test_source_data, test_target_data = data

    titles = ('MNIST predicted source images.', 'SVHN predicted
    target images.',

    'MNIST reconstructed source images.', 'SVHN reconstructed
    target images.')

    dirs = ('mnist_source-%s' % postfix, 'svhn_target-%s' %
    postfix)
# generating SVHN images, which are the predicted targets and
# the MNIST images, which are the source
    if g_models is not None:

    g_source, g_target = g_models

    other_utils.test_generator((g_source, g_target),
    (test_source_data, test_ target_data),
```

```
        step=0, titles=titles, dirs=dirs, show=True)

        return

# build the cyclegan to perform the shift

        models = build_cyclegan(shapes, "mnist-%s" % postfix,
        "svhn-%s" % postfix, kernel_size=kernel_size,
        patchgan=patchgan)

# Because the input will be downscaled we need to divide the patch
size by 2^n

        patch = int(source_data.shape[1] / 2**4)

        if patchgan else 1

        params = (batch_size, train_steps, patch, model_name)

        test_params = (titles, dirs)

# train the cyclegan

        train_cyclegan(models,  data, params, test_params,

        other_utils.test_generator)
```

That's it! Using the same methods you already implemented, we now have generated images that follow the style of the SVHN dataset. However, the digits haven't been fully transferred. For instance, if you look at the third row, you will see that some of the digits still follow a different style. Furthermore, the results from the backward cycle differ as well. For instance, the generated images in this case respect the style of the MNIST dataset, but they aren't properly translated. You will see digits like 5 and 2, stylized as 7, 8 and 3.

This problem that we detect in the translation from the MNIST dataset to SVHN where digits from the source are translated to the target is referred to as label flipping. Even if the CycleGAN predictions are consistent from a cycle point of view, they are consistent from the semantic perspective. This means that some of the digits lose their meaning during the translation process. In order to solve this problem, we can improve the CycleGAN by implementing a CyCADA algorithm, which stands for Cycle Consistent Adversarial Domain Adaptation. The main difference between the two is that the semantic loss will guarantee that the prediction will be consistent from a semantic point of view and not just from the cycle one.

Keep in mind that CycleGAN is cycle consistent which means that if we have "x" source, the model will rebuild that source as "x'". The same thing happens to the "y" target. Now if we look at the MNIST digit reconstruction inside the forward cycle, we will see that they are nearly the same as in the source MNIST. The SVHN digits are rebuilt in the backward cycle and most of the target images are successfully reconstructed. However, some of the digits are identical and some of them are blurred. Others are translated to different digits even though the style doesn't change. The model isn't perfect, but by implementing other corrective algorithms like the CyCADA algorithm, this issue can be constrained.

Summary

In this chapter we have focused on the CycleGAN algorithm which is used mainly for the translation of images, where the source and target images don't have to be aligned. You have worked through two examples that translate grayscale images to color image, or back, as well as translate the digits style from one dataset to another. Even though there are many other translations you can perform with this mode, these two examples clearly show how CycleGAN works and how you can implement it to solve real world problems.

In the next chapter, you are going to learn about another advanced deep learning generative model, namely the Variational Autoencoder. Their purpose is similar to that of learning how data can be generated. The latent vector is modeled as a Gaussian distribution, but you will notice several similarities with

Chapter 6

Variational Autoencoders

———————◆———————

Variational Autoencoders are in many ways similar to GANs because they belong to the same branch of generative models. Variational autoencoders have a generator which is meant to produce outputs while going through its latent vector, which is continuous. We can explore the decoder's features by examining the latent vector. With GANs however, the focus point was placed on how to construct a model which can perform an approximation of the input distribution. Variational autoencoders, however, need to model the distribution by working with a decodable latent space which is continuous. This is the main reason why variational autoencoders can't create as many realistic data items compared to GANs.

For instance, when it comes to image generation, GANs can generate highly realistic images. The main issue with variational autoencoders is that when compared to GANs, they cannot generate such sharp results because the focus is on the variational inference instead. The purpose of variational autoencoders is to create a framework devised for learning by using latent variables. For instance, we have variational autoencoders that use disentangled representations which enable the reuse of latent code for the purpose of transfer learning.

When it comes to the architecture of this type of autoencoder, it follows the same rules and structure of the autoencoder, at least on a basic level. The structure is made from an encoder, in this case also referred to as an inference model, and a decoder, also referred to as the generative model. Variational autoencoders, as well as autoencoders, seek to rebuild input data at the same time as learning the latent vector. The difference, however, is that variational autoencoder have a continuous latent space and the decoder is used as a generative model.

In addition, in a similar way as GANs, the decoder of the variational autoencoder can be conditioned. For instance, if we use the MNIST dataset we have the ability to select which digit we want to create a one-hot vector. In this case, however, we have to deal with a conditional variational autoencoder where the latent vectors can be disentangled with a hyperparameter that can regularize itself on top of the loss function. Again, if we use MNIST as the example, we can confine the latent vector in order to establish various features of the digits, such as thickness or tilt angle.

With that being said, in this chapter we are going to focus on the implementation of variational autoencoders amd work with the Keras library

Concept and Implementation

Because we're discussing a generative model, most of the time our focus lies in the ability to approximate the real distribution of inputs with the help of advanced neural networks. As mentioned earlier, the variational autoencoders is constructed from an encoder, a decoder, and a loss functions. This type of autoencoder actually refers to an approximate inference in a latent Gaussian model.

Let's say we have a dataset that contains the faces of certain famous people. In this case, the purpose is to explore a distribution that is capable of drawing faces. This concept is similar to that from the MNIST dataset where we sought to generate real handwritten digits that could be recognized. In deep learning, we have to perform a particular grade of inference in order to discover a common distribution between the inputs and the latent variables. Keep in mind that the latent variables aren't a component of the dataset. They actually encode various features that can only be seen from the inputs.

Going back to our celebrity example, when it comes to faces, we have to focus on various attributes such as hairstyles, gender, eye color, facial expression, and everything else that makes up a face. If we go back to the MNIST dataset with the same focus, the latent variables are simply the digits and the styles in which they are written. Once we examine all the features, the result will be a distribution that can describe every single input. If we take into account all the facial expressions, gender, and other attributes, the distribution that describes the faces is obtained. Similarly, when we look at the MNIST dataset with all the digits and handwriting styles in mind, we will obtain a distribution of digits. One problem, however, exists in the implementation because the optimization process through a neural network cannot be achieved, or at the very least it is not viable.

Modelling with Keras

As mentioned earlier, the architecture of the variational autoencoder is almost the same as that of the basic autoencoder. However, we have a sampling of Gaussian random variables during the reparameterization process. You will notice that the encoder, decoder, and the entire variational autoencoder are implemented with the help of a multilayer perceptron. Furthermore, the latent vector will be a 2-dim one in order to preserve simplicity.

The encoder will be constructed as a multilayer perceptron with two layers, where the second layer will generate the log, as well as the mean variance. The reason why we have a log variance in this scenario is to simplify the processing of the KL loss and reparameterization. In addition, the encoder has a third output which represents the sampling of the latent vector by relying on the reparameterization process. Take note that in the sampling function we have a standard deviation of the Gaussian model.

As for the decoder, it is also a multilayer perceptron with two layers, which accepts the samples of the latent vector in order to be able to calculate the inputs approximately. As long as both the decoder and encoder rely on a 512-sized dimension, the variational autoencoder network is simply the combination of those two components. At the same time, we also have the loss function which can be calculated as the KL loss and the reconstruction loss. In addition, we will use a simple Adam optimizer in order to obtain accurate results. Keep in mind that our variational autoencoder will have over 800,000 parameters.

With that being said, let's go through the code. Remember to always examine it thoroughly because the comments describing each step are included in the code.

```
# reparameterization

#instead of sampling from Q(z|X), sample eps = N(0,I)

# z = z_mean + sqrt(var)*eps

        def sampling(args):    z_mean, z_log_var = args

        batch = K.shape(z_mean)[0]

# K is the keras backend

        dim = K.int_shape(z_mean)[1]

# by default, random_normal has mean=0 and std=1.0

        epsilon = K.random_normal(shape=(batch, dim))
```

```python
        return z_mean + K.exp(0.5 * z_log_var) * epsilon

# we are using the MNIST dataset

    (x_train, y_train), (x_test, y_test) = mnist.load_data()

    image_size = x_train.shape[1]

    original_dim = image_size * image_size

    x_train = np.reshape(x_train, [-1, original_dim])

    x_test = np.reshape(x_test, [-1, original_dim])

    x_train = x_train.astype('float32') / 255 x_test =
    x_test.astype('float32') / 255

# neural net parameters

    input_shape = (original_dim, ) intermediate_dim = 512
    batch_size = 128 latent_dim = 2 epochs = 50

# variational autoencoder model = encoder + decoder

# creating the encoder model

    inputs = Input(shape=input_shape, name='encoder_input')

    x = Dense(intermediate_dim, activation='relu')(inputs)

    z_mean = Dense(latent_dim, name='z_mean')(x)

    z_log_var = Dense(latent_dim, name='z_log_var')(x)
```

```python
# use reparameterization in order to push the sampling out as an
input

    z = Lambda(sampling, output_shape=(latent_dim,),
    name='z')([z_mean, z_log_var])

# instantiating the encoder model

    encoder = Model(inputs, [z_mean, z_log_var, z],
    name='encoder') encoder.summary()

    plot_model(encoder, to_file='vae_mlp_encoder.png',
    show_shapes=True)

# creating the decoder model

    latent_inputs = Input(shape=(latent_dim,),
    name='z_sampling')

    x = Dense(intermediate_dim,
    activation='relu')(latent_inputs)

    outputs = Dense(original_dim, activation='sigmoid')(x)

# instantiating the decoder model

    decoder = Model(latent_inputs, outputs, name='decoder')

    decoder.summary()
```

```python
    plot_model(decoder, to_file='vae_mlp_decoder.png',
    show_shapes=True)

# instantiating the variational autoencoder model

    outputs = decoder(encoder(inputs)[2]) vae = Model(inputs,
    outputs, name='vae_mlp')

    if __name__ == '__main__':

    parser = argparse.ArgumentParser()

    help_ = "Load h5 model trained weights"

    parser.add_argument("-w", "--weights", help=help_)

    help_ = "Use mse loss instead of binary cross entropy
    (default)"

    parser.add_argument("-m", "--mse", help=help_,
    action='store_true')

    args = parser.parse_args()     models = (encoder, decoder)

    data = (x_test, y_test)

# variational autoencoder loss = mse_loss or xent_loss + kl_loss

    if args.mse:

    reconstruction_loss = mse(inputs, outputs)
```

```python
    else:
        reconstruction_loss = binary_crossentropy(inputs, outputs)
        reconstruction_loss *= original_dim
        kl_loss = 1 + z_log_var - K.square(z_mean) - K.exp(z_log_var)
        kl_loss = K.sum(kl_loss, axis=-1)     kl_loss *= -0.5
        vae_loss = K.mean(reconstruction_loss + kl_loss)
        vae.add_loss(vae_loss)
        vae.compile(optimizer='adam')
        vae.summary()
        plot_model(vae, to_file='vae_mlp.png', show_shapes=True)
        if args.weights:
            vae = vae.load_weights(args.weights)
        else:
# training process for the autoencoder
            vae.fit(x_train, epochs=epochs, batch_size=batch_size,
            validation_data=(x_test, None))
```

```
vae.save_weights('vae_mlp_mnist.h5')

plot_results(models, data, batch_size=batch_size,
model_name="vae_mlp")
```

We are using the plot results function in order to display the latent vector's continuous space after 50 epochs have passed. To keep things simple, the plot will contain two images, test labels and the generated handwritten digits. The last two elements are part of the latent vector's function. You will see that the plots conclude the way the features of the digits are determined by the latent vector. By passing through the space there will always be a result as an output that looks nearly identical to the handwritten digits supplied by the MNIST dataset. For instance, if we navigate through the area of digit nine, we will see that it is close to the area of digit seven. If we simply move from the nine close to the center and go to the left, it will transform the digit to a seven. Then if we switch from the central region and go downwards we will notice how the digit changes from a three to eight and then lastly to a one. This transformation becomes even more obvious the further you navigate. Furthermore, if you look at the plot, you will also see the output of the generator, as well as the digit distribution in latent space. Because the distribution is the densest in the middle of the region, you will see that the changes occur rapidly in the center and slower as the values of the mean increase.

Working with Convolutional Neural Nets

So far we have implemented a variational autoencoder with a multilayer perceptron, however, we can also use a convolutional neural network instead in order to boost the performance and efficiency. With the help of a convolutional neural net, you will also notice a positive impact on the quality of the generated handwritten digits. Furthermore, the number of parameters will also go down from approximately 800,000 to just over 130,000, which is also a significant change.

In this section we are going to look at the code where we will have an encoder constructed from two convolutional neural network layers, as well as two multilayer perceptron layers that will create the latent code. The architecture of the output will be nearly identical to that of the multilayer perceptron version which we analyzed in the section above. The decoder, on the other hand, is built using three transposed convolutional neural network layers, as well as one multilayer perceptron. Furthermore, the chosen optimizes for this model will be the RMSprop because it will cause a lower loss when compared to the Adam optimizer.

Keep in mind that in this code you will not see some of the operations that are identical to the previous model. Therefore, make sure to fully analyze the variational autoencoder in order to understand the basis of this implementation. With that being said, let's take a look at the convolutional variational autoencoder with the following code:

```python
# neural net parameters

    input_shape = (image_size, image_size, 1) batch_size = 128
    kernel_size = 3 filters = 16 latent_dim = 2 epochs = 30

# VAE mode = encoder + decoder

# creating the encoder model

    inputs = Input(shape=input_shape, name='encoder_input') x
    = inputs

    for i in range(2):

    filters *= 2

    x    =    Conv2D(filters=filters,    kernel_size=kernel_size,
    activation='relu', strides=2, padding='same')(x)

# In order to create the decoder model we first need the shape info

    shape = K.int_shape(x)

# creating the latent vector

    x = Flatten()(x)

    x = Dense(16, activation='relu')(x)

    z_mean = Dense(latent_dim, name='z_mean')(x)

    z_log_var = Dense(latent_dim, name='z_log_var')(x)
```

The sampling needs to be pushed as an input with the help of reparameterization

Keep in mind that the "output_shape" isn't needed when using TensorFlow backend

```python
z = Lambda(sampling, output_shape=(latent_dim,),
name='z')([z_mean, z_log_var])
```

Encoder model instantiation

```python
encoder = Model(inputs, [z_mean, z_log_var, z],
name='encoder') encoder.summary() plot_model(encoder,
to_file='vae_cnn_encoder.png', show_shapes=True)
```

creating the decoder model

```python
latent_inputs = Input(shape=(latent_dim,),
name='z_sampling')

x = Dense(shape[1]*shape[2]*shape[3],
activation='relu')(latent_ inputs)

x = Reshape((shape[1], shape[2], shape[3]))(x)

for i in range(2):

x = Conv2DTranspose(filters=filters,
kernel_size=kernel_size, activation='relu',    strides=2,
padding='same')(x) filters //= 2
```

```
    outputs = Conv2DTranspose(filters=1,
    kernel_size=kernel_size, activation='sigmoid',
    padding='same', name='decoder_output')(x)

# decoder model instantiation

    decoder = Model(latent_inputs, outputs, name='decoder')

    decoder.summary()

    plot_model(decoder, to_file='vae_cnn_decoder.png',
    show_shapes=True)

# instantiation the variational autoencoder model

    outputs = decoder(encoder(inputs)[2])

    vae = Model(inputs, outputs, name='vae')
```

If you analyze the generated plot you will notice the continuous latent space of the variational autoencoder with the convolutional neural network model after thirty epocs. Take note that the area where every handwritten digit is assigned differs, however the distribution itself is nearly identical. If you compare this implementation with the one modeled with a multilayer perceptron, you will see that there is a smaller number of handwritten digits that aren't clear. This implementation is superior in quality.

The Conditional Variational Autoencoder

The conditional variational autoencoder is in many ways similar to the conditional GAN. If we continue with the MNIST dataset as the example, we will see that if the latent space undergoes random sampling, the variational autoencoder loses the control over the generation of specific digits. Conditional variational autoencoders seek to resolve this problem with the introduction of a condition in the form of a one-hot label. This condition is meant to set a limit to the digit which is produced and it is imposing itself on the inputs of the encoder as well as the decoder.

In order to have a maximum output in this implementation, we need the two losses to be minimized. Like in the previous mode, we are referring to the reconstruction loss that is attached to the decoder, and the KL loss that resides between the encoder and the previous distribution. With that being said, let's go through the Keras implementation of the conditional variational autoencoder. Keep in mind that we are still going to use convolutional neural network layers here as well.

processing the number of labels

        num_labels = len(np.unique(y_train))

neural net parameters

```python
input_shape = (image_size, image_size, 1) label_shape =
(num_labels, ) batch_size = 128 kernel_size = 3 filters = 16
latent_dim = 2 epochs = 30
```

The encoder and decoder make up the variational autoencoder model

creating the encoder model

```python
inputs = Input(shape=input_shape, name='encoder_input')

y_labels = Input(shape=label_shape, name='class_labels')

x = Dense(image_size * image_size)(y_labels)

x = Reshape((image_size, image_size, 1))(x) x =
keras.layers.concatenate([inputs, x]) for i in range(2):

    filters *= 2 x = Conv2D(filters=filters,
    kernel_size=kernel_size, activation='relu', strides=2,
    padding='same')(x)
```

In order to create the decoder model we need to obtain the shape info first

```python
shape = K.int_shape(x)
```

creating the latent vector

```python
x = Flatten()(x)
```

```python
x = Dense(16, activation='relu')(x)

z_mean = Dense(latent_dim, name='z_mean')(x) z_log_var
= Dense(latent_dim, name='z_log_var')(x)
```

The sampling needs to come out as an input,

therefore we need to apply reparameterization

keep in mind that the "output_shape" is optional

if you are using the TensorFlow backend

```python
z = Lambda(sampling, output_shape=(latent_dim,),
name='z')([z_mean, z_log_var])
```

encoder model instantiation

```python
encoder = Model([inputs, y_labels], [z_mean, z_log_var, z],
name='encoder') encoder.summary()

plot_model(encoder, to_file='cvae_cnn_encoder.png',
show_shapes=True)
```

creating the decoder model

```python
latent_inputs = Input(shape=(latent_dim,),
name='z_sampling')

x = keras.layers.concatenate([latent_inputs, y_labels])

x = Dense(shape[1]*shape[2]*shape[3], activation='relu')(x)
```

```python
x = Reshape((shape[1], shape[2], shape[3]))(x) for i in range(2):

x = Conv2DTranspose(filters=filters,
kernel_size=kernel_size, activation='relu', strides=2,
padding='same')(x) filters //= 2

outputs = Conv2DTranspose(filters=1,
kernel_size=kernel_size, activation='sigmoid',
padding='same', name='decoder_output')(x)
```

decoder model instantiation

```python
decoder = Model([latent_inputs, y_labels], outputs,
name='decoder')

decoder.summary()

plot_model(decoder, to_file='cvae_cnn_decoder.png',
show_shapes=True)
```

instantiating the variational autoencoder model

```python
outputs = decoder([encoder([inputs, y_labels])[2], y_labels])

cvae = Model([inputs, y_labels], outputs, name='cvae') if
__name__ == '__main__':     parser =
argparse.ArgumentParser()
```

```python
help_ = "Load h5 model trained weights"
parser.add_argument("-w", "--weights", help=help_)

help_ = "Use mse loss instead of binary cross entropy
(default)"

parser.add_argument("-m", "--mse", help=help_,
action='store_ true')

help_ = "Specify a specific digit to generate"
        parser.add_argument("-d", "--digit", type=int,
help=help_)

help_ = "Beta in Beta-CVAE. Beta > 1. Default is 1.0
(CVAE)"

parser.add_argument("-b", "--beta", type=float, help=help_)

args = parser.parse_args()     models = (encoder, decoder)

data = (x_test, y_test)

if args.beta is None or args.beta < 1.0:

beta = 1.0

print("CVAE")

model_name = "cvae_cnn_mnist"

else:    beta = args.beta
```

```python
print("Beta-CVAE with beta=", beta)

model_name = "beta-cvae_cnn_mnist"
# VAE loss = mse_loss or xent_loss + kl_loss

if args.mse:

    reconstruction_loss = mse(K.flatten(inputs),
    K.flatten(outputs))

else:

    reconstruction_loss=binary_crossentropy(K.flatten(inputs),
    K.flatten(outputs))

reconstruction_loss *= image_size * image_size

kl_loss = 1 + z_log_var - K.square(z_mean) -
K.exp(z_log_var)

kl_loss = K.sum(kl_loss, axis=-1)     kl_loss *= -0.5 * beta

cvae_loss = K.mean(reconstruction_loss + kl_loss)

cvae.add_loss(cvae_loss)
        cvae.compile(optimizer='rmsprop')

cvae.summary()

plot_model(cvae, to_file='cvae_cnn.png',
show_shapes=True)
```

```python
        if args.weights:

            cvae = cvae.load_weights(args.weights)

        else:

    # the training process for the autoencoder

            cvae.fit([x_train, to_categorical(y_train)],

            epochs=epochs, batch_size=batch_size,
                    validation_data=([x_test, to_categorical(y_test)],
            None))          cvae.save_weights(model_name + '.h5')

            if args.digit in range(0, num_labels):

            digit = np.array([args.digit])

        else:

        digit = np.random.randint(0, num_labels, 1)

        print("CVAE for digit %d" % digit)

        y_label = np.eye(num_labels)[digit]

        plot_results(models, data,     y_label=y_label,
        batch_size=batch_size,

        model_name=model_name)
```

The conditional variational autoencoder implementation essentially requires a number of modifications to the original variational autoencoder. Don't forget that with this model we are using convolutional neural networks.

Our encoder input can be summarized as a concatenation of the original image together with the one-hot label component. The decoder input, on the other hand, is represented by the sampling of the latent space, together with the target image's one-hot label. In this implementation we also have a much smaller number of parameters ($\sim$170,000) than with the basic model, however, there are more when compared to the convolutional model. You will also notice that we made no modifications to the loss function. However, the one-hot labels are provided during the training, testing, and plotting phases.

When compared to the other implementations you will notice that the label is not focused on a single region. Instead, it is spread over the entire plot. This is caused by the fact that the latent space sampling generates specific digits. By navigating this space, the feature of a certain digit will change. For instance, let's say that the specified digit is zero. If we navigate the space, we will still have a zero, however some of the features, like the writing style and thickness, will be different from the original.

In addition, you will notice that with the change of the latent vector from left to right, the width, as well as the roundness if it exists, will change. At the same time, the tilt angle will also change with the vector moving downwards. Once we shift from the middle region of the distribution, you will see that the image starts falling apart. This degradation is normal in this case because the space is in fact a circle. Other features that can vary exist, however they depend on the particular handwritten digits. For instance, one of the strokes of a specific digit may only be seen in the upper left section.

Summary

In this chapter we have analyzed the most important variational autoencoder implementations. You learned about the core concepts behind them and how they are similar to GANs in creating manufactured outputs from the latent space. Furthermore, you have seen through practical examples that networks built from variational autoencoders are easier to train when compared to GANs.

Conclusion

———————◆·———————

C ongratulations for making it to the end of this deep learning, hands on guide for experts! If you started from the beginning of this series, you have come a long way. Take your time to absorb all of the information provided and even go through the book one more time. The concepts and techniques explained here are advanced and sometimes difficult to implement. However, after going step by step through the material you should feel confident enough in implementing the advanced deep learning models we discussed.

Remember that deep learning is a relatively new field and some of the concepts and models you explored in this book are only a few years old. This field is ever-evolving and practical applications like the generative adversarial networks and autoencoders are constantly changing and evolving. Take what you have learned with the help of this series and practice thoroughly by implementing these algorithms and creating your very own deep learning models.